a complete guide to
FAMILY FINANCE

roderick millar

TESCO
Every little helps

KOGAN PAGE

First published in Great Britain in 2004 by Kogan Page Limited

120 Pentonville Road
London N1 9JN
www.kogan-page.co.uk

British Library Cataloguing in Publication Data

A CIP record for this book is available from the British Library

ISBN 0 7494 4203 4

Typeset by Saxon Graphics Ltd, Derby
Printed and bound in Great Britain by Bell & Bain, Glasgow

Contents

TESCO

Tesco Personal Finance offers loads of great value, straightforward financial products to help you make the most of your money. That's why over 4million people have bought one of our products.

So if you are looking for a credit card, loan or motor insurance, or even wanting a new mortgage, all from a name you can trust-we can help.

Just pick up a leaflet in store or visit **www.tesco.com** to apply online.

But there's more to Tesco Personal Finance than just great value products. We also have lots of services and information to help you manage your money, and make your life a bit easier.

That's why we've developed our online help and information site, Smarter Money.

We know, from speaking to customers, that lots of you feel you could get smarter with your day to day money and you know that you should be planning for your financial future. But we also know that it can be difficult to know where to start.

Smarter Money is an online service, giving you all the straightforward information, money saving tips and tools you need to help you get smarter with your money and start planning your financial future.

So why not visit **www.tesco.com/smarter** to find out more?

Foreword

Britain is at a crossroads when it comes to family finances. On the one hand, politicians from all the main parties are telling us we can no longer rely on the State for financial support. The welfare state is increasingly merely a safety net, providing the bare minimum in times of crisis. Anyone who wants to enjoy a comfortable life – both today and in the future – must learn to take financial responsibility for themselves. On the other hand, many people have lost their trust in the financial services industry. A series of scandals, from the mis-selling of personal pensions to the collapse in the endowment mortgage sector, has destroyed people's trust in banks, building societies, insurers and investment firms. Financial advisers, to whom we should be able to turn for help, are often held in particularly low regard, whether they are independent or employed by our biggest banks. The launch of this book could therefore not have been better timed. It covers everything you need to know in order to save, invest and insure for the future without being duped by cowboys. Even better, it explains the facts in plain English, without using any of the jargon that financial services companies too often rely on. Whatever the professionals would like us to believe, the truth is that personal finance is not a complicated subject. Everyone can get to grips with the concepts explained in this book, once they have got past the mystifying language into which the experts too often descend. That's not to say you will never need expert help with your money again. Armed with this book, however, you should be able to develop a strong working relationship with a financial adviser, rather than worrying about whether or not you are being conned.

Above all, remember that personal finance is a means to an end. There is no point in saving for the future, for example, simply for the sake of saving. Private medical insurance does not exist so that you can buy a new type of cover. Never forget that taking responsibility today will mean an easier life tomorrow – whether that means retiring in the sun or keeping your family safe.

David Prosser
Personal Finance Editor
Daily Express, Sunday Express

Introduction

*Money can't buy you happiness but it does bring you
a more pleasant form of misery.*

The comedian Spike Milligan

In the long term we are all dead.

The celebrated economist J M Keynes

*There are two types of forecasters, those 'who don't know'
and those 'who don't know they don't know'.*

The equally celebrated economist J K Galbraith

A warning

Guides to personal finance are peculiar beasts. If we write something that only describes the mechanics of the finance industry, so providing the reader with a basis of understanding, he or she will only get half the picture, at best an outline drawing. If we add in some history and interpretation, the picture gains better perspective and depth, but inevitably the presentation will be more opinionated and less objective.

This guide will try to give you the 'added colour' required to make the book more informative and yet not be too subjective. This problem is not limited to personal finance books. It is, as we shall see (in Chapter 1), even more of an issue when we examine the motivations of financial advisers and the money industry at large.

Two significant facts in favour of the book are first that we can give no 'investment advice' either legally or actually, as all people's circumstances are different and therefore an individual's financial requirements require an individual assessment; and second that we have no 'axe to grind' as we cannot profit from any financial decision you make (other than in buying this book!).

As a consequence of this we recommend that you take action in the following order. Read the book to learn about the financial mechanics of the area you are interested in, discover our views on what affects these processes, then go to speak with a certified adviser who can suggest current options tailored to your particular needs. By that stage, we hope, you will be able to assess whether you agree or disagree with that advice based on your new-found knowledge and understanding.

Financial phobia

The online bank Egg, which is predominantly owned by the insurance giant Prudential, commissioned a recent survey from the Faculty of Social and Political Science at Cambridge University. The research examined the extent of negative feelings people had about their personal finances. Oddly, it seems no other research had been done on this specific area. The marketing departments of all retail banks and financial institutions have spent many millions of pounds over the years assessing how customers will react to certain products and campaigns, but no one had ever assessed what our general attitude to dealing with our own finances was like. The results make interesting and, for many, reassuring reading.

The compelling discovery of the report was that a genuine psycho-logical condition, which the author Dr Brendan Burchell called financial phobia, really exists. Dr Burchell suggests that 'Financial Phobes can be intelligent people who are high achievers in most areas of their lives; they are not irresponsible, feckless or spendthrift.' Like sufferers from dyslexia, the real problems these people experience are often scoffed at by non-

TESCO
Smarter money

Want to see if you can get smarter with your money, or need help planning your financial future?

Smarter Money is a website providing help and information from Tesco.

It's packed with information, quizzes, calculators and money saving tips.

Smarter Money is divided into 6 sections so it is easy to find what you need.

- **Day to day money**
- **Borrowing money**
- **Getting insured**
- **Planning your retirement**
- **Saving and investing**
- **Protecting your loved ones**

Every little helps

Did you know?
Over 33%
of UK adults have no savings.
And 57% have less
than £1,500.*

To find out more visit
www.tesco.com/smarter

sufferers, but as Dr Burchell makes clear the effects of financial phobia are not caused by laziness, defiance or negligence but through a more complex psychological trigger. The bad news is that the report estimates that up to 20 per cent of the UK adult population are financial phobes, with a further 30 per cent showing certain symptoms of the condition. The good news is that it can be relatively easily overcome.

The symptoms of financial phobia are many and various. At their most benign they are probably not checking your bank balance, increasing through not opening statements promptly to not opening them at all. In the most extreme sufferers these actions (or non-actions) are accompanied by physical feelings of apprehension, ranging from dizziness to nausea.

While there is no clear group of people who are 'high risk' of becoming financial phobes, the younger and poorer members of the population are slightly more prone to making irrational financial decisions. The study also showed that more women than men scored as financial phobes; however, more women than men were in the top 20 per cent of financial ability, which may suggest that women just filled in the questionnaire more fervently than their male counterparts.

The importance of all this information is to illustrate that fear of managing your personal finances is perfectly normal. What is more, it has no bearing on your expertise in other areas. You may be a wizard at computing while being less than magical at pensions; or an artist in the world of human relations and rather cack-handed when it comes to debt management. Financial phobia, at whatever level, can strike anybody.

In order to eradicate these financial gremlins it is important to realize that while managing your personal finances may not be the peak of your year's excitement, with a little thought it can really be quite easy and straightforward. Whether you are a phobic, mildly confused, or just looking for some reassurance on some aspect, it can only help to familiarize yourself with some simple ground rules – which is what you will find in this book.

A change of perspective

Writing this book in early 2004 is to be doing so in a very different economic climate to that which existed only three years ago. At the turn of the century although we had passed the peak of the current stock market cycle, we had not really detached ourselves from the reckless optimism that took us there. The Millennium bubble had still not been burst. As a result we still believed that vast fortunes were relatively simple to make from the stock market. This belief that by sticking with the stock market we could, with only a little luck and wisdom, become millionaires very quickly, affected not just investors but nearly every part of our financial lives. If you assume that your assets will only increase in value you can take greater risks with the rest of your finances, or even worse, ignore any further financial planning altogether.

In part the belief is still with us. This book will emphasize the importance of changing that belief, and will take you through the various stages of your financial life, examining how to achieve a balance between gaining the greatest rewards and not risking your current level of security. It is still possible to make a vast amount of money from successful investment, but it is almost impossible to do this in normal times without taking on a high level of risk. The truth is that following the bursting of the Millennium bubble, we are now in much more 'normal' times than we were three or four years ago. That means lower growth rates and longer economic cycles. The Millennium bubble was just that: it basically lasted only four years, from 1997 to 2001.

Of course, what 'normal' means is open to a wide range of interpretations, and not all aspects of personal finance have returned to normal. The year to December 2002 saw the average house price rise by 22.24 per cent (according to the Land Registry for England and Wales, *Property Price Report*, February 2003), and this had more effect on private individuals' total wealth than the stock market bubble ever did. You are going to have fewer worries about your credit card debt, paying off your mortgage, university top-up fees or your pension if you know your house is worth £25,000 more this year than it did last year. However, this rate of increase is clearly 'abnormal' and will not continue forever. It is wise to remember that it is perfectly possible for house prices to decrease by the same amount in a 12-month period.

There are an infinite number of 'indicators' that people watch that let them know what is going on in the economy, including house price growth, stock market rises, interest rate levels, general inflation, and more complex ratios such as stock and bond yields. Professional investors spend enormous sums of money on sophisticated computer programs that monitor all these changes. The average individual cannot realistically do this. And we would strongly argue that you should not even try – there are better things to do with your life!

This book will try to guide you with its feet firmly based in reality. There is no advantage in making financial decisions based on unrealistic assumptions; they will only make you feel good about yourself for a short-lived, optimistic period. Our approach is a more cautious and, we feel, more sensible one. We shall travel through a financial life, covering all aspects likely to be encountered from birth to death. We shall, however, examine the issues not in chronological order but in three segments based on financial caution.

The three levels of financial competence

We have identified three distinct categories that need to be attended to in your journey towards financial comfort. The three quotations that opened this chapter give a flavour of each of these three levels of financial competence.

Level 1

> Money can't buy you happiness but it does bring you a more pleasant form of misery.
>
> *Spike Milligan*

While money clearly does not buy you happiness, it can take away a lot of stress and worry if you have a sufficient amount of it. This level is the bare minimum of financial planning you should do to ensure that you do not run out of money, either from overspending or failing to provide for your basic requirements.

Level 2

> In the long term we are all dead.
>
> *J M Keynes*

Lord Keynes, when he pointed out that 'in the long term we are all dead', was noting that usually most financial objectives can be achieved if we wait long enough. However, you may not be around to appreciate that moment when it arrives. This level of financial caution is about maximizing your resources so that you can also enjoy them. There is little use in working hard at your finances if you never get to enjoy their benefits. Organizing your finances is a balancing act between planning for the future and living for today.

Level 3

> There are two types of forecasters, those 'who don't know' and those 'who don't know they don't know'.
>
> *J K Galbraith*

Having ensured your financial foundations in Level 1 and carefully managed your assets to maximize your risk/reward return through Level 2, only now should you consider increasing the level of risk you take on through more adventurous savings and investment. This is the level that the world at large has come to think of, incorrectly, as the core of personal finance, whereas to our minds it is the icing on the cake. As John Kenneth Galbraith remarked, forecasting what investments are going to do is a very uncertain game and will take a mixture of time, skill and nerve.

In terms of actual areas of finance, Level 1 will focus on broad financial planning, especially debt and how to avoid it and how to get out of it; the role of insurance to protect your current assets and standard of living; and finally pension provision to provide for your non-earning future.

While the different components that comprise the first level of financial competence will all apply to the vast majority of readers, those of the second level of financial competence are more diverse. Depending on readers' situations, needs and aspirations you can pick and choose which elements are relevant to your own situation. The single most important element will probably be choosing and managing your mortgage. Other areas we look at are private healthcare, long-term care for the elderly, and taking out loans for one-off expenditure items such as cars, building projects and special holidays. For those who have children we look at the costs associated with their arrival, their education, especially further education, weddings, and finally good tax planning and management.

When you feel that you are happy that you have ordered all these elements to enable you to live your life fully and relatively stress-free, you can look to set aside money that will increase your total wealth through various forms of savings and investment. Our third level of financial competence looks at the opportunities and pitfalls you may encounter when you choose to delve into this exciting arena.

We hope you do not find organizing your personal finances too stressful – with a little planning and slightly more discipline it should really not be that complicated. Above all don't obsess about it, as it is only a means to an end – the end being to enjoy yourself in the long term.

Part 1

Financial Competence: Level 1

Money can't buy you happiness but it does bring you a more pleasant form of misery.

The comedian Spike Milligan

This first section of the book introduces the subjects of financial intermediaries and financial planning, then deals with three areas that everyone needs to master before they can contemplate more interesting and enjoyable areas of personal financial management. They are dealing with debt; providing for your future retirement and providing for catastrophe. For simplicity we call these chapters:

- Debts and loans.
- Pensions.
- Essential insurance.

Planning for your childrens future?

...don't ask the piggy bank!

...find a highly qualified independent financial adviser

SOFA "Find an Adviser"

The Society of Financial Advisers (SOFA) is offering a free **'Find an Adviser'** service on the internet. Only those advisers who hold SOFA's professional designations MSFA (Members), ASFA (Associates) and FSFA (Fellows) are on the website.

- All advisers are **Independent**
- All advisers have the Advanced Financial Planning Certificate (AFPC) as a minimum qualification
- You can search by postcode, town or name
- You can select how you wish to pay for the advice either by fees, commission or a mixture of both

Make sure that your money is in expert hands.

 Visit our website at **www.sofa.org** or call 020 7417 4442 for your FREE guide to Financial Planning

The Society of Financial Advisers (SOFA) 20, Aldermanbury, London, EC2V 7HY

1

Financial intermediaries

The truth is that at some stage or another you ought to consult a financial intermediary, which might be a financial adviser, an accountant, a stockbroker or just your bank or building society. There is something a little unsettling about speaking to an expert about your financial affairs; you are inevitably having to put your trust in someone you probably do not know, and the decisions you take will involve your hard-earned cash and your future security. Added to this, the financial advice industry has created a bad name for itself in the last few years, with a series of scandals, most prominently on pensions and endowment mortgage mis-selling. It is no wonder that plenty of people put off the moment they make these decisions for many months, sometimes years, sometimes forever. But delaying making financial decisions is probably the worst choice you can make.

Types of financial intermediary

There is a range of different financial intermediaries that you may come across. For general financial information on planning, budgeting and financial product selection you will need to speak to a financial adviser. For more specific investment advice a stockbroker will be able to guide you, but a stockbroker cannot recommend pension or insurance products. An accountant can help with your budgeting and tax problems but again will not be able to recommend other financial products unless he or she is a certified financial adviser as well. An insurance broker will only be able to suggest insurance products to you. Finally your bank branch will have financial advisers it is more than willing to put you in touch with, who will be different people from the tellers or your normal branch manager.

Choosing a financial adviser

For general advice you will probably want to speak to a financial adviser. However, choosing which adviser requires two more decisions – what type of adviser you need, and how you wish to be charged. Financial advisers come in three varieties: tied, multi-tied and independent.

Tied

When you go to your bank and ask to see a financial adviser it will arrange a meeting with a bank employee, who will be trained in giving financial advice. However, he or she will be limited to recommending products supplied by the bank or its partners. This is a tied financial adviser. Tied advisers work directly for large financial companies and only sell their own products. It is important to bear in mind that these are agents, working for a company, and strictly speaking not advisers working for you.

Multi-tied

A multi-tied adviser is a rarer beast, and these have only been allowed by the Financial Services Agency (FSA) in recent years. The multi-tied agent markets products from several different financial institutions. This is really a cost-sharing exercise by large financial corporations, allowing them to cross-sell each other's products. Ultimately, though, the multi-tied adviser is still limited to recommending a product from a small selection of companies.

Independent financial advisers (IFAs)

For a truly impartial opinion that allows you to be offered the most suitable products from the whole financial services industry, you should consult an independent financial adviser (IFA). This is someone who has no connection with any product supplier. His or her continued income comes from a reputation of giving 'best advice', so that clients come back for more.

Paul Boateng, the Treasury minister, stated in a parliamentary question in August 2003 that of the 5,574 complaints upheld regarding advice on 'other investment products' in the year 2002/3, 89 per cent involved tied advisers and only 11 per cent IFAs. The figure was even higher regarding mortgage endowment products specifically.

People go to tied agents because they are easily accessible through their normal financial services, banks and building societies. If you have built up a good relationship with one of these companies you are likely to trust it. Clearly, tied advisers are not all going to give you bad advice, and with new government-rated CAT products (products that meet basic standards on cost, access and terms: see Chapter 16) you can have more certainty that your purchase will at least be sound, even if it is not the optimum for you. We advocate using an IFA, though.

Charging system

If you decide that an IFA would be best to advise you, you still need to make a further decision – how do you wish to pay for his or her services? There are three options. You pay the adviser a fee based on hours worked, or fixed in advance; you pay the adviser a commission based on your purchases; or you pay part fee and part commission. The FSA recently considered disallowing the commission system, but backed down after a storm of protest from the industry.

Commissions

When you buy a financial product, whether it is a mortgage, life insurance or pension, part of the initial sum you invest is often separated out immediately and paid to the adviser. There are two drawbacks to this system. First, it makes the impartiality of the advice less clear. An adviser might be inclined to offer you a product that offers a good rate of commission, rather than a lower-commission one that would be more appropriate for you. Second, because the commission is typically deducted from your initial payment, it reduces the value of your investment. For example, if you pay £1,000 as an initial lump sum towards a new pension fund, a commission of £350 might immediately be deducted, so only £650 would actually be invested on your behalf. The adviser is legally bound to tell you what deductions will be made, but when there is a lot of paperwork involved you might not take this fully into account.

Fees

A fee-paying system is usually much clearer for the investor. It can be structured in a number of different ways. One alternative is for the adviser to charge by the hour: £75–150 per hour would be a reasonable expectation, depending on the adviser's experience and expertise and the type of product. Alternatively, if you are entering into an ongoing contract, a fixed monthly fee may be agreed. For investment products a percentage of the sum invested is often charged: somewhere between 0.1 per cent and 2 per cent is not unusual.

Although the fee system should be established clearly at the outset of any discussion, this method does have the downside that if you do not purchase a product you still have to pay for advice. With commission-based charges you will only pay if you make a purchase.

Commission and fees

Many IFAs will offer a combination of the two charging systems. A fee rate is agreed (say per hour), and once you have received the advice and agreed on a product, the adviser receives a commission which is offset against the fee. If the product carries a large commission, as do some life insurance products, the commission might be larger than the IFA's fee, and the difference is reinvested in the product. If the commission is less than the fee, you pay the difference. You might be given advice on a range of different products, and find that the commission on just one of them pays for all of it. This will not always be so, but so much the better when it is!

Trust and understanding

So why should you go and discuss your finances with an expert? You have just bought this book, after all; surely it will tell you all you need to know? This book will tell you the mechanics of how the financial world works. It explains the problems and pitfalls that you are likely to encounter and it highlights the options available to you. What it cannot do is understand your individual circumstances, your own unique set of needs and restraints, and so it cannot recommend any tailor-made solution.

Of course, the person who understands your personal situation best is yourself. You will be constrained by two things, however. Firstly and most importantly, it is very unlikely that you have a comprehensive knowledge of all the financial products currently on the market; and second, by definition you cannot take an objective view of your situation. A good financial adviser should help you through the decision process, and with specialist knowledge of the sector, point you in the direction of appropriate products.

Once you have established that you should discuss your affairs with an expert, the difficult bit comes next. How do you find an IFA and how do you know you can trust him or her? Trust is the core to your having a successful relationship with an adviser, and to a large extent it will be built on your knowledge of who the IFA is and how he or she operates.

Identifying your starting point

There are two likely scenarios when you are looking for a financial adviser. One is that you are aware that you have done nothing about organizing your finances in recent years, if ever, and need to overhaul them. The other is that you are relatively happy with the majority of your finances but there is a specific area you would like to discuss. The first scenario is easier to deal with, and once you have built a relationship with an adviser and are happy with him or her, further specific discussions will be easier.

The second scenario presumes you do not already have a trusted adviser, and here the situation becomes more complex. Many financial advice books state that before you start looking for an adviser it is essential that you should be clear in your own mind what you want advice about. This is good advice as far as it goes, but very few financial decisions can be taken without considering your situation as a whole. For example, a decision about pension provision would need to consider your savings, your mortgage costs and other monthly expenses, and your health and life expectancy. For an adviser to suggest a pension plan without enquiring about these aspects would be irresponsible, negligent and these days illegal.

However, although most financial discussions will be far-ranging, you should still be clear why you want to see an adviser. If it is pensions you are going to discuss, then by all means discuss your other financial products, but do not let the agenda change to a wholesale reorganization of your financial affairs.

Finding an IFA

To work out your figures – get the right letters first

So what are the basic requirements in looking for an adviser? There are some very simple rules that must be followed. The first and the most critical is to ensure that your adviser is registered with the FSA. If he or she is not registered with the FSA, he/she will not legally be allowed to give financial advice, and indeed to do so is an offence. If he or she is registered with the FSA, he or she will have some professional qualification to further assure you of his or her expertise.

Find out what qualifications and experience your adviser has. The minimum and mandatory qualification is the Financial Planning Certificate (FPC), but the IFAs' own promotion body (IFAP) admits that this is really only equivalent to a 'challenging GCSE or 'O' Level'. Table 1.1 sets out other well-recognized qualifications that a financial adviser may have. The possession of further qualifications does not mean that the adviser is necessarily better than one who does not have those qualifications – experience and being able to get on with the client are also important – but it does show that the adviser has taken the extra time

Table 1.1 IFA qualifications

Initial	Name	Awarding body	General (G) or specialist (S) qualification
MAQ	Mortgage Advice Qualification	Chartered Insurance Institute (CII)	Mostly specialist
AFPC	Advance Financial Planning Certificate	CII	G
ACII	Associate, Chartered Insurance Institute	CII	G
FCII	Fellow, Chartered Insurance Institute	CII	G
MSFA	Member, Society of Financial Advisers	Society of Financial Advisers (SOFA)	G
ASFA	Associate, Society of Financial Advisers	SOFA	G
FSFA	Fellow, Society of Financial Advisers	SOFA	G
ALIA (dip)	Associate, Life Insurance Association	Life Insurance Association (LIA)	G
FLIA	Fellow, Life Insurance Association	LIA	G
CFP	Certified Financial Planner	Institute of Financial Planning (IFP)	G
FIFP	Fellow, Institute of Financial Planning	IFP	G
MSI	Member, Securities Institute	Securities Institute	S
FSI	Fellow, Securities Institute (Securities Inst Diploma)	Securities Institute	S
CertIM	Certificate in Investment Management	Securities Institute	S
IMC	Investment Management Certificate	UK Society of Investment Professionals (UK-SIP)	S
IMAAQ	Investment Management Asset Allocation Qualification	UK-SIP	S
CeMAP	Certificate in Mortgage Advice and Practice	Institute of Financial Services (IFS)	S
BSc Hons, ACIB	BSc Hons in Financial Services and Associateship	IFS	G
PIC	Professional Investment Certificate	IFS	S
ACIBS	Certificate in Mortgage Advice and Practice Associateship, Chartered Institute of Bankers in Scotland	Chartered Institute of Bankers in Scotland Chartered Institute of Bankers in Scotland	S S G

and effort to acquire these letters, and that indicates commitment and diligence.

Routes to finding an IFA

- The best method is to rely on recommendations from friends and associates you know well and trust.
- The Society of Financial Advisers (SOFA) has a search facility on its Web site at www.sofa.org, which enables you to search for IFAs by name, postcode or town.
- IFAP is a not-for-profit company run by an independent executive to promote the IFA industry and help put clients in touch with local IFAs. It is funded at arm's length by 27 large and well-known financial product companies, on the basis that the easier it is to find IFAs, the more people will do so, and therefore the more likely they are to buy financial products. It offers a Web site (www.unbiased.co.uk) with a search facility, and a hot line (0800 085 3250).
- If you know of an IFA close to you, you can check out his or her credentials on the FSA Web site (www.fsa.gov.uk) or on its hot line (0845 606 1234).
- Many IFAs advertise in Yellow Pages and local papers, but choosing one this way is more of a lottery.

These methods should enable you to shortlist some IFAs who fit your criteria: they are based near you and easily reached, have the right expertise and qualifications in the areas you require advice about, and have a reasonable amount of experience (they have practised in the trade for enough time to understand it). You will probably need to talk to them to find out about their charging structure, and will certainly need to do so to find out if you have a good rapport with them. Some of the things you discuss with your adviser will be complicated, some will be highly personal and most will be confidential. If you do not feel comfortable talking to your IFA you will not be getting the best out of him or her. It is essential that you are relaxed with the individual, so speak to a few over the phone and try to gauge whether this will be the case or not.

When you arrange a meeting the IFA is obliged to discover as much about your circumstances as he or she can, so as to be able to give appropriate advice. This is called the 'fact find'. Ask the IFA to send you a 'fact find' questionnaire for you to fill in and return before the meeting, so that expensive time is not used up during your meeting filling in the forms. The IFA can ask any necessary follow-up questions when you meet. Also establish your preferred charging system before you meet up. This way everyone is clear on what basis the meeting is proceeding.

Generally the more explicit the adviser is about costs and the more eager to explain things in writing, the better he or she will be. Do not, however, let the adviser bamboozle you. If you do not understand something, ask. If you do not know what happens next, ask. If you do not like something, say so. Remember you are the paying client, and it will help the adviser if you are straightforward with him or her. Finally, the more information you can provide an IFA with, the better service he or she will be able to provide you. If you know what you want to talk about and understand how the product works, that will get you off to a great start. That is partly what this book is here to help you do.

When you should not use a financial adviser

Financial advisers are not always the right solution. If you have done your own research and are happy with your findings, if you know exactly the product you are after, or if you have a specific problem that another specialist can deal with, then there is little point in adding in the expense of an adviser.

If any of these situations are familiar, you are likely to need the services of a professional who can give limited, specific advice, or will act on an 'execution only' basis: that is, he or she will just carry out your instructions. The likely areas in which you will meet these situations are buying and selling investments (for which you will need someone with access to a stock exchange or dealing room, generally a stockbroker); purchasing insurance (an insurance broker) and tax matters (an accountant). Below we briefly examine approaching each of these professionals.

Choosing a stockbroker

If you want to buy or sell shares or bonds you will need to employ someone who has access to the appropriate market places, whether that be an exchange or a dealer. The same applies for buying unit trusts and OEICs (see Chapter 16), although these can also be bought and sold direct from the managers of these investments. In most cases you will need to contact a stockbroker.

These days the Internet has made stockbrokers much cheaper at a basic level – they are no longer just for millionaires. Essentially there are two types of stockbroker for private individuals, the traditional office-based companies and the Internet ones. The traditional companies are the most varied, in terms of size, location and range of services they can provide. The Internet companies provide essentially similar services although their level of reliability and user-friendliness may vary. (See Chapter 21 for more information.)

When looking for a stockbroker you must decide what you want the broker to do for you. There are three levels of service: execution-only, advisory and discretionary.

Execution only

If you know exactly what you want to buy or sell, execution only is the cheapest option, and very well covered by the Internet companies. You can generally buy or sell investments valued from as little as £25 (although because of the charge the brokers make, such small amounts are unlikely to be profitable). The broker will charge either a fixed flat fee or a percentage of the investment. The minimum charge is likely to be around £10.

Advisory

If you would like to discuss your purchases and sales with a professional, and would also like to be notified of investment opportunities and changes to shareholdings in companies in which you own shares (splits, mergers, cash repayments and so on: see Chapter 16 for more information), you will want an advisory service from your broker. This is an ongoing contract between you and the broker, and means the firm will probably also send you quarterly or half-yearly portfolio statements. This service tends to only be provided by 'traditional' brokers, and they will charge you a yearly fee for the service plus commission on any sales or purchases.

Discretionary

Finally, there is discretionary management (also known as 'full service' or 'portfolio management') where the stockbroker manages your investments (that is, buys and sells shares and other instruments) at his or her own judgement and timing. This service is usually only provided to people with a significant minimum amount available to invest, generally from £50,000 upwards depending on the broker. Again only 'traditional' brokers offer this service, and the cost will generally be a percentage of the portfolio value plus buying and selling commission, although the commission rates are likely to be much lower than for an advisory service.

For information on Internet brokers and how to find them see Chapter 21. Traditional brokers come in all shapes and sizes, from vast multinational banking firms (like Citigroup and HSBC) to country-wide firms of brokers (such as Hargreaves Lansdown and Brewin Dolphin) to solicitor investment managers and regional stockbrokers. Which one best suits you will depend on how often you will want to use the firm and what type of relationship you expect to have with it. As with financial advisers, you must check that the broker is registered with the FSA to ensure you will be covered by the Financial Services Compensation Scheme. You may also want to know whether it offers share management schemes, nominee schemes, 24-hour trading, and so on. See Chapter 16 for more information on these. However, the most important factor may well be how well you get on with the broker!

Choosing an accountant

Finding an accountant is a similar process to finding an adviser, but should be simpler. It is perfectly possible to manage your financial affairs without the help of an accountant, but if there are any complex tax issues involved, accountants are there to help. Many firms of accountants do not have the time to deal with private finances as they focus on business accounts. You will need to find a company that is small enough to be interested in having you as a client, or a larger one with a department that specializes in personal taxation and the like.

The best way to find an accountant is once again personal recommendation. Failing that, the trade bodies for accountants have search facilities. Beware: anyone can call him or herself an accountant, but to be professionally recognized the individual must have qualified as either a chartered or a certified accountant. Chartered accountants are regulated in England and Wales by the Institute of Chartered Accountants for England and Wales (ICAEW: www.icaewfirms.co.uk) and in Scotland by the Institute of Chartered Accountants of Scotland (ICAS: www.icas.org.uk). Membership of the ICAEW allows the accountant to put the letters FCA or ACA after his or her name, and members of the ICAS use just CA. Certified accountants are regulated by the Association of Chartered Certified Accountants (ACCA, www.acca-business.org/dom/) and put FCCA or ACCA after their name. The Web sites listed above all have search facilities by location.

Choosing a bank

There are still many people in the UK who do not have a bank account. A study by the FSA in 2001 discovered that 17 per cent of the adult population do not have bank accounts, and amongst the poorer sectors of the population this figure rose to over one quarter. In response to this and because it wanted to pay social security benefits directly into bank accounts rather than by giro cheque, the government launched its Universal Bank at the Post Office in April 2003. However, this basic account does not provide a cash card or direct debit facilities. Most of the high street banks have also set up basic bank accounts for people with no previous credit history, or a poor one. To manage your finances properly it is essential that you have a bank account – and nowadays there is no excuse not to.

Banks have been through a rough time in the last decade. Their reputations have been knocked as they have tried to balance being profitable for their shareholders and useful to their customers. They still have an ability to get things wrong – and your eventual choice of bank will be as much to do with reliability and friendliness as the exact services it offers.

In today's environment people have less need than ever before to visit their bank branch. They can get money and check their balance at cash machines, have their wages paid in directly to their account by their employer and manage their bills by direct debits. With access to the Internet they can also transfer money by computer from their office or homes, and see their transactions on screen within moments of their occurring. So what is to choose between one bank and another? It is when things go wrong that the differences between banks or even branches become clear. If you see that an item in your statement is wrong, does your bank make it simple to call someone to rectify this? Do you speak to the branch or a call centre? If you can have personal recommendation that a particular branch is well run, and it is convenient for you, that is probably the best route to take. More likely you will find people warn you off certain branches and banks.

If you do not have an account already, go to all the main high street banks and see which is friendliest, has the shortest queues, and the most staff behind the counter. Then find out what types of account it would be happy to open for you straight away, and what facilities come with those accounts (such as cards, overdrafts and interest rates). Do not be persuaded to join a bank because it offers you a free gimmick, such as a CD voucher or kitbag – in a month's time that will be of little importance to you, but you will be lumbered with its services.

You can, of course, change banks easily if you are unsatisfied with the service. If you already have an account and a reasonable amount of money in it, the rates of interest payable (or charged on overdrafts) become more important. It is always worth checking these interest rates a couple of times a year, and considering whether your money would be better served in another account or with another bank. (See Chapter 15 for further information.)

2

Financial planning

The core of successfully managing your finances is not being a brilliant identifier of financial products and outwitting the financial markets, it is much more mundane than that. Successful managers of their finances are people who have sat down and worked out their likely financial wants and needs as early in their lives as possible. Personal financial success all comes down to long-term planning. This planning will produce the best results if you have an understanding of the probable way your lifestyle will develop, and combine this with a basic understanding of how the financial markets and products work.

For this reason it is well worth taking a quick look at some basic economic facts and figures that affect people's finances. With some solid information as background knowledge it is much easier to judge the merits or problems of any particular financial product, so you can decide whether it is appropriate for you or not. This will also enable you to 'see' the patterns that affect your finances in relation to your life. Finally it will help to put in perspective the importance of time in choosing a financial product.

This is usually the point that most people 'switch off' – but bear with us, it is worth doing and not as complex, or boring, as you might expect!

The basic rules

We all like to think that there is a magic formula to having enough money instantly. In fact there is: if you win the lottery, the pools, the premium bonds jackpot, have an unknown Great Aunt Doris with untold millions in her will, or discover a Rembrandt in your attic. If you think the odds on any of these actually happening are stacked against you, you have taken your first sensible step towards sorting out your finances. Most of us, it is hoped, will have decided this a long time ago.

Rule One is that money does not arrive instantly or by magic. If it does not arrive instantly, then how does it arrive? Simple: it arrives slowly. The only reliable, low-risk way to collect money (that is, to have savings) is to do it slowly, little by little, over a long period of time. If you need money today to buy something substantial, such as a house deposit or a car or a new central heating system, the very best way to pay for it is to use money you started saving years ago. Before you cry out, 'That's all very well, but I didn't start saving years ago, and I do need the money now', there are plenty of other ways to find money now – but they are not the best (that is, the cheapest) ones. We shall see why this is so in more detail later on.

Rule Two is to try to start saving as early in your life as you can. The sooner you start, the better it will be. This is to do with the 'time value of money' and 'compound interest rates'. If you do not know about these, they may sound off-putting, but you should understand the concepts by the end of this chapter. Once you know about them, you will realize the benefit of starting to save today and the drawbacks of putting it off until tomorrow.

Life cycles

The famous economist Franco Modigliani, who died in September 2003, described the relationship between a person's income and his or her will-ingness to save. As economics textbooks would have it, 'the standard life-cycle model as presented here is firmly grounded in expected utility theory and assumes rational behaviour'. Whatever that means. What the person in the street needs to visualize is that over the course of your working life your income generally increases until you retire, after which your income will come from savings you made while you were working. This is obvious when you think about it from a distance, but it is easy to do nothing about it when you are earning most.

See Figure 2.1. The top curve represents a typical income – minimal in childhood, increasing until retirement, then falling off – and the bottom curve represents the amount that can be saved. The gap between the two curves is the amount of expenditure, which is taken to be minimal in childhood, when parents (hopefully) carry your costs.

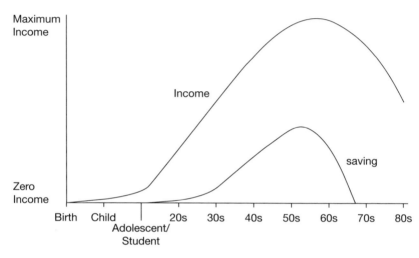

Figure 2.1   Savings and income chart

In a perfect world your income would increase steadily throughout your working life, and for the majority of that working period you would be saving a part of your annual earnings to provide for you when you retire. In reality things are never as smooth as in the graph. We almost all experience large or small increases and decreases in our income and expenditure, for example when we change houses, change jobs, or get a salary increase. Our savings pattern alters to reflect these changes, but generally the rule holds that as your income increases, so should the amount you save.

Figure 2.2 suggests what a more 'real' savings and income pattern might look like. Part of the 'savings' line in this graph is below the x (horizontal) axis, representing points at which instead of saving, the individual is incurring debt. The figure assumes that up till the late teens – where the vertical line is drawn – parents will in fact cover costs, so the notional 'debt' is written off at this age. When the savings line is above the horizontal line you are actually starting to save. The savings area minus the debt area to the right of the vertical line then represents the amount of money this individual can save over his or her lifetime.

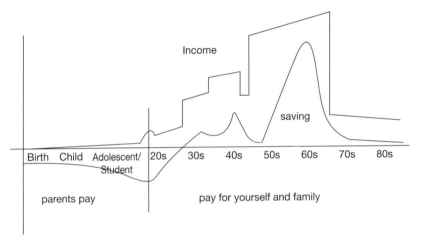

Figure 2.2   Real savings and income chart

Your aim in drawing up your own graph should be to make the savings area as large as possible while still enjoying a good life. There is little point in going to meet your maker with your bank balance at bursting point if you have had a miserable time while alive because you have just been saving. Figure 2.2 emphasizes that while the window of opportunity to save is quite extended, it *is* generally limited. Someone with an income and expenditure pattern similar to the one in the chart has approximately 35 years to accumulate savings. This is good news if you start saving in your late twenties to early thirties, as 35 years is a long time in savings! The bad news is that this is also the period when the pressure to spend is at its highest.

Let's now take a look at expenditure patterns. Figure 2.3 suggests how much an individual might 'cost' at certain ages. It is based on an individual's personal expenditure as a proportion of the whole household's expenditure. Obviously this is a very inexact model, but hopefully it will help to build the picture we are after. The figures are based on the household being made up of four people, with both parents working. When you are a baby or child your food and drink bill is likely to be small in comparison to your parents', as will be your leisure expenses. The reason the tallest column in the chart is for people in their twenties is that at this point the example expects them to have left the family household and started to share accommodation. The rent for this will probably be more than a quarter share in a £100,000 mortgage (at today's low rates), and car and food costs will probably not be shared as efficiently as they would be between a married couple or per head of family.

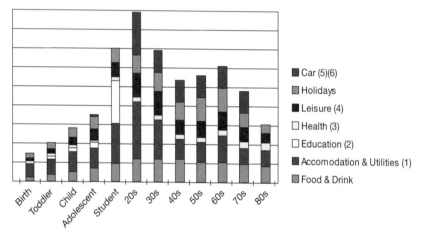

Figure 2.3   Individual life cycle expenditure by age group

Assumptions used:
1. Accommodation based on average mortgage of £100,000 at 5 per cent, and divided by the space taken up by the individual as part of the household: baby = 0.1666 of household; toddler = 0.2 of household; child and adolescent = 0.25 of household; student = shared below-average rent (£65/wk); 20s = shared above-average rent (£100/wk); 30s = 0.5 of household; 40s = 0.25 of household; 50s = 0.25 of household; 60s = 0.33 of household; 70s = paid off mortgage; 80s = paid off mortgage. Utilities based on average gas and electricity figures (£800), plus a telephone charge (£500), plus £2,000 of repairs/insurance/council tax, divided by household size (total = £3,300).
2. Education includes books, uniforms, kit and student fees.
3. This figure presumes a health insurance premium plus incidental medicines.
4. Meals out, cinema, theatre, sport expenditure plus presents, clothes, incidental expenditure.
5. £20,000 loan repayment at 12 per cent (£2,500), insurance (£600), servicing (£500), petrol (£20 × 52 = £1,040) = c £4,600.
6. Increased insurance for extra driver.

Although the individual's peak costs are greater in his/her twenties, this is not to say that life gets cheaper for most people after they are in their twenties, because this is the stage at which many of us acquire dependent children. Figure 2.4 charts likely total household expenditure by the age of the main wage earner, and shows how life gets progressively more costly until children start leaving home. This might not occur until the parents are in their late fifties these days. Finally the chart suggests that although total *household* expenditure falls when people are in their sixties, *individual* expenditure increases at this point – it is just that there are fewer individuals! (The notes to the figure explain the example's assumptions more fully.) It is as well to have the pattern clearly in your mind as you consider planning your finances.

So we are left with the situation where your opportunity to save increases as you progress through your working life, but if you have a family to support, then so does your expenditure. None of this is rocket science, but it is as well to have the pattern clearly in your mind as you consider planning your finances.

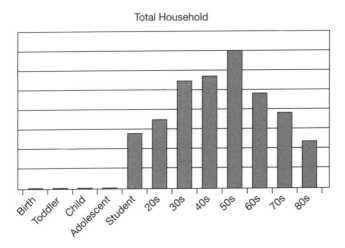

Figure 2.4   Household expenditure chart by age group

Economic cycles and recent economic history

If you draw up projected income and expenditure charts on these lines, you will have an idea of when you should start saving, how long you should be saving for, and roughly how much you should save at each point. The next big question is where and how to invest your savings. (Part 3 of this book covers this in more detail.) A worry many people have is finding the right moment to put their hard-earned money into an investment. It is very irritating to buy an investment and see it go down in value straight away, whether it is shares, a pension fund, or a house. However, the critical factor is not an investment's value at any given moment, but its value when you want (or need) to sell it. In essence your motto ought to be 'time rather than timing'.

In the introduction we mentioned various indicators that financial professionals monitor, such as house price growth, stock market rises, interest rate levels, general inflation, and more complex ratios such as stock and bond yields. We shall briefly look at these, but first let us examine how the UK economy as a whole has performed in recent decades.

Every government likes to say that it has created an economic marvel, either in creating consistent above-average growth or alternatively by preventing the economy from slowing down more than it might otherwise have done 'were it not for the government's management'. At the same time the opposition parties always suggest that the country's economy is being bungled by a bunch of incompetent ministers. The truth only becomes clear some time later, when the country's economic statistics are published and the course the economy has taken can be seen.

The main measure of the country's economic performance is the Gross Domestic Product (GDP): how much the country creates in monetary terms in a given time period. (Exactly how this is calculated is a complicated process and the minutiae of how it is done are not important to us here.) Figure 2.5 shows the economic rate of growth, or the year-on-year increase in GDP. Each bar of the chart represents one year's growth, while the line indicates the year-on-year increase, measured against the scale on the right. Figures 2.6 to 2.11 provide some more standard financial indicators.

Of course all graphs and statistics can give false impressions. Figure 2.5 suggests that 1975 had an amazing growth spurt of over 26 per cent, but when we look at the inflation statistics for that year (Figure 2.6) we see 1975 had average inflation of 24.2 per cent and the real growth was only just over 2 per cent (Figure 2.7). It is Figure 2.7 that gives us a truer indication of how the economy performed.

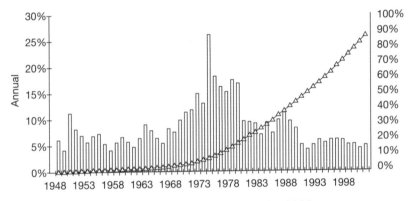

Figure 2.5   UK GDP growth 1948–2002

Compiled with data from the ONS

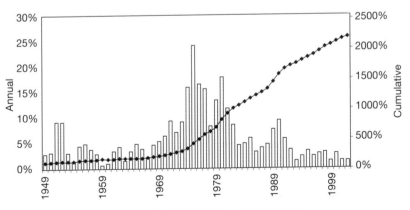

Figure 2.6   UK inflation 1949–2002

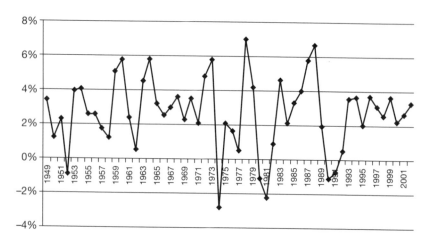

Figure 2.7 UK real GDP growth 1949–2002

Compiled with data from the ONS

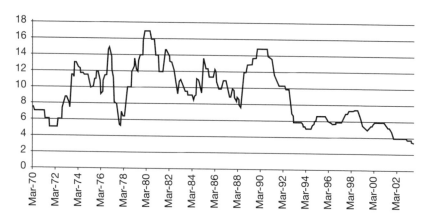

Figure 2.8 Bank of England base rates 1970–2004

Compiled with data from Bank of England and ONS

The current Chancellor, Gordon Brown, is much taken with the concept of economic 'prudence' and is inclined to roar out during his budget speech that under his Chancellorship 'there will be no return to boom and bust'. When we look at Figure 2.7 we can see clearly what he is referring to. From 1965 to 1971 the country's economic growth as

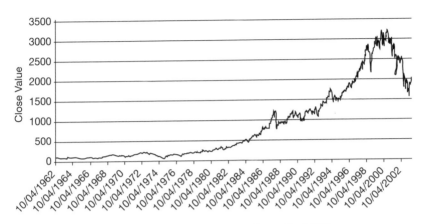

Figure 2.9 FTSE All-Share Index 1962–2003

Compiled with data from FTSE.com

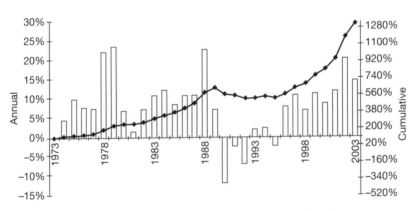

Figure 2.10 UK House Price Index 1973–2003

Compiled with data from the ONS

measured by changes in real GDP was relatively stable, remaining around 3 per cent per year, and always between the 2 per cent and 4 per cent lines. With the entry to the EEC growth shot up, and then with the 1973 oil crisis, growth disappeared. This was the first and most savage of the recent 'boom and bust' cycles, which lasted four years from 1971 to 1975.

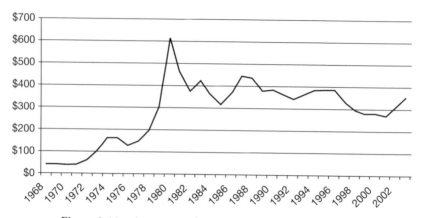

Figure 2.11   Average yearly London gold price 1968–2003

Compiled with data from kitco.com and goldinfo.net

In 1975 economic growth returned to more or less the same rate it had had in 1971. These rates continued for the next two decades, with North Sea oil coming online, and the trade union unrest at the end of the Callaghan government, which was followed by the 1980s booms and busts as the new Tory government struggled with union reform and new types of economic management focusing exclusively on the money supply. In fact, the period of Mrs Thatcher's prime ministership was marked by wild swings in economic growth. It was not until John Major's time that the UK economy gained a more stable footing, possibly as a result of the dramatic restructuring of the years before.

Since 1993, however, the UK's economy has been remarkably stable, once more maintaining a position somewhere between 2 per cent and 4 per cent growth per year. Whether through good management, good timing or good luck (probably a mixture of all three) Mr Brown has indeed kept the economy stable, despite financial crises in the Far East, the Internet bubble, massive financial scandals in the United States and the war against terrorism.

One of the main tools the Treasury used during this period to control the economy was the base rate, the interest rate that the Bank of England charges. Figure 2.8 shows that since the economy stabilized in the early 1990s the swings in the level of the interest rate have also moderated. In the last decade the base rate has stayed within a 4 per cent band, with a maximum at 7.5 per cent and the minimum at the end of 2003 of 3.5 per cent, a 30-year low. After the 1997 election the Treasury gave the Bank of England responsibility for base rates – and so far this appears to have been wisely managed.

Figures 2.9, 2.10 and 2.11 show the performance of three different types of investment, as opposed to economic results: the two major investments private individuals are likely to make, in the stock market and the housing market, and the price of gold for comparison. In an ideal world all investments would increase in value at a steady and sustainable rate, producing a chart that rises gently from left to right.

Figure 2.9 shows the performance of the FT All-Share Index, which represents nearly all the companies on the London stock market, and more importantly is the longest-running of the current indices. It is slightly less volatile than the FTSE 100 index of leading shares. Figure 2.10 shows the annual and year-on-year increase in average house prices. As with the stock market this has been a pretty bumpy ride in the last few decades. With good luck and good timing great increases in wealth have been available in both sectors, but equally those who caught the bandwagons late and did not stay on them have lost a lot of cash. The important pattern to note is that over extended periods of time both these graphs are on rising curves. If you have invested in either the stock market or the housing market for over a decade you will always have made money, and the longer you have held 'average' investments for, the more you will have improved your financial position in relation to the alternative of just holding money in a savings account.

The lesson we can draw from looking at economic history is that regardless of inflation peaks and interest rate changes, the two main investment categories have historically continued to rise in value. We have just witnessed a large and prolonged stock market slump, but history suggests that within 10 years the market will have recovered and once again be profitably above its previous high. The All-Share Index was at its peak (3167) in September 2000; we shall have to see if it exceeds this level by September 2010.

As an aside it is worth also looking at some of the less popular investment types. Although Figure 2.11 features gold prices, it could equally show the price trends for antiques, art or any other collectible or commodity. These markets are smaller than the housing and stock markets (that is, fewer people trade in them) and are therefore more volatile. They are also prone to non-financially based 'fashions'. (The stock market and housing are also prone to 'fashions' but these tend to be grounded in some sort of financial rationale.) This makes trends in these minor markets much more difficult to predict, even over an extended period. Those who invested in gold in 1980 are still waiting for the price per ounce to return to the same level nearly a quarter of a century later. Obviously it is possible to make a lot of money in these sectors, but it requires more specialist knowledge.

Time value of money and compound interest rates

In this chapter we have seen that we have a reasonably large but still limited period in which to accumulate our life's savings. We have also noted that our expenses tend to increase as we get older, at least until we are into our late fifties or sixties if we have a family. In the previous section we saw that the performance of the economy is beyond our (and often anyone else's) control, but that investments in the two main private investment sectors have tended to perform well over 10 years or more. All these ideas point to starting to invest or save as early as possible to allow you to reap the most benefit.

Part of the reason that time is so important is the 'magic' of compound interest. If you put £1,000 into a savings account which pays 5 per cent interest every year, you will have £1,050 at the end of year one, but at the end of year two you will have earned your 5 per cent not on £1,000 but on £1,050. 5 per cent of £1,050 is £52.50, so your savings total will be £1,102.50. This does not seem like a huge extra increase, but if we carry on the process for 10 or 15 years the difference becomes quite noticeable, and substantially larger each year. Table 2.1

Table 2.1 Compound and simple interest compared for an initial investment of £1,000 with a notional interest rate of 5%

Year	Non-compounded annual interest	Compounded annual interest	Total Investment (non-compounded)	Total Investment (compounded)
1	£50	£50.00	£1,050.00	£1,050.00
2	£50	£52.50	£1,100.00	£1,102.50
3	£50	£55.13	£1,150.00	£1,157.63
4	£50	£57.88	£1,200.00	£1,215.51
5	£50	£60.78	£1,250.00	£1,276.28
6	£50	£63.81	£1,300.00	£1,340.10
7	£50	£67.00	£1,350.00	£1,407.10
8	£50	£70.36	£1,400.00	£1,477.46
9	£50	£73.87	£1,450.00	£1,551.33
10	£50	£77.57	£1,500.00	£1,628.89
11	£50	£81.44	£1,550.00	£1,710.34
12	£50	£85.52	£1,600.00	£1,795.86
13	£50	£89.79	£1,650.00	£1,885.65
14	£50	£94.28	£1,700.00	£1,979.93
15	£50	£99.00	£1,750.00	£2,078.93
16	£50	£103.95	£1,800.00	£2,182.87
Total interest earned	£800.00	£1,182.87		

gives an example. By the sixteenth year the compounded interest total is nearly half as large again as the non-compounded interest total, making the whole investment over 20 per cent larger than it would have been otherwise. The critical part to notice is that the big extra increases gained by compounding occur after a few years have gone by. In years 1 to 4 the investment is only gaining a few pounds more than it would otherwise have done, but from year 5 onwards the compounded investment is earning over 20 per cent more than the non-compounded version, and by year 16 it is over double the rate.

Compound interest can therefore work its 'magic' for your savings – but it requires a little time before the benefits can really be seen.

Beware, however: compound interest can also work against you. If you are borrowing money rather than saving it, the compounded interest rate piles up in favour of the lender. Tables 2.2 and 2.3 give examples of someone borrowing £10,000 at 7 per cent compound interest and paying

Table 2.2 Repayment of a £10,000 loan at 7 per cent compound interest, at £2,000 per year

1 Year	2 Loan Outstanding (column 2 minus column 6)	3 Interest on Loan Outstanding	4 Total Outstanding (2 plus 3)	5 Yearly Repayment	6 Capital Repayments (5 minus 3)
1	£10,000	£700.00	£10,700.00	£2000.00	£1,300.00
2	£8,700.00	£609.00	£9,309.00	£2000.00	£1,391.00
3	£7,309.00	£511.63	£7,820.63	£2000.00	£1,488.37
4	£5,820.63	£407.44	£6,228.07	£2000.00	£1,592.56
5	£4,228.07	£295.97	£4,524.04	£2000.00	£1,704.03
6	£2,524.04	£176.68	£2,700.72	£2000.00	£1,823.32
7	£700.72	£49.05	£749.77	£749.77	£749.77
Total interest paid		£2749.77			

Table 2.3 Repayment of a £10,000 loan at 7 per cent compound interest, at £1,000 per year

1 Year	2 Loan outstanding (2 minus 6 from row above)	3 Interest on loan outstanding	4 Total outstanding (2 plus 3)	5 Yearly repayment	6 Capital repayments (5 minus 3)
1	£10,000.00	£700.00	£10,700.00	£1000.00	£300.00
2	£9,700.00	£679.00	£10,379.00	£1000.00	£321.00
3	£9,379.00	£656.53	£10,035.53	£1000.00	£343.47
4	£9,035.53	£632.49	£9,688.02	£1000.00	£367.51
5	£8,668.02	£606.76	£9,274.78	£1000.00	£393.24
6	£8,274.78	£579.23	£8,854.01	£1000.00	£420.77
7	£7,854.01	£549.78	£8,403.79	£1000.00	£450.22
8	£6,922.06	£484.54	£7,406.60	£1000.00	£481.73
9	£6,406.60	£448.46	£6,855.07	£1000.00	£551.54
10	£5,855.07	£409.85	£6,264.92	£1000.00	£590.15
11	£5,264.92	£368.54	£5,633.46	£1000.00	£631.46
12	£4,633.46	£324.34	£4,957.81	£1000.00	£675.66
13	£3,957.81	£277.05	£4,234.85	£1000.00	£722.95
14	£3,234.85	£226.44	£3,461.29	£1000.00	£773.56
15	£2,461.29	£172.29	£2,633.58	£1000.00	£827.71
16	£1,633.58	£114.35	£1,747.93	£1000.00	£885.65
17	£747.93	£52.36	£800.29	£800.29	£800.29
Total interest paid		7800.29			

back either £2,000 a year or £1,000 a year. If half as much is paid back each year, the total cost of the loan nearly trebles because of the compound interest.

The effect of compound interest is seen in a huge range of financial products, both those that work for you (savings and investment) and those that work against you (loans and mortgages). We will return to the concept throughout this book.

Budgeting

All this information guides us in one direction. It is very important to plan for your personal finances, and plan for them as early as you possibly can. This is not easy, as you cannot know what your future wants and needs will be, or how much they will cost. For example, if you started your working life in the mid-1980s when the average house cost around £35,000 and the average income was about £12,500, you probably did not expect house prices to more than treble in price in the next 20 years, while average income would only double. You would not have known when or if you would get married or have children, and you would not have realized that if your children were to go to university they would need substantial financial resources to do so. Planning your future finances is an endeavour that requires you to make predictions not only about your own personal aspirations and desires but also about economic trends in the world at large. This makes it impossible to plan with any accuracy. So what can you do?

For long-term planning your only sensible course of action is to try to save a little money on a regular basis from as early as possible. As you cannot accurately know the timing or amount of your future monetary requirements, you will have to save according to your current situation. If you put aside as much cash each month as you can possibly afford without severely affecting your current standard of living, you will be doing as much as you can to prepare yourself financially for your future. In the rest of this book we look in detail at the many demands on your resources that you might encounter, and we also look at the range of alternatives you can use to maximize your investment returns.

Before you start to examine these options it is necessary to discover what 'as much cash each month as you can possibly afford without severely affecting your current standard of living' actually amounts to in your particular case. In order to do this you must draw up a statement of your current financial position: that is, a list of your income and outgoings.

This will be easy to do if you are reasonably confident and happy about your finances. If you are on the path to financial phobia, as discussed in the introduction, or if you are well ensconced in it, then this exercise will be difficult, both from a point of steeling yourself to do it and also because you are unlikely to have all the information that you will require easily to hand. But it is absolutely vital to understand what your personal income and outgoings are if you want to have your money under control. Look at drawing up the list as a form of therapy – once you have done it you will see the real situation, and you can then make definite decisions based on your findings. Without drawing up your list you will remain in ignorance until the inevitable crisis arrives, and it will be much worse to sort out.

To establish a picture of your financial position you need first to look at all your income. This should be relatively straightforward if you have a main single form of employment with a regular weekly or monthly wage. It will be more difficult if you are self-employed, only occasionally employed – in which case your income may vary from month to month – or have several sources of income (two or more jobs or income from benefits, rent or other investments). If you do have several sources of income it is likely that you will be filling in a self-assessment income tax form, which will need to have all this information on it in any case.

Once you have thought through where your income comes from and how much and how regular it is, note the month-by-month details down on one side of a piece of paper, as in the example in Table 2.4.

Then comes the trickier part – to work out your typical monthly expenses plus any occasional extra costs you incur. Some regular expenses will be simple to identify: mortgage payments or rent, council tax payments, insurance premiums for your house, contents and car, and perhaps health and travel insurance. Utility bills are more difficult to assess as they vary from bill to bill, but you should be able to make a

Table 2.4 Budgeting example: estimating your income

Month	Income description	Net income amount	Expenditure description	Expenditure amount	End of month balance
January	Salary 1 Salary 2	£2,000 £1,050			
February	Salary 1 Salary 2	£2,000 £1,050			
March	Salary 1 Salary 2	£2,000 £1,050			
April	Salary 1 Salary 2	£2,000 £1,050			
May	Salary 1 Salary 2	£2,000 £1,050			
June	Salary 1 Bonus 1 Salary 2	£2,000 £1,000 £1,050			
July	Salary 1 Salary 2	£2,000 £1,050			
August	Salary 1 Salary 2	£2,000 £1,050			
September	Salary 1 Salary 2	£2,000 £1,050			
October	Salary 1 Salary 2	£2,000 £1,050			
November	Salary 1 Salary 2	£2,000 £1,050			
December	Salary1 Bonus 1 Salary 2	£2,000 £1,000 £1,050			

reasonable approximation (especially if you have copies of your last year's bills – if not contact your utility company and see if they can provide them for you).

Other normal expenses to consider include car and travel costs, daily or weekly food bills, and occasional expenses such as holidays. The most difficult part to judge is your leisure and occasional expenses. Amongst other things these include clothes, trips to pubs and restaurants, cinema tickets, small purchases, presents and treats plus a mass of one-off items that are bought throughout normal life. It is very important to try to work out your expenditure on these items, for it is these costs that are the ones that tend to spiral out of control – precisely because they are hard to quantify.

If you have a credit card, looking at its statement and also your cash withdrawals from the bank will help identify how much you are spending in this area. If you do not have these cards or do not have a record of your statements, it is worth writing down all your purchases for a short time – ideally a month, but probably a week is more practical. If you cannot manage this then just do it for random days here and there. Eventually you will build up a picture of your occasional purchases and discover the true pattern of your spending.

Table 2.5 gives you an example of these figures added to the spreadsheet started in Table 2.4.

In this example our household has managed to save £3,880 from its disposable income of £38,600 a year. The table shows that while for most months the family kept to their regular spending pattern, some months inevitably strayed from that, for either unavoidable but foreseeable events such as the occasional boring bill (like the two insurance instalments), or unexpected ones like the new boiler they required in November. In June they spent £2,000 on a family holiday, and at Christmas with presents, extra travel and whatever they spent an additional £1,500 to their normal monthly costs. Both these two 'happy' extra expenditure events luckily took place when the main earner received a bonus. Should the bonus not have been forthcoming the family could have spent less on these events or alternatively saved less. Either way, because they knew their incomings and outgoings reasonably well they were in a position to make a well-informed choice. This is the great strength of understanding your 'cash flow', and it is as important for individuals as for businesses.

Any well-run household needs a reserve of easily accessible money to manage its cash flow ups and downs, and help with unexpected costs (like that boiler), but the family did not need to keep all its £3,880 savings readily accessible – and it could make more money putting at least some of this money in a savings scheme that provides better returns

Table 2.5 Budgeting example: estimating your expenditure

Month	Income description	Net income amount	Expenditure description	Expenditure amount	End of month balance
January	Salary 1 Salary 2	£2,000 £1,050	Mortgage Council tax Utilities Car & travel Food Leisure & purchases Monthly total	£500 £85 £150 £150 £350 £1,000 £2,235	£815
February	Salary 1 Salary 2	£2,000 £1,050	Monthly total	£2,235	£815
March	Salary 1 Salary 2	£2,000 £1,050	**Insurance** Monthly total Extraordinary monthly total	£450 £2,235 £2,685	£365
April	Salary 1 Salary 2	£2,000 £1,050	Monthly total	£2,235	£815
May	Salary 1 Salary 2	£2,000 £1,050	Monthly total	£2,235	£815
June	Salary 1 Bonus 1 Salary 2	£2,000 £1,000 £1,050	**Holiday** Monthly total Extraordinary monthly total	£2,000 £2,235 £4,235	−£1,185
July	Salary 1 Salary 2	£2,000 £1,050	Monthly total	£2,235	£815
August	Salary 1 Salary 2	£2,000 £1,050	Monthly total	£2,235	£815
September	Salary 1 Salary 2	£2,000 £1,050	**Insurance** Monthly total Extraordinary monthly total	£450 £2,235 £2,685	£365
October	Salary 1 Salary 2	£2,000 £1,050	Monthly total	£2,235	£815
November	Salary 1 Salary 2	£2,000 £1,050	**New boiler** Monthly total Extraordinary monthly total	£1,500 £2,235 £3,735	−£685
December	Salary1 Bonus 1 Salary 2	£2,000 £1,000 £1,050	Christmas expenses Monthly total Extraordinary monthly total	£1,500 £2,235 £3,735	−£685

than a bank current account. It is the basic principle of this book that the best way for most people to do this is to set up a regular monthly savings system, where a sum is 'spent' automatically and money is not saved as an afterthought. This type of regular investment is easy to arrange, but it should only be done when all more expensive debt has been paid off.

The second part to budgeting draws together most of the elements already discussed in this chapter. It is a reinforcement of the lesson that to start putting aside regular savings as early as possible is the best route to successful financial management. This element of budgeting is longer-term and concerns having money for future events, whatever they maybe.

Figures 2.12, 2.13 and 2.14 show 'timelines' for three people: Ms Cautious, Mr Livefortoday and Captain Sensible. They all have three high-cost expenses over a 15-year period, to purchase a car (£5,000), to pay for a wedding (£10,000) and to pay for a hip operation (£5,000). Plainly all three items could be done more cheaply (or more expensively), but we are presuming these are the amounts they wish to spend; and that the interest rate on their savings is again 7 per cent.

Figure 2.12 shows the value of the regular monthly savings that Ms Cautious started making 10 years ago, and also shows what her situation would have been had she started saving only five years ago. The figure does not show her 'spending' any of the money required for the three

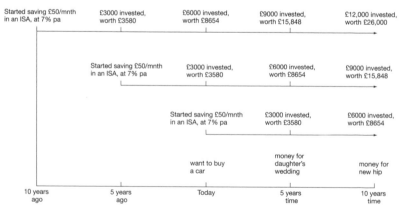

Figure 2.12   Timeline for Ms Cautious

expenses, but it does show what she has available to spend: and you can see that the regular monthly investments build up over time to a considerable sum.

Figure 2.13 shows what the cost would be for Mr Livefortoday, who has made no savings and takes out loans to meet each of the three expenses. Although the basic cost is £20,000, he will pay £36,468 once the interest charges are added in. Figure 2.14 shows our hero, Captain

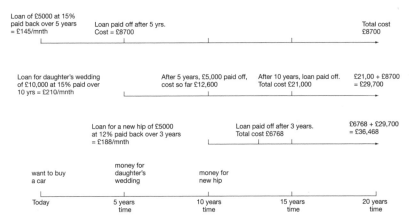

Figure 2.13   Timeline for Mr Livefortoday

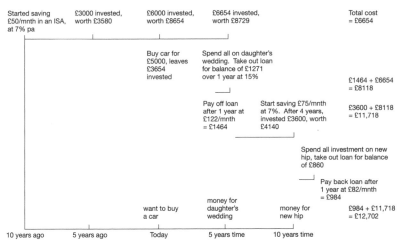

Figure 2.14   Timeline for Captain Sensible

Sensible, who has started investing early like Ms Cautious, but spends his savings when he needs the money. He then pays off any small loans he needs and continues saving.

By the '10 years time' stage, Ms Cautious has amassed £26,000 in savings but has not bought a car, her daughter has had no wedding (at least not paid for by her!) and her hip goes on aching. Mr Livefortoday has paid for these three items but is mired in debt and still has another 10 years of repayments to make. Captain Sensible has his car, a happily married daughter and walks with a spring in his step with his new hip, as he has only a year's worth of repayments to make before he can start saving again. His balanced approach has been unexciting but it has provided nicely for him.

What is worth noting is that if Captain Sensible had put aside a further £10 a month since he began saving (making £60 a month in total), he would never have needed to borrow money and would have still had over £1,500 in savings after his hip operation. Such is the power of compound interest and the passing of time. (Before we get too carried away with this route to riches, it must be pointed out that our example, for reasons of simplicity, has not included the effect of taxation on these savings, which depending on how the savings were invested to achieve the 7 per cent per annum rate, will have reduced the totals shown.)

3

Debts and loans

Taking on debt to invest in your business is considered to be good practice. In business if you want to grow quickly you are most likely to borrow money to fund your growth. So why is debt such a problem for individuals?

The problem with debt

The problem with debt is to be able to distinguish profitable debt from unprofitable debt. Businesses use debt to invest in their growth. The money they borrow is used (or should be used!) to fund new projects that will increase the business's turnover or its value. With individuals this also happens – but by no means always. Problems with debt arise when people use debt to fund their daily expenses, or worse, to purchase unnecessary but costly items.

We can categorize individuals' debt in two ways. First, is it secured? That is, does the lender have a claim on the item that is purchased with the borrowed money? The classic example of this is a mortgage on a house. The bank or building society has a legal claim on the house until the mortgage is paid off. For this reason it will be prepared to lend the money at a more attractive rate to the borrower. The second question to ask is whether the money borrowed is being used for a profitable purpose. That is, is the money being spent on something that should grow in value, or on something that will ultimately just be consumed with no monetary value left behind? Again buying a house is a good example of something that should grow in value. Spending money on a party or a holiday, however, will mean that there is nothing left (of monetary value at least) after the event.

Generally, the more security and the greater the potential growth in value of the purchased item, the cheaper the loan will be. (See Figure 3.1.)

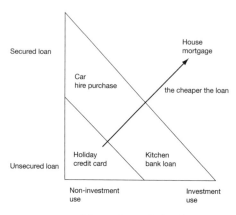

Figure 3.1 Debt chart

The other general rule is that the larger the amount you borrow, the cheaper the loan will get. There are two reasons for this. First, the lending company makes more money on larger amounts, even with lower interest (as 10 per cent of £1,000 = £100, which is still less than 5 per cent of £10,000 = £500) although the paperwork involved in adminis- trating the loan is probably the same; and second, larger loan amounts are usually, but plainly not always, more likely to be either for investment purposes (home improvements or capital goods) or securable.

Returning to the question in the opening paragraph, 'why is debt such a problem for individuals?', in recent years there has been an enormous increase in lending to individuals, the bulk of which has been secured on housing (which is fine as long as people can continue to afford their repayments if interest rates go up, and the value of their property does not fall). Figure 3.2 shows that in the last 10 years net consumer debt, which is unsecured and mostly not for investment purposes, has

TESCO
Smarter money

Need help with day to day money?

Smarter Money is a website providing help and information from Tesco to help you get smarter with your money.

It's packed with lots of straight forward information, quizzes and calculators.

We've got sections on:

- **Day to day money**
- **Borrowing money**
- **Getting insured**

Every little helps

Did you know?
The average borrower could **save over £700** a year by shopping around for mortgages, loans and credit cards.*

To find out more visit
www.tesco.com/smarter

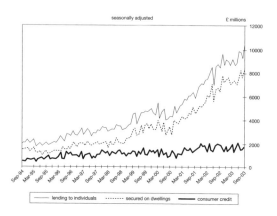

seasonally adjusted   £ millions

lending to individuals   ········ secured on dwellings   —— consumer credit

Figure 3.2 Net lending to individuals 1994–2003

Source: Bank of England

increased almost fourfold, from around £500 million a month in September 1994 to nearly £2 billion in September 2003. What is even more dangerous is that two-thirds of this debt is on credit cards – the most expensive of the debt options available to individuals.

In an ideal situation you will not have any consumer debt. This is not such an impossible position to achieve. This chapter looks at the different ways to reduce the costs of any debts you do have, and what to do if your debts have reached a crisis point. First it is important to be clear why having debt is best avoided.

Why you should not have unsecured debt

In Chapter 2 we looked at why it was so beneficial to your long-term finances to start saving as early as you can. We saw that the effects of compound interest built up over the years to enable savers to purchase the things they wanted more cheaply (that is, without having to pay interest on extra borrowing). We used in our examples in Chapter 2 a savings return rate of 7 per cent. This is the highest rate which the FSA suggests you should consider using as a long-term average for savings calculations. It is perfectly possible to earn more than this each year from your savings, but with each further increase in rate of return you are increasing the risk of the investment, and the likelihood of getting low to medium-risk returns of over 7 per cent a year on a continual basis is very small (while the base rate and inflation rate are at their current levels of around 4.5 per cent and 2.5 per cent respectively). The 7 per cent return is better than the long-term average in the stock market, even for those reinvesting their dividends (this is explored in more detail in Chapter 16).

So say your best average savings return is 7 per cent. If you are a standard rate tax payer you will pay 22 per cent on any income from your savings, or 40 per cent on any profit from selling your investments. A higher rate taxpayer will pay 40 per cent on both. This means that the maximum likely rate of return on your savings is actually going to be either just under 5.5 per cent or just over 4 per cent once you deduct tax – that is, unless you have the savings wrapped up in a tax-free vehicle like an ISA.

If you also have an unsecured loan you will be paying interest on it. The current lowest rate for an unsecured loan (with base rates at 4.5 per cent, just above their lowest level for over 30 years) is around 6 per cent per year (for a loan with conditions). The current average loan rate is 8.5 per cent. This means that on a loan of £5,000 the minimum you would pay in interest charges is £425 each year. If you were also sitting on an investment valued at £5,000, the maximum gross (that is, before tax) return you could reasonably expect would be £350. The net return (after having paid tax) would be £275. So you would be £150 worse off by keeping the savings and taking out the loan than if you cashed in the savings to provide the money you need. And this is with interest rates at historically cheap levels. The lesson here is clear: it is better to pay off expensive debt before you start accumulating savings.

How banks arrange loans

This may seem an irrelevant question, but it is helpful to understand the process from 'the other side' in order to work out how best to approach lenders yourself.

Banks know that they have got money to lend, but they worry about whether the person they lend it to is a good or bad risk. When a customer approaches a bank asking for a loan, the bank assesses the customer for his or her 'credit-worthiness' – see the box below for more information on credit scoring – to measure how likely that particular customer will be to repay the loan in full. If the customer has an acceptable credit score, the required loan amount, the length of the loan and the current interest rate applicable is fed into a computer to calculate the monthly repayment amount. This is a standard calculation that you can do yourself – see the box on page 53.

Credit scoring

Banks generally use information provided by the credit referencing agencies, principally Experian and Equifax, to assess whether someone is a good or bad risk. These companies state that they only collect facts (dates, age, marital status, amounts, addresses, missed payments, late payments and so on), not opinion, and they make this information available to banks and other lenders.

Which facts the banks use, how much weight they attach to different pieces of information, and where they set their 'pass' and 'fail' levels are usually closely guarded secrets. This means that if a lender has refused you credit you will not know which element of your credit history has caused the problem. This does have the benefit that if you try another lender it might use a different set of criteria and accept you. The downside is that the referencing agencies also record all your attempts to gain credit, and lenders may mark you down if they see you have multiple applications.

You are entitled to view the information the rating agencies hold on you, and if you do not agree with it you can apply to have it corrected. You can also add a 'Notice of Correction', a personal statement up to 200 words long that appears with your file when a lender sees it, if you feel this might help to redeem a particular impression about your credit history.

You can contact:

- **Experian** at www.experian.co.uk or on 0800 656 9000, or write to them at: PO Box 7710, Nottingham, NG80 7WE;
- **Equifax** at www.econsumer.equifax.com/consumer/uk/ or write to Equifax Credit File Advice Centre, PO Box 1140, Bradford, BD1 5US.

Things to consider to improve your credit rating

- Ensure your name is on the electoral roll.
- If companies have searched your file more than once for a single application, ask them to delete one of the searches.
- If your credit file links you to addresses you no longer have any connection with, ask the agency to correct this.
- If other people who live in your home are listed on your credit file and you have no financial connection with them, ask the agency to remove their names.

How to work out your monthly payments

There are a variety of ways to calculate the likely monthly payment amount for a loan. Before you start you need to know:

1. The amount you want to borrow (the Principal, P).
2. The time you want to pay it back over, usually in months (m).
3. The rate of interest being offered to you (i).

Option 1: If you have access to the Internet the easiest way is to look up 'loan repayment calculator' on a search engine. Make sure you find a site where you can enter the interest rate, as many sites only offer you their own interest rates. A good calculator can be found on http://money.msn.co.uk

Option 2: If you have access to a computer with a spreadsheet, you can use the future payments function. Type into a spreadsheet cell (in Excel or any spreadsheet that works similarly):

$$=\text{PMT}(\text{rate,nper,pv})$$

where *rate* is the monthly rate (the annual percentage rate (APR) divided by 12, expressed as a decimal, so that 8.3 per cent APR is $0.083/12 = 0.0069$)

nper is the number of payments: if the loan is to last four years, there will be $4 \times 12 = 48$ months of payments

pv is the present value of the loan, that is, the amount you are borrowing.

So if you want to borrow £5,000 for four years at 8.3 per cent, you would put in $=\text{PMT}(0.0069,48,5000)$ and press Return to give you the monthly payment of £122.72.

Option 3: Finally if you are handy with equations you can always try to crank the equation yourself.

$$\text{Monthly payment} = \text{Principal} \times \frac{i}{1 - (1 + i)^{-m}}$$

where i = monthly interest rate (APR/12) and m = number of payments.

Debt – how to get it and how to get rid of it

There are times when you do need to borrow money. The examples in Chapter 2 show that even if you have been diligently saving for many years, occasions can arise where you still do not have enough salted away. Those of us who have not been so disciplined will find that these occasions come up more regularly.

The first question to ask yourself is whether you really need to spend the money. Is a new kitchen essential? Does your daughter require as expensive a wedding as all that? Can you struggle on for a few more months and get your hip replaced by the National Health Service? Only you can make these decisions and choices.

If you do decide that you need to take out a loan, there are some more specific questions to ask yourself:

- How much will it be for? Obviously the less, the better.
- How much can you afford to pay back each month? The more quickly you can repay the loan, the cheaper it will be in the long run.
- What borrowing options are available to you? There are a number of different ways to borrow money. The most widely available, from cheapest to most expensive, are mortgages, bank loans, hire purchase and similar lease products, credit and store cards, and overdrafts.
- Can you secure the loan against something? You do not have to secure the loan against whatever you are going to use it for, and often cannot: new kitchens, daughters' weddings and new hips are not securable, for instance. But you might be able to pay for one of these by taking out a further loan on your property, which is securable. This is likely to be cheaper. Be aware though that the downside of securing loans is that if you fail to meet the repayments, the lender can force you to sell the secured asset.
- What is it actually going to cost you? This depends on a number of factors:
  - the amount you want to borrow;
  - the rate of interest being charged;
  - your personal credit rating, which might enable you to get better rates of interest;
  - the length of the loan, as mentioned above.

Some lenders impose other charges in the small print or as 'extras'. Typically these include:
  - administration charges;
  - repayment insurance (which more often than not is hugely expensive);

- early repayment penalties;
- fines for missing payments.

Table 3.1 shows the approximate current rates of interest applied on different loan products in early 2004.

Table 3.1 Typical interest rates on loans, early 2004

Type	Detail	Typical APR applied	Typical loan amount	Annual interest per £1,000
Mortgage (cheapest)	2 year discounted	3.1%	£25,000 upwards	£31
Mortgage (standard)	Standard variable rate	5.75%	£10,000 upwards	£57.50
Bank loan – secured		6.9%	£1,000 upwards	£69
Bank loan – unsecured		8.5%	£1,000 upwards	£85
Credit cards	VISA/Mastercard etc	14%	£1 upwards	£140
Overdraft	Interest-paying current account	17.9%	Over £100	£179
Unarranged overdraft	Interest-paying current account	33.7%	Over £100	£337

It is clear from the table that you should try to have your loans secured if possible (that is, if you are confident that you can repay them, and that you will not be forced by the lender to sell up your security, which will probably be your house or car). However, the other forms of credit available to you do have their advantages.

Unarranged overdrafts

OK – not all of them have advantages! These charge astronomical rates of interest. The banks will argue that unarranged overdrafts are not financial products as such, and the interest is a tool to make people aware of their spending and ensure they communicate with the bank. So think of it more as a fine than a rate of interest. Unarranged overdrafts are purely for financial ostriches – those who resolutely keep their heads in the sand for fear of knowing what is really going on. There is no excuse for using an unarranged overdraft with your bank. It is likely to be the result of not opening your bank statements, not knowing how much you spend, and not knowing what you are doing. The only people to benefit from your taking out an unarranged overdraft are the bank and its shareholders. If you are reading this book you are showing more than enough interest in your financial affairs to be well past this stage.

Arranged overdrafts

Most banks will give you a small overdraft amount, usually up to £100, if you ask. This can act as a cushion if a payment you anticipate is paid out early or paid in late. Over this amount you should only arrange an over-draft facility if you know that you will only need it for a few days, perhaps a fortnight at maximum. This type of credit is not cheap, but it is easy to set up: a phone call to your bank is often all that is required. Remember that you are paying for this simplicity and convenience – if you think you are going to need the money for more than a limited 'tiding over' period you should be looking to get the loan through some other means.

Credit cards and storecards

Credit cards are very useful – they are fairly easy to get, they are accepted nearly everywhere and they make life much easier when you want to buy something. In addition they now come with all sorts of attractive additional 'extras' – like cashback, air miles and bonus points. However, it is this attractiveness and simplicity that is so dangerous. Storecards are similar to credit cards except for the crucial difference that they can only be used in a single chain of stores, and that the rate of interest charged is frequently even more expensive than the rate on credit cards.

Credit cards are an enormous business these days. There are over 61 million in use in the UK alone. That is more than one for every man, woman and child – which means that most people who have them have at least two. Two-thirds of consumer debt is held on credit cards, some £100 billion. All this means that there is a lot of profit in it – and the credit card companies are out to get hold of it in any way they can.

The best way to use a credit card is to gratefully accept the free credit period (the time between your purchasing an item and the 'pay by' date on the statement on which it appears, which can be up to two months) and then pay your bill in full each month, preferably by direct debit. The credit card companies do not feel too cheated by this as they get paid around 2 per cent of every transaction you make by the shops – so they still make money from you.

If you do not repay your credit card bill in full you will be charged interest. Here it becomes complicated, because different companies charge interest in different ways.

The date the interest is charged from

- Some companies charge interest from the day you actually spent the money. This can be two or three days before it appears on your statement.
- Some companies charge interest from the date the transaction appears on your statement.
- Some companies only charge interest from the date your statement is issued, which could be up to a month later.

Clearly the less time interest is being charged, the better.

The period before the statement has to be paid

Some companies expect you to pay your bill within a fortnight of the statement date, while others give you as much as 25 days. If you are paying off the whole amount, you will want to be given as long as possible before you have to pay (which could amount to a 56-day interest-free loan). If you are not paying off the whole amount, you will just be adding to your interest cost by waiting until the last minute to make your monthly payment.

Choosing a card that is best for you

If you are sure you will pay off the whole balance each month, first check that the card issuer allows you to set up a direct debit to pay off the whole amount each month. Some do not allow this, while others have a standard procedure that only pays off the minimum by direct debit, and you have to specifically ask for the whole balance to be repaid. Then go for a card that has useful or valuable 'extras':

- Cashback – where a (small) percentage of what you spend is deducted from your bill. This is to encourage you to spend as much as possible on your card.
- Points – where you are awarded points for each £10, £25 or £100 you spend, which can be redeemed in certain shops or for gifts from a catalogue. Again this is to encourage you to spend as much as possible on your card.
- Air miles – as with points, but just for collecting air miles.
- Affinity cards – these cards are issued in association with a charity or organization (football club, university, museum and so on) and the card company donates a certain (small) percentage of your bill to the chosen organization.
- Premium/gold/platinum cards – these usually carry a fee, for which you get a range of 'special services', almost always including a form of travel insurance, and sometimes theatre booking services, discounts at certain shops and so on. And the prestige of flashing a metal-coloured card around!

If you are not going to pay your full balance off each month, you must compare the interest rates of the different cards to see which offers you the best deal. Also compare their charging structure, as noted above:

- Zero per cent interest cards are now widely available. These come in a variety of packages. They are generally trying to attract new customers who might have two or three cards already, all with outstanding balances. The issuer wants you to transfer all your debt to its card, which has a lower rate – it must be lower because it is 0 per cent. However, the 0 per cent rate will only be for a limited period (typically six months, although some are longer), then it will revert to a high interest rate.

- A trick to watch out for is that the 0 per cent interest might only be for the 'balance transfer', the amount you initially transfer from your other cards. Any new purchases you make on the 0 per cent card could have a different interest rate, so check the small print.

- Many 0 per cent card issuers also pay off your transfer balance first, so you are left with your new purchases which are being charged a higher rate of interest for longer.

- By no means everyone who applies for a 0 per cent card gets one. Surveys suggest that substantially fewer than half of applicants are approved.

- Most card issuers offer interest rates based on your individual credit rating, and set an interest rate to suit that level of risk (so called 'risk pricing'). Frequently they do not make clear what rate of interest they will be charging, or that it will be different from the rate advertised. You must get your card issuer to confirm clearly the rate it is charging you.

- You should always try to pay off as much as you can afford and not just the minimum amount – it will all have to be paid some day, and the sooner you pay it the cheaper it will be.

Finally, most issuers will offer you 'card protection' for what appears like a small fee each month. This purports to pay off a certain percentage of your outstanding balance should you be unable to do so through accident, sickness or unemployment (known as ASU in the trade). Read the small print very carefully for these services. Some now only pay off 3 per cent of your outstanding bill, others perhaps 10 per cent, and often only for a limited period or to a certain maximum amount. If you want this type of cover you are almost certain to be able to find it cheaper through an insurance broker than from your card issuer.

Bank loans – secured and unsecured

Short of taking out or extending your mortgage this is the most efficient way to borrow money on the open market (but see 'Family and friends' below). These loans are similar in many respects to mortgages, in that they are for fixed periods and the rates charged can be discounted, fixed or variable depending on the lender's policies. (For more information on these options see Chapter 6 on Mortgages.)

Secured loans are regulated loans of less than £25,500 secured against your property. They are only available to you if you own a property. They give you lower interest rates than unsecured loans, and are relatively easily approved, but they tend to take a relatively long time to be processed (as title to your property has to be checked).

Your bank might be able to provide you with this type of loan. If it will not, there are a host of companies that do offer them. You can find them through an Internet search, or in the Yellow Pages. All firms and individuals that provide credit commercially must be registered with the Office of Fair Trading as Licensed Credit Brokers. This, however, just means they are registered, and does not guarantee that they comply with best practice standards or any codes of conduct. A variety of trade bodies involved in the industry do have codes of conduct and complaints procedures that their members must follow (including the Consumer Credit Trade Association, www.ccta.co.uk or 01274 390380; the Finance and Leasing Association, www.fla.org.uk or 020 7836 6511; the Credit Services Association (for debt collectors, www.csa-uk.com or 0191 213 2509) and the Consumer Credit Association (for home credit, www.ccauk.org or 01244 312044)), but still there is no clear logo or mark that assures borrowers of good service and reasonable rates.

Unsecured loans are even more widely available. Most banks, building societies and mortgage providers offer them. Many insurance and mortgage brokers also have products available. A large number of specialist firms offer loans to those with poor credit histories who the high street companies will not lend to. The main factors to bear in mind are again the rate of interest and the reputation of the lending company.

Always read the small print very carefully in loan agreements, as the level of service and reputations of companies offering loans, particularly those in the 'debt management' sector, can vary widely from best-practice companies to cowboys.

Unsecured loans in their turn are more expensive than secured loans, and more stringent criteria are applied before the loan is granted. Despite that they can be more quickly available.

Mortgages

See Chapter 6.

Friends and family

Often the cheapest source of borrowing money is from a friend or relative. He or she may well be able to lend the money interest free, and you can avoid all the bureaucracy and complications that come with borrowing money through a professional business. For many this is an ideal situation. Over half of all start-up companies are funded in this way. It does have its drawbacks, though. If things go wrong and you cannot repay the loan, either on time or at all, there will be no set procedure for the lender to get back some or all of the money. This can lead to ugly scenes and unforeseen consequences. Be very careful before you borrow money from a friend or relative. You should be confident that you will be able to pay it back. Make sure you draw up a simple agreement, including the amount of the loan and the date and manner in which it is to be paid back, and have both parties sign this. At least then you will both understand the terms of the agreement and know when it has been broken.

Debt now is problem debt later

With consumer debt running at its highest ever level, and interest rates at or around their historically lowest level, it is not surprising that over half the adult population in the UK is currently repaying a loan of some sort. Although base rates are currently low and have been stable for some time, history suggests that they will rise from this level, and this could happen at a quicker pace than many expect. The occasional quarter percentage point increase in rates will probably not make a huge difference to most borrowers. A series of quarter-point increases, as occurred in the second half of 1997 when there were five in six months, will make a difference. The finance industry is fearful of a 'credit crunch' as they call it, where people suddenly find that interest rate rises have increased to a level where they can no longer pay their monthly charges, let alone pay off the loan itself.

The best time to solve this problem is before it arises – which is right now! So if you have a high three-figure or any four-figure sum on your credit card, and/or a loan on a variable rate, it is well worth trying to reduce it now while you can afford it, rather than later when you cannot.

How to reduce your debt

Reducing your debt is not easy; it requires you to be strong-willed and to adopt some rather boring (in as much as they are repetitive and controlling) habits. This might not be how you like to see yourself, but you must also ask whether you see yourself as a poor and indebted person, which is not very glamorous either!

The first thing you must do to get out of debt is to make sure you know how much in debt you are. Write down on a sheet of paper all your debts (who they are from, how much they are for, when the next payment is, how much it is for, and crucially what rate of interest is being charged). Table 3.2 gives an example.

You also need to know what your monthly budget looks like. (Follow the guidelines on budgeting in Chapter 2). Once you have discovered how much you have left over at the end of each month after paying for your basics and essentials (rent, rates, utilities, food and travel), you will be in a good position to decide how much you can afford to set aside towards paying off your debt. The more you can pay each month, the quicker it will go.

Table 3.2 Current debts: an example

Lender of	Amount	Next payment date	Next payment amount	Current rate interest
1 yr bank loan of £5,000	£2,467 left to pay off	21 November	£209.30	8.5%
Credit card A	£1,266	10 November	£225.50	16%
Credit card B	£5,523	18 November	£510	10.5%
Overdraft	£250	N/a	£22.85	19%
	£9,506		£967.65	

Now order your debt by how expensive it is. This means which has the highest interest rate, not which one you are paying out most for each month. Table 3.3 continues the earlier example.

Table 3.3 Debt ordered by interest rate

	Lender	Rate
1	Overdraft	19%
2	Credit card A	16%
3	Credit card B	10.5%
4	Bank loan	8.5%

Consolidating your debt

If you can transfer your more expensive debts to a cheaper loan, then you should do so. In this example you could either try to increase your bank loan and transfer all your debt to that, or better still start a new account with a 0 per cent credit card. You would certainly be able to transfer your two credit card balances, and you might be able to transfer the bank loan and overdraft as well. In this best-case scenario you would find your monthly repayments had reduced from £967 to £792 a month for a six-month period. If you paid this off by paying the same amount per month as you had been paying previously (that is, £967 a month), you would get rid of your debt within a year. (Note though that 0 per cent interest rates often have hidden catches to them, as outlined above.)

Pay off the most expensive debt first

If you cannot consolidate all or at least some of your debts, you should create a scheme for yourself where you focus all your efforts to paying off one debt at a time. You must, of course continue to pay the minimum sums on your other debts while you do this, but all left-over available money should go to just one debt. Start with the most expensive (highest rate) first, which in our example is the bank overdraft. Luckily it is also the smallest, so you could probably clear it in a month. Then once you are back in the black in that account, you move on to the next most expensive debt, credit card A in the example. The advantage of this system is that you can see that you are making progress, as the number of debts reduces. It should be clear that having eradicated the first debt you will then have that amount more to put toward eradicating your next targeted debt, so it should reduce more quickly. By the time your credit cards are paid off in the example, and you are only left with the bank loan, you will have £758.35 more to put towards it than at the outset of your payback scheme, and should be able to pay it off in a couple of months.

Other essential tips

All this takes discipline, as we noted earlier. It is likely that you will make a few slips along the way (perhaps buying something not strictly necessary and failing to keep to your schedule for a month or two), but try not to let them put you off. There are plenty of debt advice chat rooms on the Internet if you have access to it, and also some agencies will help you with advice, encouragement and understanding, such as National Debtline (0808 808 4000 or visit www.nationaldebtline.co.uk), Consumer Credit Counselling Services (0800 138 1111 or visit www.cccssecure.co.uk) and Citizens Advice Bureaux (www.nacab.org.uk or check the telephone directory for your nearest office).

The most important rule, however, is that once you have decided to deal with your debt, you must not add to it. Cut up your credit cards – you will still get the bills even if you are not using the cards! Avoid going to the high street with its temptations. Cut back on your usual nights out and other costly expenditure. The pattern to adopt is by necessity an unglamorous one, as we stated above – but it is well worth the effort. You might even enjoy trying to achieve a frugal existence for a while, especially if you can see that a debt-free status is the reward.

Do not ignore other ways of raising money. You might consider taking some of your unwanted clutter to a car boot sale, and put the proceeds towards your repayments. Lodgers and second jobs are other possibilities for some people. Finally, try to manage your money so that when your pay cheque arrives you do not splurge it, but put some of it straight towards the repayments.

The whole debt repayment process is easier if you do not have any children, but often having children is a source of debt (they are not cheap to run). With some imagination you can make the whole family help in the cost-cutting exercise, but if you are finding it especially difficult, do go and talk to someone at an advice centre. Remember it is always better to tackle debt sooner rather than later.

When it has all gone horribly wrong

Some people find that events overtake them and there is just not time to sort out the problem before debtors come knocking at the door and lawyers start to be involved.

The important thing to do if this situation does arise is to keep talking to the lenders. If you appear reasonable and show good intentions to pay off your debts, they are more than likely to be accommodating. It is very expensive to take formal action to collect debt, and often lenders will get little or none of their money back, if they pursue the claim through courts, after legal expenses and the like have been deducted. As a result, if they are approached by a debtor, at any stage, it is always worth their while to try to reach a mutually acceptable agreement for repayment, which could involve a longer time for repayment with smaller monthly amounts, a reduction in interest rate, or even writing off some of the debt.

Credit blacklists

If you are not well organized about your finances, you might not be aware that things are getting out of control until you find yourself being refused credit. You might think that this means you have been put on a 'credit blacklist', but no such thing exists. It could mean that your file at one of the credit rating agencies (see page 52) has incorrect information on you (although this is rare), or that the information paints a poor credit history which means you fail to make a 'pass' score with lenders. The box on page 52 explains how to contact the agencies to see your file, and how you can try to improve your rating.

Credit unions

Improving your credit rating will take time. If you are in urgent need of money and high street banks and building societies will not lend to you, then rather than go to a disreputable lender or answer a small ad in the newspaper that offers money, a good place to look is at a local credit union.

These are not very well known, but they have been around for many years and are being encouraged by the government to help prevent 'financial exclusion'. A credit union is a financial cooperative that is owned and controlled by its members. The members save in a common fund, and the money saved can be used to make low-interest loans to other members. Successful credit unions pay an annual dividend of up to 8 per cent, so they are a good savings option too.

Only people who come within the 'common bond' of the credit union can join it and make use of its services. The four main 'common bonds' are 'community or residential' – people who all live in a certain area; 'live or work' – people who all live or work in a certain area; 'employment or industrial' – people who all work in the same group or company; and 'associational' – people who all work in the same trade or for the same union. Credit unions provide a very effective way of borrowing. The maximum rate of interest they can charge is 12.68 per cent APR, all loans are insured, and your current ability to pay is their guiding factor, not your credit history. Credit unions are non-profit making so they are there to help, not to profit from you. For more information contact the Association of British Credit Unions (ABCUL) on 0161 832 3694 or at www.abcul.org.

County court judgements (CCJ)

In England and Wales the first legal step in recovering a debt is to serve a county court judgement on the debtor. As a debtor the first you will know that your debt has got to this level is when a notification letter is sent to you. You will have one month to pay the debt off before the debt is 'registered'. Once registered it remains 'on file' for six years and the credit ratings agencies will also know of it. Having a CCJ on your credit file means you will find it much more difficult to get credit – so it is best to avoid it in the first place.

If you are unable to repay the debt within the month you have two options. First, you can let the court know that you can repay the debt, but it will take longer than one month; or second, you can let the court know that you cannot repay the whole debt. In both cases you *must* tell the court what you plan to do. Ignoring the notification will only worsen your situation.

In the first case, when you have repaid the debt after a few months (either through the court system or direct to the lender) you should let the court know. If you have paid it directly to the lender the court will need proof that it has been fully repaid, after which it can issue a 'Certificate of Satisfaction' which shows on the register that the debt has been repaid in full. This certificate will cost you £10 for processing.

If you cannot repay the debt the court will ask you to fill in a Form N245 (available from the court), which will set out your current income and expenditure. From this the court will decide how much you can repay and 'vary' the debt accordingly. Processing the N245 will cost you £30.

Note that the process the court uses is very similar to the one we advise you to use yourself (that is, assess whether you can repay the debt, contact the lender to discuss different repayment terms and so on), so it is very much in your interest to repay the debt *before* the courts are involved. The procedure will be the same but the after-effects are much better – you will not have a CCJ against your name.

Insolvency

If you have run out of luck and time and there are a mountain of debts to repay, not just one or two, maybe it is time to take some action to give yourself a fresh start. You could consider becoming 'insolvent'. You will need professional advice, and should see a licensed Insolvency Practitioner, who will be either a lawyer or an accountant.

There are two routes available to an individual in these circumstances. The first is to opt for an Individual Voluntary Arrangement (IVA), where under the guidance of a licensed Insolvency Practitioner the debtor agrees to 'vary' the debts with his or her lenders. The proposal must be approved by at least 75 per cent, by value, of the lenders for the IVA to be accepted. It will usually take between two and five years to complete the repayments, and the debtor has to pay the Insolvency Practitioner for his or her work. If this is the route you feel might work for you, check out the rates you will be charged first. With an IVA you retain a certain degree of control, and are unlikely to be forced to sell your house and/or personal belongings.

The ultimate option is to declare bankruptcy. It is unusual for an individual to do this; usually a lender makes the court order. You can be declared bankrupt for owing as little as £750, although it is usually done for more substantial sums. An Official Receiver or Insolvency Practitioner will be appointed by the court to manage all your finances, and it is likely that he or she will sell everything you own to pay off the debts – often including your home. The only things you can keep are a few basic belongings in order that you can eat, sleep and clothe yourself, any tools you need to be able to continue working, and the contents of your pension scheme – all other savings will be long gone.

Bankruptcy used to last for three years. However, since April 2004 when the new Enterprise Act 2002 came into law, most bankrupts are discharged by the court after only one year. After the discharge you are no longer liable for any of your debts. However, if the court is unhappy with your behaviour during that time it can refuse to discharge you.

Scotland has a slightly different system from the rest of the UK. The most obvious differences are that IVAs are known as trust deeds, and bankruptcy as sequestration.

For more information on insolvency see www.insolvency.gov.uk or call 020 7291 6895.

4

Pensions

Introduction

Pensions are complex, filled with jargon and often reported as not giving good value for money. Is it any wonder that many of us go to great lengths to avoid thinking about them? Look at the box if you think you know all about pensions, and see how many of those acronyms and terms you can confidently explain!

Pension jargon

APP	appropriate personal pension
APPSHP	appropriate personal pension stakeholder pension
ARR	age-related rebate
ASCN	appropriate scheme number
AVC	additional voluntary contributions
BRP	basic retirement pension
COD	contracted-out deduction
COMB	contracted-out mixed benefit
COMP	contracted-out money purchase
COMPSHP	contracted-out money purchase stakeholder pension
COSR	Contracted-out salary related
DB	defined benefit

DC	defined contribution
ECON	employer's contracting-out number
EPP	executive pension plans
ERI	employer-related investments
FSA 86	Financial Services Act 1996
FSAVC	free-standing additional voluntary contribution
FURBS	funded unapproved retirement benefit schemes
GMP	guaranteed minimum pension
GPPP/GPPS	group personal pension plans/schemes
HRP	home responsibilities protection
ICTA 88	Income and Corporation Taxes Act 1988
IPA	individual pension account
IR (#)	Inland Revenue Practice Notes (with the relevant number)
LEL	lower earnings limit
LPI	limited price indexation
MFR	minimum funding requirement
MIG	minimum income guarantee
MND	member nominated directors
MNT	member nominated trustees
NRD	normal retirement date
OMO	open market option
OPRA	Occupational Pensions Regulatory Authority
PA 95	Pensions Act 1995
PAYG	pay as you go (funding of pensions from current contributions)
PIBS	permanent interest bearing shares
PPP	personal pension plan
PPPRP	personal pension protected rights premium
PT	pensioner trustee
RAC	retirement annuity contracts
RPI	retail price index
S2P	State Second Pension
SERPS	state earnings-related pension scheme

SIP	statement of investment principles
SIPP	self-invested personal pension
SPA	state pension age
SSA 86	Social Security Act 1986
SSAS	small self-administered schemes
Annuities	
Flexible	
Non-Profit	
Phased	
With Profit	
Carry Back	
Concurrency	
Contracting in	
Contracting out	
Defined benefit	
Defined contribution	
Income drawdown (or just 'drawdown')	
Money purchase	
Preserved benefits	
Segmentation	
Transfer values	
Underfunded	

But do not give up on pensions yet. Give them a chance, because they are there to help. More importantly if you do not have one, or have not given proper consideration to whether you should have one, you are in for a nasty shock when you stop working.

This chapter attempts to explain how pensions work, what is available to you, and how you can choose from those options to obtain an adequate pension to make your and your spouse's retirement comfortable and enjoyable. Armed with this knowledge you can then approach a qualified pensions adviser to discuss your situation in further detail. The options can be complicated and the decisions confusing, so getting professional advice is essential.

Because pensions are complex and confusing this chapter is in four parts. The first three parts describe and explain how the main types of pensions work and the factors that affect them. The final part draws all these ideas together, and considers the questions you need to address to find an appropriate pension solution for you and your spouse.

How a pension works

At its simplest a pension is an investment fund. Over a long period of time, hopefully most of your working life, money is put into a fund. With occupational and personal pensions, on retirement the fund is made available to buy another product that will pay out an income for the rest of your life.

The trick is that pensions have special tax advantages over most other investment funds – as the government really wants you to have a pension so it does not have to pay to support you. The sacrifice you make for receiving the tax advantage is that the government limits the way you can spend the money in the fund. First, it does not let you spend the funds until you retire, and second, it ensures the bulk of the fund is spent on an annuity.

An annuity is a particular type of financial product that is very low-risk but will pay out a steady amount of income for whatever period it is designed for. The problem with annuities is that as they are low-risk they are also low-reward – that is, you could get a much better return in other types of product, but you are not allowed to. There is a solid reason for this: if people were allowed to invest in riskier but more profitable products they might lose their pension savings, and then the government, having given them all these tax advantages, would again find itself having to support them in their old age, which is exactly what it is trying to prevent.

Types of pension

Pensions can be split into three different basic types. In all of them it is you who pays out the money that goes into the 'pension fund', although it might not seem so. The difference is in who is responsible for managing the fund. The three types of pensions are:

- **State pension** – this is managed by the government and you pay money into the 'pension fund' through your National Insurance (NI) contributions. (See the box on how state pensions are funded.)
- **Occupational pensions** – these are managed by your employer, and money is paid into the 'pension fund' through deductions from your wages/salary, and also through an 'employer's contribution'.
- **Personal pension plans** (PPP) – these you manage yourself, or at least you employ someone to do so. How much you contribute and when is your decision.

State pensions

The state pension is in two parts, the basic state pension and an additional state pension commonly known as State Earnings Related Pension Scheme (SERPS) or from 6 April 2002 the State Second Pension (S2P). People who worked at any time during the period April 1961 to April 1975 may also be eligible for graduated retirement benefit.

How state pensions are funded

The major problem with the state pension is that its 'fund' is only theoretical. In fact, the government pays pensions out of current NI contributions. This is the method used by most state systems internationally, and is known as pay-as you-go or PAYG. This situation is fine as long as there are many more people employed and paying NI than receiving pensions. The proportion of working people to retired people is called the 'dependency ratio':

the lower the figure, the more workers per pensioner. In the UK in 2000 the figure was 24 per cent, or nearly four workers for every pensioner. In 2030 it is expected to be about 35 per cent, approximately three workers for every pensioner, and by 2050 over 40 per cent, only 2.5 workers for every pensioner. This means each worker will have to support nearly double the number of pensioners he or she does currently, or alternatively each pensioner will only have half the support he or she currently gets. If you think it is bad in the UK, the situation is much worse in Germany, France, Italy and Japan.

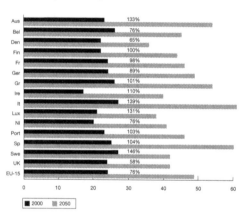

Source: Eurostat. Defined as persons over the age of 65 as a percentage of working age population (aged 15 to 64). The percentage figure on the right refers to the percentage change between the 2000 ratio and the projected figure for 2050.

Figure 4.1   The dependency ratio in different countries

How much you get from the state as your pension depends on a wide range of different factors. This is because over the years different governments have brought in different pieces of legislation, which entitle you or do not entitle you to different pension benefits. The older you are, the more complicated the picture becomes, as you will have been making contributions through several different pension regimes.

You can find out what your state pension is likely to be, based on your contributions so far, by getting a Standard State Pension Forecast from the Pension Service, the part of the Department for Work and Pensions (DWP) that deals with all pension matters. You will need to fill a form BR19: to get one call the Pension Service on 0845 3000168 or go to www.thepensionservice.gov.uk and type BR19 into the search facility.

There are two critical factors in calculating your state pension entitlement. The first is your age, and when you will become eligible to claim your pension: that is, your state pension age or SPA. At the moment this is different for men and women. The male SPA is 65 and due to remain so. The female SPA is currently 60, but from 2010 it will start to rise, until by 2020 it will also be 65. (See Table 4.1 for a ready reckoner.) The second factor is the amount of your NI contributions. To be entitled to a full state pension you must have had sufficient qualifying years of contributions. (See the box for an explanation of qualifying years.)

Table 4.1 Ready reckoner for state pension age

Year of birth	Year of retirement (men)	Year of retirement (women)
1939	2004	already achieved SPA
1940	2005	already achieved SPA
1941	2006	already achieved SPA
1942	2007	already achieved SPA
1943	2008	already achieved SPA
1944	2009	2004
1945	2010	2005
1946	2011	2006
1947	2012	2007
1948	2013	2008
1949	2014	2009
1950	2015	2010*
1951	2016	2012*
1952	2017	2014*
1953	2018	2016*
1954	2019	2018*
1955	2020	2020*
1956	2021	2021
1957	2022	2022
1958	2023	2023
1959	2024	2024
1960	2025	2025
1961	2026	2026

1962	2027	2027
1963	2028	2028
1964	2029	2029
1965	2030	2030
1966	2031	2031
1967	2032	2032
1968	2033	2033
1969	2034	2034
1970	2035	2035
1971	2036	2036
1972	2037	2037
1973	2038	2038
1974	2039	2039
1975	2040	2040
1976	2041	2041
1977	2042	2042
1978	2043	2043
1979	2044	2044
1980	2045	2045
1981	2046	2046
1982	2047	2047
1983	2048	2048
1984	2049	2049
1985	2050	2050

* Women born on or after 6 April 1950 and before 6 April 1955 will reach pension age at age 60 plus one month for every month or part-month their date of birth is after 5 April 1950. For these women retirement pension will always be awarded from the 6th of the same month.

National Insurance contributions and qualifying years

NI is a charge that the government takes from your wages each week or month. The charge entitles people to state benefits including an old age pension. There are six classes (or types) of contributions, confusingly numbered 1, 1a, 1b, 2, 3 and 4.

Class 1 is paid by all employed earners (employees) and their employers. The employees' part is deducted from their wages or salaries. It is calculated as a percentage of earnings, currently 11 per cent, but is only charged on earnings up to £31,720 a year (2004/5 figures). Above that figure NI is charged at only 1 per cent. Employers also pay a NI contribution for each employee.

Class 1 contributions entitle those eligible to incapacity benefit, jobseekers allowance, maternity benefit, state pension and widow's pension.

Class 1a is paid by *employers* who provide directors and employees with certain benefits in kind that are available for private use, such as cars and fuel.

Class 1b is paid only by *employers* who enter into a special PAYE Settlement Agreement with the Inland Revenue.

Class 2 is paid by the self-employed. It gives them rights to incapacity benefit, maternity benefit, the state pension and widow's pension. Class 2 contributions must be paid within six years of their falling due, although it is clearly better to make payment regularly and on time.

Class 3 is the only voluntary contribution, and is paid by people who have not earned enough in a year to make it a 'qualifying year' (see below) and wish to make up the difference. You can make up payments up to six years after the tax year in which the shortfall occurred.

Class 4 contributions are paid by self-employed people, on profits or gains from any trade, profession or vocation, if those profits or gains are above the Class 4 lower profit level. This is in addition to Class 2 NI contributions. However, there are a few exceptions – for more information contact the Pension Service.

Earnings limits and qualifying years

NI contributions are only payable by people who earn over a certain level, known as the lower earnings limit (LEL). In the tax year 2004–05 the LEL was £79 a week or £4,108 a year. If you earn this amount or more, you must make NI contributions of the appropriate class for your employment status.

A *qualifying year* is a tax year in which you have either paid, or been credited with, Class 1 contributions on earnings of at least 52 times the LEL, *or* paid 52 Class 2 contributions, *or* paid or been credited with Class 3 contributions.

There is also an upper earnings limit above which you only pay 1 per cent of earnings to NI. This is currently set at £31,720 a year (tax year 2004/5).

Basic state pension

The basic state pension is a flat-rate benefit based on the number of years (known as qualifying years) in which you paid or were credited with a minimum amount of standard rate contributions.

To get any basic pension, one of these qualifying conditions must apply:

- Before 6 April 1975 you must have paid 50 flat-rate Class 1, 2 or 3 contributions.
- Between 6 April 1975 and 5 April 1978 you must have paid in any one tax year before you reached the SPA, Class 1 contributions on earnings of at least 50 times the weekly LEL, or equivalent Class 2 or Class 3 contributions.
- After 5 April 1978 you must have paid in any one tax year before you reached the SPA, Class 1 contributions on earnings of at least 52 times the weekly LEL, or equivalent Class 2 or Class 3 contributions.

To get basic pension at the full standard rate (100 per cent), about 9 out of every 10 years in your working life need to be qualifying years. The maximum number of qualifying years you can have is 44. Less than that, and you only get a pension equivalent to the proportion of qualifying years. For example if at retirement age you have 33 qualifying years of NI payments, you get 33/44 or 75 per cent of the full basic pension. You get no state pension at all if you have not managed to make at least 11 qualifying years of payments, that is 25 per cent of the maximum possible. There are exceptions to this rule: see the section on 'Home responsibilities protection' below.

Additional pension

Unlike the basic pension, the additional pension will not depend on your having paid contributions for a certain number of qualifying years. Your rights will build up year by year, and your additional pension will be based on your earnings in your working life from 1978–79 to the year before the one in which you reach the SPA. The more you earned, the higher your additional pension will be, up to a prescribed maximum.

To get the additional pension you must have made NI payments above the LEL. Since 2000 the government complicated the system even further. Your additional pension contributions are taken on earnings above a new figure, the earnings threshold (ET), which is slightly greater than the LEL (for 2004/5 it is £91 per week or £4,732 per year). The LEL still exists and is still used for basic pension calculations. The gap between the LEL and the ET is ignored when calculating entitlement to the additional pension. If this all sounds very confusing – it is! Fortunately employers generally make the necessary calculations.

Graduated retirement benefit

Between 1961 and 1975 the additional part of the pension was based on payment of graduated contributions. If you worked during this period and paid these contributions, you will be paid graduated retirement benefit in addition to any other pension you are eligible for.

Home responsibilities protection

If you are unable to work because you are looking after children under 16 years or caring for a dependent relative, you are probably eligible for home responsibilities protection (HRP). This is a system where the maximum number of qualifying years is reduced for each year you have HRP, so it increases your final basic pension percentage.

If someone had only made 33 qualifying years of contributions, but he or she also had eight years of HRP, he or she would get 92 per cent of the basic pension instead of 75 per cent (44 years minus 8 years equals 36, so the percentage will be 33/36 = 91.66 per cent, rather than 33/44 = 75 per cent). HRP can reduce the maximum number of qualifying years to a minimum of 20 years for a woman and 22 for a man. (Women born after 1955 are restricted to 22 years due to the change in SPA.) You must have made at least five years of qualifying contributions to be eligible at this level.

You are automatically awarded HRP if you are claiming child benefit and are not working. For carers the eligibility rules are more complex. If you are receiving carer's allowance this automatically compensates you for lost NI contributions, and if the person you are caring for receives disability benefits this will also affect your entitlement. Carers are advised to contact their local Contributions Office for specific information on their situation.

You can also get credits towards your NI contributions if you are registered for jobseekers allowance or are unfit for work. For more information contact your local Contributions Office, listed under Inland Revenue in the phone book.

Contracting out

You cannot opt out of the basic state pension, but in some circumstances you can choose to opt out of the additional state pension scheme and join a private scheme instead. This is called 'contracting out'. The replacement scheme is called an appropriate personal pension (APP), or (if it is stakeholder-based) an appropriate personal pension stakeholder pension (APPSP). In either case the scheme must fulfil certain criteria to be approved as 'appropriate' by the Inland Revenue.

If you choose to join an occupational pension scheme run by your employer, contracting out means that you and your employer pay lower NI contributions, known as minimum contributions. Minimum contributions are the payments made up to the LEL. Any amount above this normally goes towards your additional state pension, but once you contract out the payments go towards your occupational pension. This contribution above the minimum contribution is called the 'contracted-out rebate' when it is paid towards a contracted-out scheme. When you retire, your second pension then comes from your employer's scheme and not from the additional state pension.

You can also contract out of the additional state pension to join a stakeholder pension scheme or a PPP. Instead of paying lower NI contributions, once a year the Inland Revenue pays directly into your PPP account an amount equal to what you would have paid towards your State Second Pension. This is called the contracted-out rebate.

You can join a stakeholder pension scheme or a PPP scheme without contracting out of the additional state pension but in this case you will not get the rebate. You do, however, usually get tax relief on your contributions to a private pension scheme. With a basic rate of income tax of 22 per cent, every £100 that goes into your pension costs you £78 (based on the tax year 2004/05). If you pay income tax at the higher rate of 40 per cent, every £100 that goes into your pension fund costs you £60 (based on the tax year 2004/05). Some occupational schemes and some PPPs are organized on a 'rebate-only' basis. This means that the only money being paid into the scheme is your NI contributions rebate. If you have chosen this sort of second pension, it will give you roughly the same size of pension as you would get from the additional state pension. You still need to consider whether it will be enough to support the lifestyle you want when you retire.

The State Second Pension gives employees earning up to £25,600 from 6 April 2003 a better pension than SERPS, whether or not they are contracted out to a PPP. Most help goes to those who earn less than £11,200 from 6 April 2003. A person contributing to a contracted-out PPP and earning less than £11,200 (from 6 April 2003) in a tax year will also get a State Second Pension top-up for that year. The top-up reflects the more generous additional state pension provided by the State Second Pension.

Getting your pension paid abroad

An increasing number of Britons retire abroad in search of some year-round sun or to be nearer families. The state pension is currently paid to around 900,000 people overseas. It can be paid abroad fairly simply. In the European Economic Area and some other countries, including Israel, Jamaica and the United States, all annual increases are paid. In the rest of the world the pension is only paid at its initial rate. If, however, you return to the UK it will jump to the correct current rate – but it will fall back to the initial rate if you go abroad again. Contact the Pension Service for more details.

Pension credits (minimum income guarantee)

Regardless of how little you have paid in NI contributions throughout your working life, the government will not let you become totally impoverished. There is a minimum income amount to which everyone is entitled. If your income does not reach this level the government will top it up. A few years ago this was done through income support. In 1999 a specific scheme directed at pensioners was introduced, called the minimum income guarantee (MIG). In October 2003 this was replaced by pension credits.

The MIG was considered unfair in that if you had built up some savings during your life this counted against you: you were expected to use them up before you became entitled to the benefit. The government correctly believed that this penalized savers and encouraged people on low incomes not to save. The pension credit actually rewards people on low incomes who have also managed to build up some savings.

In 2004/05 the pension credit guarantees single people aged 60 and over at least £105.45 a week, and couples £160.95 a week. Further payments up to a maximum of £14.79 for singles and £19.20 for couples are available depending on how much you have managed to save and your level of income. See the Pension Service for more details.

Married women's pensions

The government does not pay married couples twice as much as single people. When both husband and wife are eligible to collect their state pension the wife will only receive up to 60 per cent of the full basic state pension based on her husband's contributions, regardless of her own NI contributions through her working life. She will continue to receive her own entitlement to any additional pension, however. This creates a number of anomalies that married women should be aware of.

In order to get a full basic state pension a married woman must have had at least 20 qualifying years of payments (see the section on home responsibilities protection above), or 39 qualifying years if she has no children. If she is eligible to collect a state pension and her husband is not (that is, she has reached the SPA before he does), she will be paid her full entitlement, but as soon as her husband achieves eligibility her basic pension becomes a percentage of her husband's. This is true regardless of whether she has paid any NICs. So the first anomaly is that a working wife who has paid NICs all her working life will get exactly the same basic pension (and other benefits) as a wife who has never paid any NICs at all.

The second anomaly is the reduced rate contribution. Before 1977 married women were allowed to pay reduced rate contributions, which entitled them to industrial injuries benefit and maternity allowance but nothing else. Those who paid this contribution up to its abolition in 1977 were able to carry on paying it after that date – but it not only does not earn them a pension, it prevents them from getting one! There are at least 100,000 women still paying this contribution in the UK, and they are advised to stop paying it. In order to obtain extra pension and benefit entitlements they should pay Class 3 voluntary contributions, which go towards an additional pension and jobseekers allowance amongst other things. These payments are most rewarding to women who are older than their husbands, or less than five years younger than them.

Inheriting an additional state pension

The additional state pension is only paid to an individual who has made sufficient NI contributions. If your partner was the main worker in the family and you are not eligible in your own right for an additional pension, you are entitled to 'inherit' some of the benefits should he or she die before you. Up to 2002 the maximum entitlement (entitlement depends on your own pension income) was 100 per cent. It has now been reduced to a maximum of 50 per cent. Contact the Pension Service for more details.

Deferring a state pension

It is possible to defer taking your state pension for up to five years after reaching the SPA. For each year you defer it the government will increase your eventual pension by 7.5 per cent, so if you defer it for three years your pension will increase by 22.5 per cent. After 2010 you will be able to defer it for as long as you want, with the increase rising to 10 per cent per year. Obviously this is a risky thing to do, as you do not know how long you will live for. Definitely seek advice before opting for deferment.

Current level of state pension

Clearly a mass of different factors affect entitlement to the basic state pension. What is certain is that your basic state pension will be no more than the current maximum. In 2003/04 this was £77.45 a week for a single person and £123.80 a week for a retired couple. In mid-2003 the average additional pension payment was around £15 per week per person. Thus a single male pensioner eligible for a full basic state pension plus an average additional pension received £92.45 a week or just under £5,000 a year, and a married couple about £8,000. Of the 11 million pensioners in the UK, 6.9 million currently receive additional pensions.

Occupational pensions

In the section above we indicated what an 'average' state pension might amount to if you were to receive a full basic state pension plus a 'typical' additional state pension. While the figures above are only illustrations, they are typical of the pension many people in the UK receive from the state. The 'before tax' average UK income for the full-time employed was £25,170 in April 2003, so a typical state pension represents a huge fall from this level. This underlines the idea that, if you can manage to make more provision, the state pension should only be thought of as a foundation for your retirement income, and not the whole amount. It certainly will not allow you anything to spare.

Your alternatives for supplementing the state pension are to either take out a further pension (or pensions) or build up other investments that will give you an income in retirement. We look at other investment opportunities later in the book: the two most popular are share portfolios, especially those 'wrapped' in an ISA, and buy-to-let property investments.

As women tend to get lower pensions than men they should be even more enthusiastic about building up a second pension 'pot'. Women do badly from pensions in three ways. They often have broken contribution records because of breaks for child care and the like, they still tend to be paid less than men, and when they reach pension age their annuity payments are lower as they are expected to live longer than men.

The non-state pension alternatives are to join a pension scheme run by your employer, called an occupational scheme, or to have a personal pension plan (PPP). In most situations you are probably best advised to join a company pension scheme if one is available. The main drawback to occupational schemes is apparent if or when you change jobs. The pension you have built up in the company scheme might not be transferable, and you might find you have not earned a reasonable return from your contributions. Usually reasonable returns are only achieved once you have been in a pension scheme for at least six or seven years.

The advantages of occupational schemes are:

* Your employer will contribute to the scheme. (This is the only occasion where someone else puts money into your pension fund.) Sometimes employees are not asked to contribute anything at all: this is a 'non-contributory' pension. Of course, your pay will take the employer's contribution into account, but it is unlikely that you will be paid any more if you choose not to join an occupational scheme, so if you opt out, you will just be missing out on the employer's contributions.

- Occupational schemes tend to have lower running costs than private pension schemes, and the company often covers them from funds outside the pension scheme.
- The schemes often also have additional benefits such as life assurance and widow's pensions.
- Since 1997 all defined-benefit schemes have had to index their payments to the inflation rate, up to a maximum of 5 per cent per year, although they can index above this rate if they want to.
- The company is responsible for making sure that the fund is well managed and sufficiently funded, and must make up any shortfall should it arise. In private schemes this is your own responsibility.

How much do you pay for your pension?

This is the really attractive part of occupational schemes. Not only do you make contributions but so does your employer. Typically the employer makes a larger contribution than you do. A typical arrangement, according to recent data, is for the employee to put 6 per cent of his/her pay into the scheme and the employer to add around 16 per cent (if it is a defined-benefit scheme; but only 6 per cent if it is a defined-contribution scheme), although there are no standard fixed rates.

Say you are paid £24,000 a year, or £2,000 a month, gross. You pay income tax and NI contributions of £497.62 a month, giving you net pay of £1,502.38 per month. If you join an occupational scheme and pay 6 per cent of your gross pay into the scheme, or £120 per month, this will be deducted before tax and NI contributions are charged. This means your take-home pay is reduced to £1,408.77 after reduced tax and NI contributions of £471.22 and the pension deduction of £120. However, remember the pension contribution is still your money; you just cannot get hold of it until you retire. So your actual month's pay is £1,528.77, £26.39 more than when you were not paying into a pension.

Add to this your employer's contribution and you really are in a better position. If your employer adds the equivalent of 8 per cent of your pay, £160 per month in the above example, your pension pot will increase by £280 a month or £3,360 a year.

With a private pension plan the tax is added back when you make your contribution to the scheme (see page 98), but there are no employer contributions.

You can see how these figures work with your own pay by using an income tax calculator on the Internet. There is a good one at www.moneyextra.com/tax/

Who runs occupational schemes

Occupational pension schemes are very tightly regulated these days. Following the crooked activities of Robert Maxwell at the Mirror Group, where he took money from group pension schemes to support parts of his business and was unable to repay it, the government has been very keen to make sure that this kind of activity can no longer occur.

Typically a financial institution, such as an insurance company or a fund management company, manages the occupational pension scheme. It takes the contributions and invests them appropriately. For this it charges a fee of around 1–2 per cent of the total value of the fund. The fund is controlled by a board of trustees, some of whom are executives of the company whose scheme it is, while others are independent of it. It is the trustees' duty to ensure that the managers are competent, and to control the fees they charge. The independent trustees are also obliged to ensure the fund is not being used for any purposes other than to provide pensions for employees, and that it is sufficiently well funded to be able to do so. If they feel it is not sufficiently funded, they must ensure that the company makes good its responsibility to replace the shortfall.

Defined benefit and defined contribution

There are two main types of occupational schemes, defined benefit and defined contribution. Defined benefit (which is only available from occupational schemes) means that your pension will pay out a guaranteed sum: usually a percentage, up to two-thirds, of your final salary, or an average of your salary over the last few years of your working life. (This is sometimes also called a 'final salary' scheme.) Defined contribution is more like the state system, in that you know how much you pay into the scheme but you do not know at the time what you will get out of it. (These are also known as 'money purchase' schemes.) The returns on a defined-contribution pension depend entirely on how well the funds invested have performed.

Under-funding

With the large fall in the stock market in recent years, many defined-benefit pension funds have been found to be 'under-funded': that is, the fund is not sufficient to cover the guaranteed payments. In these cases the company that supplies the pension scheme is bound to make up the shortfall. This is an honourable but strange situation, as the pension fund is supposed to be entirely separate from the rest of the company, so that if the company gets into financial difficulties it cannot use the money in the pension fund for other purposes. Robert Maxwell famously did not adhere to these rules. However, if the pension fund gets into difficulties the company must top it up with other corporate funds.

For this reason many defined-benefit pension schemes have been closed in recent years and replaced by defined-contribution schemes, where there are no payment guarantees and hence by definition no shortfall. In 2003 a quarter of existing defined-benefit schemes were closed, following the closure of 20 per cent of schemes in 2002 and 10 per cent in 2001.

The defined-benefit scheme, if fully funded, is an increasingly rare but very attractive prospect. Today it is most often found in the public sector, where the government guarantees the fund. Perhaps the best known final salary scheme is that given to MPs.

Sometimes companies that get into financial difficulties themselves do not have the funds to top up their defined-benefit schemes, and as a result the pensions paid are substantially reduced from the amounts originally promised. The government has announced it is to set up a Pension Protection Fund to insure against this, paid for by a small annual levy on all subscribing defined-benefit funds. A similar scheme operates successfully in the United States. For more information contact the Pension Service or visit www.thepensionservice.gov.uk/atoz/atozdetailed/fs1.asp.

Group personal pension schemes

A third type of pension available to people through their employer is a group personal pension scheme (GPPS). It is not an occupational pension, in that the company does not have responsibility for overseeing and managing it. The company outsources all the responsibility to a private pension scheme provider, usually an insurance company. In this way a GPPS is actually more like a private pension scheme than an occupational scheme, but it does have a couple of advantages over a standard private scheme. First, the employer must contribute something towards the fund, as with an occupational scheme (the minimum is 3 per cent of salary); and second, the company should be able to negotiate lower management costs than are typical with a private scheme. If you leave the company your pension remains your own, but you lose these two benefits.

Defined-benefit pensions: how much you get and what if you change employers

With a defined-benefit scheme you know how your pension will be calculated when you join the scheme. Typically it is described as a fraction of your final salary: often 1/60 multiplied by the number of years you have belonged to the scheme, although other fractions can be used: 1/30 or 1/45 would be very generous, 1/80 less so. These different fractions make a significant difference to your eventual pension income.

If your final salary is £40,000 and you have been paying into a scheme based on 1/60 scheme for 12 years, your yearly pension income will be £8,000 (1/60 × £40,000 × 12 years) (or £10,666 with a 1/45 multiple or £6,000 on a 1/80 multiple.) The pension is normally index-linked, so it grows in line with inflation both until you retire and throughout your retirement. (The law caps compulsory index linking at 5 per cent, although many schemes link above this rate, especially in the public sector.)

The scheme may also offer you a lump sum at retirement. Typically this is expressed as x/80 (3/80 is not unusual) of your salary multiplied by your years of service. In the example above, a 3/80 scheme would give you a one-off tax-free lump sum of £18,000 (3/80 × £40,000 × 12 years).

It should be clear that the longer you are a member of a scheme, the better you will do from it. As UK workers work on average for five different companies during their working lives, they are unlikely to receive the full potential of a defined-benefit occupational scheme. Studies suggest that moving jobs an average number of times will reduce your final pension income by 25–30 per cent. Table 4.2 shows that even when you increase your salary substantially by moving jobs you are still likely to lose on your pension scheme.

If or when you do change your employer, there are a number of options available for dealing with your occupational pension:

- The simplest is to leave it where it is. The pension will be payable to you on reaching retirement, calculated on the salary you were paid when you left the company and the number of years you worked there. The risk is that you have no control over it, and if the company should go bankrupt in the intervening period it is possible that the pension fund will not be able to pay out what it 'guaranteed'.
- Transfer it. You should be able to transfer your 'share' of the pension fund to a PPP or a new occupational scheme. The 'transfer value' is calculated on the likely benefit you would receive on retirement from your existing scheme, with factors such as inflation and your life expectancy factored in. The pension administrators work out how

Table 4.2 Changing jobs reckoner for a final-salary pension scheme

	5 years	Salary on leaving	10 years	Salary on leaving	15 years	Salary on leaving	20 years	Salary on leaving	25 years	Final salary
Company 1	£1,666.67	£20,000.00	£4,166.67	£25,000.00	£7,500.00	£30,000.00	£11,000.00	£33,000.00	£15,833.33	£38,000.00
Company 2	£2,500.00	£30,000.00	£5,833.33	£35,000.00	£9,500.00	£38,000.00	£14,000.00	£42,000.00	£19,791.67	£47,500.00
Company 3	£3,333.33	£40,000.00	£7,500.00	£45,000.00	£12,500.00	£50,000.00	£18,333.33	£55,000.00		

Example 1: You stay in your first two jobs for 5 years each and your final job for 15 years

Company 1 you leave with a pension worth	£1,666 pa
Company 2 you leave with a pension worth	£2,500 pa
Company 3 you leave with a pension worth	£12,5000 pa
Total occupational pension	£16,666 pa

Example 2: You stay in Company 1 for 20 years and then get head-hunted to a senior position at Company 3 where you stay for only 5 years but leave with a salary of £55,000

Company 1 you leave with a pension worth	£11,000 pa
Company 3 you leave with a pension worth	£4,583 pa
(not shown above; 1/60 × £55,000 × 5 years)	
Total occupational pension	£15,583 pa

If you add in possible lump-sum benefits at 3/80 of final salary times years of service:

Example 1:

Company 1 lump sum	£3,750.00
Company 2 lump sum	£5,625.00
Company 3 lump sum	£28,125.00
Total lump sum	£37,500.00

Example 2:

Company 1 lump sum	£24,750.00
Company 3 lump sum	£10,312.50
Total lump sum	£35,062.50

much money needs to be invested today to provide that future income on retiring. The contributions you have made are not relevant in calculating this figure. Always carefully consider the levels of charges and benefits in any new scheme you are thinking about joining.

- If you have less than two years with the pension scheme, you can choose (or the pension managers can decide) to have all your contributions returned to you, but you will not get your employer's contributions. These will be returned less the tax-free element unless you reinvest the proceeds in another pension scheme.

When transferring your pension:

- You can buy into a new occupational scheme. This is done by 'buying years'. The new schemes manager or actuary will calculate a value for each year of service in the scheme, and see what the amount you transfer will buy you. Even if the two schemes are similar in rates, you are unlikely to get as many years in the new scheme as you had in your old one. This is because your old scheme value is calculated on general inflation rates and the new one on wage inflation rates. Wage inflation is normally higher than general inflation.
- You can transfer the pension into an AVC or PPP (see below).
- Before 1997 you could buy a 'Section 32 Buy-out Bond' from an insurance company, which would guarantee you a fixed income on retirement, but this is no longer available.

Deciding what option to choose is complex. It is advisable to discuss your options with an IFA or actuary, who should be able to recommend a sensible course of action.

Defined-contribution pensions: how much you get and what if you change employers

Occupational pensions that are funded by a defined contribution are known as 'money purchase' schemes. They operate in a similar fashion to PPPs and stakeholder pensions (see next section). As with defined-benefit pensions you make contributions from your pay, which are similarly tax-efficient. These payments go into a fund that is invested. Historically it was usually predominantly invested in UK shares, but since the stock market collapse of 2000 many companies have reduced the proportion invested in shares and made it up with other types of investment, such as bonds and property.

When you come to retire, the size of your share of the pension fund will depend on how well the fund has grown during the time you invested with it. There is no way of knowing in advance what the value will be. If you had retired in late 1999 or early 2000 when the stock markets peaked, you would have been rewarded with a very healthy pension. However, if you had retired a year later your pension fund could have been up to 30 per cent smaller, as the stock market crashed in the intervening period. You are unlikely to retire on the spur of the moment, so it is not really possible to choose the moment when your pension fund payout is likely to be at its optimum, but if your planned retirement comes in the wake of a crash in investment values, you could choose to continue working, or at least not draw on your pension straight away and wait for a better moment to take it. But this is risky, as values could continue to go down.

If you move jobs you have the same options as with defined-benefit pensions, but the transfer value is calculated simply as your contributions multiplied by the fund's growth (or reduction) during your membership, less any charges.

Hybrid pensions

These pensions are calculated on both a defined-benefit and defined-contribution basis, and pay you whichever is the greater. They offer you the best of both worlds at the end of the scheme, although the rates used in the calculations may not always be the most advantageous.

Topping up your pension

Most occupational pension schemes issue you with a 'benefit statement' each year that itemizes your contributions to date and forecasts your pension at retirement age. By law all money-purchase schemes must provide you with an annual statement, and you have a right to receive one from defined-benefit schemes if they do not automatically provide it. This applies equally to schemes you no longer contribute to, if you have changed jobs but still retain a scheme from your old company. The government hopes to roll out 'combined pension statements' where both your occupational pension and your state pension forecasts will be stated together, over the next couple of years to 2005. Your scheme adminis-trator will organize this.

From these statements you will be able to see whether your future pension is in line with your expectations. If it is less than you had hoped for there are a number of ways to top it up.

AVCs and FSAVCs

Occupational pension scheme members are able to take out additional voluntary contributions (AVCs). Like occupational schemes, AVCs are set up and run by the company. It pays the charges and administration costs, and the scheme is overseen by trustees. All companies that provide occupational schemes must also provide an option to pay AVCs.

There are two types of AVC. 'Added-year' schemes are only available in companies that offer defined-benefit pensions. As in transferring your pension (see above), you can 'buy' extra years. If you had worked in a company for say 12 years, your pension would be calculated using the multiple 12/60, but you could make AVCs to buy four extra years, and this would increase the pension to 16/60 of your final salary.

It is possible for a defined-benefit scheme to use the alternative defined-contribution method, and a money purchase scheme will have to do so. This is an additional fund that works in the same manner as the main defined-contribution scheme described above.

You can also top up your pension by using a free-standing AVC (or FSAVC). This is a direct-contribution pension that is not run by your employer; you will probably get it from an insurance company. It works in exactly the same way as other direct-contribution funds, but has the advantage that it is not tied to your company so you can take it with you when you change jobs. As we shall see with all PPPs, it has the disadvantage that the charges to manage it have to be paid by you.

How much you can top your pension up

The government sets limits to how much people can put into their pensions each year. The levels change depending on your age, and are calculated on a percentage of your salary: see Table 4.3.

Table 4.3 Maximum pension top-up amounts

Age at 6th April	Maximum percentage of earnings allowed
Below 35	17.5
36-45	20
46-50	25
51-55	30
56-60	35
61 or over	40

The government also caps the maximum level of earnings these figures apply to. Currently the limit is £99,000. That is, any earnings over this figure will not attract tax relief when used towards your pension.

The government is also to introduce a total pension fund maximum level. This will apply from April 2005 and is currently expected to be a total fund value of £1.5 million, rising to £1.8 million by 2010. There is some controversy about how many people this will affect. The Treasury states that only 5,000 people have pension funds of this size or larger, while industry specialists claim it is nearer 600,000. If you have a large pension being built up it is definitely advisable to discover if or when you might reach this level, as the tax penalties on any 'excess' are nearly 60 per cent.

You can top up your pension to these percentages each year. All you need to know is how much you have paid into each pension you have (excluding state pension contributions).

Regardless of your earnings level, everyone can contribute (or have someone contribute to) a PPP up to a maximum of £3,600 each year. This means that non-earning spouses, students, children, the unemployed and so on can all theoretically build up a pension if they are able to put the maximum amount into their private pensions. If you put the maximum amount of £300 a month into a fund from the age of 20 until retirement at 65, you would be forecast to receive around £500 a week from your pension, or just over the average wage.

Tax advantages of pensions

As was mentioned at the outset of this chapter, pensions are given many tax breaks to encourage people to take them out. The main tax advantages for appropriate personal pensions, both occupational and private, are:

- The contributions to your pension, both your own and your employer's where they occur, get tax relief. In occupational pensions your contributions are deducted from your salary before tax is charged. This is an advantage because it has the effect of adding 22 per cent or 40 per cent (depending on your highest tax rate) to what you otherwise would pay. (The contribution made by your employer is considered to be a legitimate business expense and not a perk, so it is not taxed.) When you pay into a PPP out of your taxed income, the government reimburses the amount of tax. People paying the basic tax rate of 22 per cent receive only 78p in each pound after tax has been deducted, so the government adds 22 pence to make the amount up to £1. To put it another way, for every £1 you put into your pension fund the government adds a further 28 pence (note *not* 22p, because 28p is 22 per cent of £1.28). Similarly the government adds 67p for every £1 those on the 40 per cent tax rate put into their pension fund.

- If your occupational scheme also offers other benefits, such as life assurance, these are also tax free.
- You pay no NI on your pension contributions.
- The capital growth that your pension fund achieves is not taxed.
- Income earned by pension fund investments is not taxed, except for share dividend income which is taxed at 10 per cent. This tax was introduced by Gordon Brown in his first budget, and raises £5 billion a year for the Treasury, but equally removes £5 billion a year from the UK's pension funds, which over the years makes a large impact in the funding of pensions.
- When you retire you can take up to 25 per cent of your total pension fund as a tax-free lump sum.

The government does tax you on the income from your pension. This means that currently a pension's tax advantage over an ISA (where the money that is put in is taxed but the money that is taken out is not, the reverse of how a pension works) is only marginal, especially as currently ISA share income is not taxed, although this is due to change shortly.

Private pensions

Private pensions, or personal pension plans (PPPs), are the third category of pension available. They are the most flexible of the categories but they are also the most costly, and leave all the responsibility of managing, monitoring and maintaining them to the individual pension holder.

Private pensions have a variety of different styles but they are all based around the core concept of defined contributions as described in the previous section. The different styles come down to who manages your fund (a professional company, in which case it will be a PPP, or you personally, when it is called a self-invested personal pension or SIPP) and whether the manager adheres to a set of rules governing charges and access. If it does it is a stakeholder pension, and if it does not it is just a regular personal pension.

In 2001 the government overhauled the existing pension rules and introduced two new concepts, the stakeholder pension and the DC regime.

Stakeholder pensions

A stakeholder pension is a personal pension plan that meets certain criteria set out by the government and overseen by the Occupational Pensions Regulatory Authority (OPRA). OPRA is to be replaced by a new pensions regulator in the future: for more details visit www.thepensionservice.gov.uk/atoz/atozdetailed/fs2.asp or contact the Pension Service.

The criteria include:

- Low charges (annual administration and management charges must be 1 per cent or less of the funds managed).
- Low and flexible contributions (minimum contributions must be at most £20, and there should be no requirement for regular contributions).
- Transferability (there should be no penalties for moving your pension out of a stakeholder scheme to another scheme).
- A default option. Personal pensions have a range of ways they can invest your money, but a stakeholder scheme for simplicity must offer a 'standard' or default option for those unwilling to choose for themselves.

There are other criteria that stakeholder pensions must meet, which you can find at the OPRA Web site. To call itself a stakeholder pension the fund must have met the criteria and been registered with OPRA, so you can always check with OPRA (01273 627600 or at www.opra.gov.uk) whether a pension fund is properly registered or not.

Generally stakeholder pensions are just as good as non-stakeholder ones: there is little sacrificed for the guaranteed low cost. Should a pension fund not meet all the criteria laid down by OPRA, it does not automatically mean it is not worth having. Some non-stakeholder personal pension plans are reliable and good value, but do not meet the government's criteria because they are trying to achieve something extra to a normal stakeholder plan. They may specialize in investing in areas that are more expensive to administer, and so need to charge a higher management fee. They may offer greater depth of advice and personal service than a stakeholder scheme is set up to do, and again charge more for this. Some group personal pension plans may not be stakeholder registered, but the extra contributions made by the employer outweigh the risks of their not being so.

The DC regime

This is a grand name for a fairly simple idea. The DC (defined contributions) regime applies to most defined-contribution pensions:

- stakeholder pensions;
- other personal pensions;
- occupational money purchase schemes that have 'opted in' to the regime.

The regime allows anyone regardless of earnings to put up to £3,600 a year into one of the above pensions. The £3,600 is calculated before tax relief is applied, so if you pay tax at 22 per cent you will only have to give the pension fund £2,808 and the government will make up the remaining 22 per cent or £792. What is more, even if you are not earning anything, and therefore not paying tax, the government will still apply basic rate tax relief, in effect adding 22 per cent to your own contribution as a bonus. Higher rate tax payers receive the tax relief through their income tax payments, either self-assessment or PAYE.

Another aspect of the regime is that the pension contributions do not have to be paid by the pension holder. Anyone can put money into anyone else's DC regime pension. This could be your employer, a family member or a rich friend! This means that DC regime pensions (which are most often also stakeholder pensions) can be held by non-working wives, children, carers and many other non-earners as well as the employed.

The DC regime also allows you to contribute more than £3,600 per tax year as long as the maximum contribution is less than the age limit earning percentages listed in Table 4.3. There is also a way to pay over the actual percentage amount. You nominate a 'basis year' from which your earnings are calculated, and this basis-year figure is then used for the following five years. If you nominate a high earnings year, you will be able to continue making contributions at that rate for a five-year period regardless of whether you have earned that amount each year. If your earnings subsequently rise you can change your basis year. However, you cannot contribute more than the earnings cap imposed by the government. Currently the maximum income from which you can take a pension contribution is £102,000 for 2004/05. It generally rises in line with inflation each year.

The DC regime also allows you to 'carry back' pension contributions if you have not made full contributions. Before the regime was introduced you could carry back for six years; however, now you can only carry back for one year of earnings.

Selecting and managing your pension

We have explored the basic elements of pension provision, and hopefully it is now reasonably clear how state, occupational and private pensions work and what benefits they provide. Now it is time to think about your personal position.

You are likely to find yourself in one of two positions. Either you do not have a pension, realize that you should have one, and want to know how much you should start putting into a pension fund, and what type, to provide for your future; or you have a pension and want to know whether it will be sufficient for you when you retire.

Unfortunately no one can give you a precise answer to these questions. Factors that no one can predict will affect your pension provision.

Foremost amongst these are the future rate of inflation (although you can build in some protection against inflation, a sudden and rapid increase in levels will severely diminish your pension income) and the age to which you live. (If you were to die shortly after or even before you reach pension age, much of the pension benefits will be wasted, although again you can build in some inheritance strategies.)

When to begin making payments

The golden rule with pensions (as with most investment products) is to start the process as early as possible. For this reason the government allows people to put money into pensions for children – if you have already accumulated, say, 15 years of private pension contributions by the time you start work it puts you in a very healthy position. However, there is an argument that children whose parents can afford to put money into pensions for them are unlikely to find themselves on the poverty line anyway!

It might be the last thing on your mind when you start work after leaving school or university, but starting a private pension at that time could well be a decision you never stop congratulating yourself on later in life. To illustrate the impact of starting a pension early, see Table 4.4. This shows how much a person is likely to have to put aside to a pension each month from four different ages if he or she is to retire at 65 with a pension paying £20,000 per year, linked to inflation. As you will see the monthly premium required doubles for every decade of delay in starting payments.

Table 4.4 The impact of age on pension fund build-up

Age when start pension contributions	Monthly pension contribution	Total contribution
25	£150	£72,000
35	£300	£108,000
45	£600	£144,000
55	£1,200	£144,000

This illustration is based on a defined-contribution stakeholder scheme and does not include any state pension contributions or benefits. It also makes the unlikely assumption that the contributor does not increase the pension premiums in line with any increase in salary throughout his or her working life. In reality someone financially savvy enough to start making payments at 25 is likely to see his or her salary increase over the next 40 years, and will be able to increase the monthly payments in line with that, so should have a final pension substantially greater than £20,000 when he or she does retire. The late starters will have much greater difficulty achieving this.

Where to go to start a pension

So starting a pension today, or preferably before today, is a clever thing to do. Where do you find the right scheme? Each pension scheme has to be judged on its own particular merits, and you should discuss the schemes that are available to you (including both any employer scheme you are entitled to join, and schemes you learn about through your own research) with a qualified adviser.

As a general rule, schemes where your employer also makes a contribution will be more rewarding than others. Your first place of enquiry is therefore at work:

- If you work for a large company it is more than likely to have an occupational scheme available to you, and you should already have been informed about it.
- If you work for a smaller company it might not manage its own occupational scheme, but it might contribute to a GPPS that is available to you.
- Otherwise, if your employer employs five or more full-time workers it is legally bound to offer a stakeholder scheme that you can join.
- Finally, if you are self-employed or work for a very small business you may need to find a pension provider yourself.

If you are not employed, again you will need to find a pension provider yourself. You are probably best advised to seek a pension through a financial adviser, although you could approach directly a provider such as an insurance company or other financial institution.

The further away from a fully fledged occupational scheme you find yourself, the greater your need to speak with a qualified adviser. See Chapter 1 for how to find one.

How much you should contribute

The first question you should ask yourself is how much money you will need when you retire. The further away from retirement you are, the more difficult this question is to answer. If you are 55 and hope to retire in 10 years' time, you will have a fair idea of where you will be living, how much mortgage you will still have to pay or how much your house will be worth should you sell it and move to something smaller, how many children you will still have to support and also your current level of normal expenditure. Trying to answer these questions if you are just out of university is an enjoyable but probably pointless exercise. So you must take a different approach at different stages in your life.

In your twenties

If you are in the happy position of addressing the pension question when still in your twenties, you are probably wiser to think in terms of how much of your monthly salary you can afford to put aside. The best answer is 'as much as you can', but only you can make the decision. Putting money into a pension is highly commendable, but at this stage probably not as important as paying off any debt. It is also advisable to have built up a small cash reserve for emergencies. After you have achieved that, try to put as much as you can into a pension fund. The maximum you can put in is 17.5 per cent of your salary.

In your thirties

In your thirties you might have started a family, and you should have a better idea where your career is going. The basic outline of what you will need in retirement will be taking shape. What is more, if you are married and have children, in the unthinkable circumstances that you die before retirement age your pension fund can be inherited by your dependants.

In your forties

By your forties you really should have started a pension plan. If not, the answer to the 'how much each month' question will almost certainly be 'as much as you can afford'. If you started a pension 10 to 20 years earlier, you can start to assess whether it is going to provide enough, and if you feel it could do with some boosting, either increase your contributions if it is a private pension, or make some AVCs or FSAVCs if it is an occupational pension.

In your fifties

In your fifties you can really make some coherent decisions about what you will need in retirement. You should carry out an expenditure analysis (see the box for a prompt on where your money might be spent), then you will be able to see if your pension is going to cover the kind of life you currently lead. The good news is that you will probably be close to paying off your mortgage, and your child-related expenditure should be diminishing, or if it has not fallen off yet (children are typically at their most expensive in the late teens and early twenties if still in education) it should do so by your retirement age.

Monthly expenditure analysis

Mortgage or rental payments
Council tax
Water rates
Gas and electricity*
Telephone (fixed, mobile and Internet)*
House insurance (buildings and contents)
Life insurance
Health insurance

House maintenance (plumbers, electricians etc)
Monthly and yearly subscriptions (magazines, clubs, television channels etc)*
Credit card
School or university fees
Other child-related expenses not included elsewhere
Car expenses (petrol, servicing, rescue organizations, tax and insurance)
Other travel expenses
Clothing
Leisure and entertainment (hobbies, sports, trips, cinema, videos, meals out, pub etc)**
Food and drink (in the house)**
Holidays (average cost of last three holidays)
Regular savings*
Loan repayments

* If you pay for things using direct debits or standing orders, ask your bank for a list of them.
** Check your recent bank statements and credit card statements to get a feel for what you spend where. If you tend to use cash, see how much you get from cash machines and how often.

In your sixties

When reaching retirement age in your sixties you will be presented with a new set of dilemmas. Principal among these is whether to take your pension straight away, defer it for a number of years or take it gradually. If you decide to take it, you may be able to take up to 25 per cent as a cash lump sum, and you will need to buy an annuity with the remainder. Either this will be provided by your pension company or you may be able to purchase one independently (this is known as the open market option or OMO). These decisions might be straightforward for you, or they might require you to weigh up various pros and cons. We look briefly at each of them below.

In your seventies

By your seventies your choices are much more limited. In all probability you will already have taken your pension decisions, and will have to live with them whether they were right or wrong. If you have deferred your pension, you will have to take it when you reach 75. If you have delayed taking it until then, it is likely that you have sufficient other income sources, so you will be looking to take as much as possible in a tax-free lump sum.

Where to invest your pension fund

Only those with private pensions can choose what type of investment product they invest their pension fund in. Occupational schemes have a board of trustees to make this decision on behalf of all the scheme pension holders.

Different pension schemes invest in a wide range of different products. The list of different types of investment fund is very similar to the different types of unit and investment trusts, for the simple reason that the fund is essentially the same as an investment trust or unit trust. What differs is the manner in which the contributions are made, and the way in which the 'pot' is distributed. Typical investments are:

- UK and international shares, managed by an 'active' fund manager: that is, one who chooses the shares based on his or her own judgement.
- UK and international shares, managed by a 'passive' fund manager: that is, one who selects the shares based on a market index. These are known as tracker funds, as they track particular markets.
- Bonds, where the fund is invested in government bonds and corporate bonds.
- Property, where the fund is invested in predominantly commercial property.
- Other themed investments. These are variations of the above but the assets are themed around a specific attribute or location, such as capital growth or dividend income, or North American or European

products. The funds do not necessarily have to restrict themselves to one type of investment product, such as just shares or just bonds.

With-profits funds are a special type of fund that makes the same kind of investments as other funds, but the profits made are 'smoothed' each year by the managing company. This means that in good years not all the profits are added to the fund, but in bad years extra sums can be added (if available from the earlier years' profits). The profits are added as annual 'bonuses', and there is usually a large maturity or termination bonus. (For more information on with-profits funds see page 278.)

The choice of which type of fund your pension is invested in is up to you for most private pensions. You must make your choice based on two factors. The first is how much risk you are prepared to accept. The more risky the investment, the greater profit it will make in a good year, but also the more likely it is that you will lose money.

The second choice is centred around who manages the pension fund: that is, which insurance company or financial institution actually provides the fund. The things to consider when choosing a provider are:

- **Financial health.** How stable is the company that is providing the pension? Is it likely to still be operating when your pension matures? This is impossible to guarantee. Better known and larger companies may be less susceptible to disappearing, but as the fall of Equitable Life shows, not even this can be certain.

- **Charges.** How much does the pension provider take from your fund each year as an administration and management charge? Differences here may have little impact when you are starting the fund and it has only a little money in it, but after a few years when you have built up a sizeable figure, small differences in charges will make much larger differences each year, and substantial differences when the growth is compounded.

- **Investment reputation.** Whether the company has a good track record in producing better than average investment returns, or is a weak performer, is often thought to be an important consideration. However, as we are constantly reminded in the small print of financial adverts, 'history is no indication of future performance'. Whether a company will continue its level of performance depends more on whether individual managers remain with the company (which cannot ever be guaranteed) and a certain degree of luck (which cannot be guaranteed either). Some people believe that no company can consistently do better than average, so if a company has had a good streak it is probably about to stumble in its performance!

At-retirement decisions

On retirement you do not get given a weekly pay packet by your pension provider. What you get is a – hopefully large – sum of money, which is the amount your fund has built up for you throughout the term of contributing to your pension fund. You have two decisions to make at this stage: when do you want to take this money, and how do you want to take it?

The question of timing we address below. The question of how you want the money is fairly simple. You are entitled to take up to 25 per cent of it tax-free to use as you wish: buy that boat, go on a round-the-world cruise or more sensibly invest in something else. We examine the questions surrounding lump sums below. The remaining 75 per cent or more, depending on how much you have taken as a lump sum, has to be invested in an annuity.

Annuities

An annuity is a fixed amount of money that is paid each year to a named individual (or sometimes more than one individual), usually until he or she dies. Insurance companies and other pension providers sell these products. They are basically a gamble on the provider's part that most people will not live long enough to use up all the money originally paid in.

Say your pension fund provides you with a sum on retirement at 65 of £340,000 (the expected return if you pay £3,600 into a fund each year for 30 years, and get an average return of 7 per cent). You can take 25 per cent as a lump sum, £85,000, to buy your retirement Ferrari. That leaves you with £255,000. This will buy you an annuity that will pay you around £1,500 per month for the rest of your life, or £1,100 per month but increasing by the rate of inflation each year, for the rest of your life. (This is based on a male non-smoker without a spouse's pension included.) If you had decided to invest the whole amount in the annuity, and forgo the Ferrari, the payments would have been around £2,000 or £1,400 per month for the rest of your life.

The company makes complex assumptions about how long pensioners will live, based on their health and average life expectancy. It then invests the money from the annuity and hopefully earns a profit on it each year. At the same time it takes from it your pension requirements. If we continue with the example of a fixed £1,500 a month until you die, in return for your payment of £255,000, at the very least (even without any profit from reinvesting), there is enough money to cover you until you are nearly 80 years old. (£1,500 × 12 = £18,000 per year. £255,000 divided by £18,000 is 14.17: so the money lasts 14 years and 2 months. If you are 65 at retirement, 14 years and 2 months later you will be nearly 80.) If you die before you reach 80, the annuity provider keeps the money left over. If you live well past 80, the provider has to pay for you out of its own resources. The provider makes money on the calculation that more people will die before their annuity purchase price runs out than will live past that time.

It is for this reason that annuity providers are so interested in your health, gender and age when you start the annuity. Obviously the younger you are when you start the policy, the longer the provider will have to make the payments, and so the less you will get each month. As women tend to live longer than men, they get lower annual returns (monthly payments) than men. Buying an annuity if you are a smoker is the only time you will receive any financial benefit for smoking, as the providers reckon you will die sooner, so they give you larger monthly payments. To win at annuities you should be a heavy-smoking man who has once had cancer – and then live until you are 104!

Other choices that affect your annuity payments are whether you would like your pension (or a proportion of it) to be paid to your spouse after you die, whether you want your pension to be linked to inflation or not, and whether you want it 'guaranteed' for a limited period or not. This means that should you take out a five-year annuity guarantee and die within that time, your inheritors will get payments or an equivalent lump sum, up to the end of the five-year period.

To discover what likely pension you will receive from your annuity, the FSA provide some easily used tables which take into account many of the variables at www.fsa.gov.uk/tables.

Table 4.5 gives some typical returns on a £300,000 annuity, depending on different variables.

Table 4.5 Typical annuity returns

Age at start of annuity	Man non-smoker	Man smoker	Woman non-smoker	Woman smoker	Man non-smoker inflation linked	Man non-smoker 5 year guaranteed
55	£1,300	£1,500	£1,250	£1,400	£800	£1,280
65	£1,800	£1,900	£1,600	£1,650	£1,150	£1,650
74	£2,300	£2,600	£2,200	£2,200	£1,600	£2,100

(c) Financial Services Authority Nov 2003, selected and averaged data

Remember that, although you get more annuity income per month by delaying purchasing your annuity, you are also losing out on actual income by not taking it earlier. The calculation whether you are better off by delaying the annuity or taking a lower annuity income earlier is complicated, and depends on how long you live after having finally taken the annuity. It is best to discuss these issues with a qualified adviser.

Your pension fund provider will probably make it very simple for you to swap your fund for one of its annuities. However, in most cases you are not obliged to purchase your annuity from your fund provider. The government (through the FSA) is very keen to get pensioners to look around for annuities from other sources as well. This is called the open market option (or OMO), where you buy your annuity in the open market. Possibly your fund providers will provide you with a more generous annuity if you buy it from them, through a 'loyalty bonus' for staying with the same company. Currently these are still quite rare, but if more OMOs are purchased, loyalty bonuses might become more popular as a way to keep customers. In any case it is worth asking your pension provider if it has a loyalty bonus scheme, and comparing the rates with other annuities on the market.

You can only buy your annuity once. Once you have purchased it you cannot transfer it, cash it in or change it in any way – you are stuck with it. So it is important to make sure you have examined all the options before you commit yourself to a purchase.

You can purchase 'extras' for your annuity:

- **Shared life,** where after you die your surviving spouse can continue to get your pension, usually at 100 per cent, 66 per cent or 50 per cent of the rate you received. The higher the rate, the lower your own pension will be.
- **Guaranteed.** You do not normally get anything back from the annuity after you die, so if you die early all your lifetime's pension savings will go to the annuity provider. You can ensure that your family gets paid, regardless of how soon you die, by taking out a guarantee, usually for 5 or 10 years, that promises to continue paying a pension for that amount of years from starting the policy, or at least an equivalent lump sum.
- **Level or linked.** A basic annuity pays a fixed amount each month that does not change until you die (known as a level annuity). You can choose to have it increase by a fixed amount each year, or have it linked to the rate of inflation. Obviously if you choose these options your initial payments will be smaller. They are only worth taking if you are confident you will live for a good many years!

Having chosen your extras you should also be aware of the different types of annuity that are available. Generally they trade increased potential returns for higher risk.

- **Standard fixed income:** this is the most secure form of annuity, where the payments are guaranteed.
- **With profits:** (see Chapter 16): this type is linked to investment performance. It should provide a better return but is also higher risk; poor stock market performance could make payments fall in the medium to long term.
- **Unit linked:** these are also linked to investment performance, but riskier again than with profits, as there is no smoothing effect. Your annuity income is likely to fluctuate with this type of annuity, which is higher risk.
- **Impaired life:** these are for people with poor life expectancy because of their lifestyle, a medical condition or family history. Consequently the annuity pays out at a better rate as the provider does not expect to have to pay it for as long.
- **Purchased life:** these are bought with a lump sum and top up any other annuity you may have. The downside is that once invested, the money cannot be passed on after you die.

Lump sums

Taking a lump sum is a decision you can only make after having worked out the levels of annuity income you would receive after having taken it and without taking it. In the example above, with a £340,000 annuity and the possibility of taking an £85,000 lump sum, the range of income available was between £1,500 a month with the full lump sum taken and £2,000 a month leaving the money in the annuity. It is up to you to decide what level of pension income you require, and whether any other income sources you have to boost your annuity income are stable and ongoing.

It is possible that if you do take the lump sum you could use it profitably to pay off your mortgage or other debts (thus reducing your monthly outgoings and so effectively increasing your income). You could reinvest it in something more risky but which produces a higher return and is also available to pass on to your inheritors, or purchase something that substantially improves your retirement lifestyle, such as a boat, a workshop and tools, or travel. The last alternative can only be considered a good idea if you reckon you have enough income from your annuity to live off anyway. There is no advantage in having a fancy boat if you cannot afford to pay the mooring charges or keep it maintained.

As with all pension decisions there are many variables to consider, and each person's circumstances and priorities will be different. It is advisable to discuss these variables with a qualified adviser.

When to take your pension

Non-state pensions can usually be taken from the age of 50 (but the government intends to raise this to 55 soon). State pensions cannot be taken early. With non-state pensions you can defer taking your pension until you are 75. However, with the state pension you can currently defer it only until you are 70, although the government is changing the system in 2005 so that you can defer it indefinitely.

If you choose to take a pension early you will clearly have fewer years to put contributions into your pension fund, and it will have less time to grow than if you continue until normal retirement age. These two factors mean that it will have built up a considerably smaller amount of money than if you did not retire early. To make matters worse your annuity income will also be considerably smaller, as the annuity provider will reckon that it will have to pay you an income for a longer time. Retiring in your early fifties is only realistic if you have amassed an unusually large pension fund by this time, or have other sources of income. It becomes a more realistic choice if you only wish to retire a couple of years or so early. Only you can tell if the annuity income available to you will be sufficient, or whether you would benefit substantially from continuing working for a few more years.

One exception to this rule is if you suffer from an illness that may affect your life expectancy. In this case your annuity provider might pay out a more generous amount, and you could then be wise to take early retirement to best enjoy it.

On reaching retirement age you have two alternatives if you do not take up your full pension entitlement straight away. You can defer it entirely or you can phase it. If you defer, your pension fund continues to grow, and you can continue to make contributions if you are still working. As a result your pension 'pot' will be larger when you do come to purchase an annuity, as will be your potential lump sum. You can also defer your state pension. This too will increase in value (see page 85), and from 2005 you will be able to take a lump sum of up to £20,000 (£30,000 for a couple) if you defer it for five years.

An alternative is to ease yourself into your pension, which is attractive if you are easing yourself out of work. Current legislation does not allow you to take a phased pension from an occupational scheme if you continue to work for the employer, even on a part-time basis, although anomalously you could do so if you worked part-time for someone else. This hiccup is being changed.

Phased retirement (also known as staggered vesting) is an attractive option. Essentially your pension fund is divided into, say, 1,000 segments and each year you can choose to take a certain number of them, some as tax-free cash, the rest to invest in an annuity. The advantage is that as you get older your annuity rates should improve, so you will be improving your potential pension income. Also, as the pension fund is still active it should be increasing in value during this period. Money in a pension fund is inheritable, while that in an annuity is not. Another option is **income drawdown**, where the pension fund provides you with an income, which can vary but will not be more than the maximum you would get were it all invested in an annuity. It has many of the same benefits as phased retirement, again giving flexibility in your income needs. **Phased income drawdown** is a mixture of the two approaches.

In all cases you must invest all your pension fund before your 75th birthday, so these options only have a limited availability.

Pensions after death

We have referred to the 'inheritability' of many of these different situations throughout this chapter. Essentially there are two inheritance issues: what happens to the assets in your pension fund if you die before you use them, and what happens to your pension income. In almost all cases the pension income is only inheritable by a spouse after death, and often at a reduced rate. This applies equally to pension funds and annuities. Typically the actual rules that apply will be set out in the 'key features' document that all pension policies should come with. If you do not have this booklet ask your IFA, company or pension provider for it.

The capital is only inheritable while it is invested in the pension fund. It is usually subject to a special 35 per cent tax rate. The exact calculations that determine how much is available after death will again vary from policy to policy. Once the fund is invested in an annuity it is not inheritable unless the pensioner has died during a guaranteed period, in which case the remaining number of years of the guaranteed income period will be available.

Pensions after divorce

Pensions, being valuable assets, are divisible between partners on divorce, especially if they are of significant value. The division is usually complex, and the calculations depend on what sort of pension exists. Defined-benefit pensions are the most complicated to divide up, as no one can tell what the eventual final salary will be at the point of divorce. Defined-contribution funds are easier to calculate as the contributions to date are known and can be divided. Occupational schemes are further compli-cated by the possibility of death in service adjustments. Finally, the state pension can also be divided, but in this case an application to the Benefits Agency is required, as a portion of the pensioner's pension is cleaved off to create a new fund for the pensionless spouse. This is a complicated area and specialist advice must be sought.

And finally...

As the length of this chapter shows, pensions are complex and can take a multitude of different shapes and forms. You should always get advice from a qualified professional. As the FSA states in its literature, in the end you should not make any decisions unless you are satisfied you understand what you are buying and the possible benefits and risks involved. To this we would add, but do not delay making that decision.

5

Essential insurance

Insurance is irritating on a number of levels. It has a certain voodoo quality to it; in the back of many of our minds is the thought that we are not paying our insurance premiums because we want to be covered should something go wrong, but rather that by paying our premiums we are warding off the evil spirits that make things go wrong. This is not a very rational approach to managing your finances. Also you have to work out where to draw the line. It would be simple but hugely expensive to insure yourself against every mishap that might occur; knowing where you are prepared to draw the line is important, but the right point is not at all clear. Finally, it is irritating because you may well find that after many years of regular premiums being paid you have never made a significant claim. If that is the case you have to console yourself with the thought that the premium payments did indeed ward off the evil spirits!

Some insurance is mandatory, some is highly advisable and some is a luxury. The mandatory insurance is generally limited to third-party car insurance, if you own a car and intend to drive it on the road (when it is a legal requirement that you be insured), and buildings and life insurance with mortgages (you are unlikely to find a mortgage that does not require these). Although these are therefore 'essential' they are not what this chapter is about.

The luxury end of the insurance range provides you with greater comfort should things go wrong. If you can afford to purchase this level of insurance then you probably should, but it is not 'essential'. The types of insurance here include fully comprehensive car insurance, private health insurance and fully insured household contents insurance.

It is the highly recommended types of insurance that we consider to be 'essential'. They do not apply to everybody, only those people with dependent families (that is, a non-working partner and/or children) and they are generally not obvious because unlike the luxury insurance which focuses on possessions, your car, your jewellery or your furniture, this level of insurance focuses on an intangible: your income.

Few people like to consider what would happen if they were to die prematurely or have an incapacitating illness or disability. While it may be interesting to consider how your partner would cope should your income disappear permanently, or at least for a prolonged period, it is critical to consider this eventuality if you have children or any other dependants unable to earn an income for themselves.

The two eventualities to be considered here are the income earner's death, and his or her inability to work through illness or disability. Financially, if not emotionally, death is the easier to deal with. There can be no question over relative levels of inability to work, and there are no extra or continued expenses to cover for the insured person. Disability or illness is much more complex. Questions of whether the insured person can do no work or some work, or can no longer earn at the previous level, and so on can be very hard to define. Extra costs might be incurred such as ramps for wheelchairs, special beds, bathing equipment and transport; these might be one-off items or ongoing expenses. At the time of taking out the insurance you will not know what eventuality you are likely to encounter. It could be a single loss of a sense such as deafness or blindness, which while distressing is at least not progressive, or it could be a progressively worsening condition. All these unknowns make insurance against loss of income through illness a much more complicated process.

Add to this the statistic that the chances of your becoming critically ill during your working life are much greater than the chances of you dying, and you find yourself in a maze of possibilities and choices with no clear route out.

To help us navigate this depressing area of personal finance we shall first of all look at the different products available, then consider how to decide which are appropriate for you.

Car Insurance

We put 100% into finding a great quote and take 10% off

£308
A typical quote

£277
Including 10% discount

We search amongst some of the UK's top car insurers to find you our best quote. Then we beat it by knocking an extra 10% off.

It's easy – sit back while we search from a panel of some of the UK's top car insurers – such as Churchill, Provident, Fortis and NIG – to find you our best deal.

It's fast – just a few short questions and a few quick clicks, and the quote is on your screen.

See how much Screentrade could save you

Company	Premium	Your saving
Screentrade	**£277.73**	It's as easy as that!
More Than	£324.87	**£47.14**
Direct Line	£406.35	**£128.62**
Elephant	£483.00	**£205.27**

Premium based on 38 year old male, married computer engineer, living in Doncaster, driving a 1998 1.6 Citroen Saxo VTR with 5 years protected no claims bonus. Data supplied by Insurance Research & Data Services in May 2004. mailirds@aol.com

See how much you could save at:

 trade.co.uk
or call 0800 032 0596 quoting LM874

We find you our best quote and beat it

ICEBERG ROAD RAGE –
A HIDDEN MENACE ON OUR HIGHWAYS

Dr David Lewis, the psychologist credited with first coining the phrase 'road rage', has discovered a new motorway menace through a nationwide survey commissioned by **www.screentrade.co.uk** – Iceberg Road Rage Syndrome.

While drivers suffering from this syndrome rarely resort to abusive words, obscene gestures or actual violence against another motorist, their angry thoughts still make them a menace behind the wheel by distracting them from the road ahead. As a result, they tend to drive much more dangerously and far less responsibly.

The survey, commissioned by screentrade.co.uk, also revealed that not only is Iceberg Road Rage Syndrome becoming increasingly widespread, but it can prove even more dangerous than the more obvious displays of fury between angry motorists.

While a low number of respondents admitted to shouting abuse through an open window, driving in such a way as to scare another motorist or resorting to physical violence, a high percentage confessed to thinking angry thoughts about an inconsiderate fellow motorist.

Eight out of ten of those surveyed said they frequently muttered angrily under their breath, four out of ten admitted to making a rude gesture but not so that it could be seen, while a third said they brooded angrily about what they considered dangerous or inconsiderate driving on the part of other motorists.

One in five said they spent the next several miles plotting about how they would take their revenge on that driver without having any intention of ever really doing so.

Such angry thoughts can occupy a motorist's mind for a considerable amount of time, with one in ten admitting that their furious broodings continued for an hour or more, and six out of ten admitted they focused on what had just happened for up to ten minutes.

Screentrade.co.uk's survey suggests that length of driving experience and personality play a major role in the likelihood of a motorist falling victim to Iceberg Road Rage.

Eight out of ten of those who had held a driving licence for ten years or more claimed that they had never felt or shown any anger towards another motorist.

Drivers who insisted that they had never felt or shown any anger towards another motorist were most likely to describe themselves as relaxed and laid back individuals who seldom allow themselves to get worked up about anything.

Respondents who admitted to brooding angrily about another driver's dangerous or inconsiderate driving or to plotting how they would like to take revenge were least likely to describe themselves as adopting either a relaxed or laid back outlook on life.

They, by contrast, were more likely to consider themselves precise, reliable and painstaking folk who hated to be hurried when making up their minds.

Those who admitted to making a rude gesture in such a way that it could be seen were the most likely to consider themselves informal and spontaneous individuals who like to laugh a lot and who never take life too seriously.

"These bitter ruminations distract drivers and prevent them from devoting their full attention to road conditions and other vehicles," says Dr David Lewis, a leading psychologist. "They may also make them drive less courteously and more riskily as they fantasise about taking their revenge on the offending motorists. Bear in mind that, if driving on a motorway, even a 10 minute distraction means someone driving at the legal limit will have covered several miles, while an hour's worth of distraction could take the driver's mind off their task for seventy miles or more. Clearly, the potential for serious errors of judgement under these circumstances is significant and extremely worrying. I have called this syndrome Iceberg Road Rage Syndrome because most of it is hidden beneath what may appear an outwardly calm surface."

Screentrade.co.uk wants motorists to be aware of the consequences of Iceberg Road Rage Syndrome. Screentrade's chief operating officer, Nigel Lombard, said: "In the past attention has focused on the visible signs of road rage. Our research demonstrates that there is a widespread, perhaps even more dangerous, form of motorist anger and frustration that can prevent drivers from fully concentrating on the road and the hazards ahead. We would urge drivers to understand the importance of being alert and fully aware of everything around them when on the road."

The main types of insurance involved are:

- life insurance;
- terminal illness cover;
- critical illness cover;
- income protection.

Life insurance

Life insurance comes in two types: term insurance, which itself has many variables; and permanent cover. Term insurance is a policy for a fixed period of years, during which a specified amount of money is paid out to the policyholder's dependants should he or she die. Should the holder not die during the term of the policy, the insurance company gets to keep all the premiums and nothing is paid back. Term insurance is therefore a gamble by the insurance company that you will remain alive throughout the policy term. If the company reckons there is a reasonable risk of your dying (if for example you are in ill health at the beginning of the policy period, or your family history suggests you might die early, or your lifestyle involves a hazardous occupation), it will reflect this in making sure you pay higher premiums.

Note that nearly all insurance policies can refuse to pay out if you fail to disclose information that could affect your life expectancy, such as current or previous illnesses, or your enjoyment of dangerous sports.

Term insurance policies come in a flurry of different shapes and sizes: see the box for a breakdown of these.

Term insurance variables

Level term insurance

This is the simplest form of term insurance. You choose a level of cover you require to be paid in the event of your death; you choose how long you want the policy to run (the 'term'); and you decide whether it is to be just for your own life or jointly (usually with your partner). The insurance company takes these variables, assesses the lives to be insured for their age, health and riskiness of lifestyle, and comes up with an appropriate monthly premium.

The 'level' element of the insurance is that the premium and the cover offered will remain static throughout the period of the term. This way you know exactly at the outset of the policy what you will pay and what you will get.

Mortgage or decreasing term insurance

If you have taken out a mortgage (or other loan) and wish to assure yourself that it will be repaid if you die, so your partner or family is not burdened with the repayments, this is a sensible type of insurance to take out. The cover provided falls in line with the outstanding amount of the loan, and although the premium remains the same throughout the term, it will be significantly lower than a level term premium.

This type of insurance can also be used to offset potential inheritance tax liabilities on any gifts. (See Chapter 19.)

Increasing term insurance

This is where the cover increases by a set amount each year, often in line with inflation, to maintain an inflation-proof level of cover. The premiums will increase at the same time. You can also get the option to increase the cover at set periods should your circumstances change (typically after the birth of a child). This is known as increasable term insurance.

Renewable term insurance

This allows you to continue the insurance period for another term once the current term ends – but without any new assessment of your health. Premiums on the second term are generally higher to reflect your increased age but not to reflect any change in health.

This could be useful should your dependants continue to be dependent on you for longer than you originally anticipated.

Convertible term insurance

This allows you to convert your term insurance into an investment-based policy. Again the converted insurance is based on your health at the outset of the original policy rather than the converted one – so the premiums should be cheaper, especially if your health has deteriorated in the meantime.

Family income benefit insurance

A variant on term insurance also exists that pays out a regular income rather than a lump sum. The income is paid out tax free, usually on a monthly basis, should you die or become terminally ill. The payments stop at the end of the policy term. Clearly the longer you live, the fewer payments the insurance company is liable to have to make. The premiums are generally the cheapest out of the types of term insurance available.

The second type of life insurance, permanent policies, is also known as 'whole-of-life' insurance and 'life assurance', as you are assured of getting something back. These are investment-based policies, which pay out a sum when you die regardless of when that happens. The upside is that you (or rather your inheritors) get something when you die; the downside is that it might not be very much if you die early in the policy period before you have a chance to build up its value. These are generally sold as 'with-profits' policies (see Chapter 16), where you get a guaranteed amount plus any profits accumulated throughout the investment period. Obviously the profit element will be small at the outset, if there is anything extra at all, but it should grow the longer you hold the policy, given reasonable investment performance. Unitized policies purchase units in an investment fund each month. Some of them are cashed in to purchase a term insurance, and the excess goes to the investment part of the policy. Every 5 or 10 years it is likely that your insurance company will review these payments, and either increase your premiums to pay for a new term policy or reduce the guaranteed cover.

Terminal illness cover

Terminal illness cover will pay out a guaranteed tax-free lump sum when you have been diagnosed by a competent medical expert or the insurance company's own medical officer as having a terminal illness or life expectancy of less than 12 months. Generally both premiums and benefits remain static for the length of the term, but increasing policies linked to the rate of inflation can also be found. The terms of when you are eligible to claim for terminal illness payouts can be quite specific, so it pays to read the policy closely and ensure you understand the cover. Many life policies include terminal illness cover, but not all, so it pays to check. With these policies, should you claim for terminal illness, the payments are normally made instead of your receiving a payment on death rather than in addition to a payment on death.

Critical illness cover

This is now becoming more popular, but has for a long time been largely overlooked by people as a useful insurance product. This is probably because when we do persuade ourselves to consider the implications of any tragedy befalling us, we are more likely to envisage a terminal and sudden end than a chronic and disabled future. Statistics tell us, however, that people are six times more likely to suffer from an illness or disablement for a prolonged period of time than they are to die during their working lives. You are therefore six times more likely to need critical illness cover than life cover.

The policy works in the same manner as other insurance policies. In return for your premiums you will receive a tax-free lump sum, of a predetermined amount, should you develop a critical illness that is on the list of illnesses covered by the policy. The box has a typical basic list of illnesses covered. These may vary from company to company, and for a higher premium you can get an extended list to cover rarer conditions. Note that if your illness is not on the list you will not receive any cover.

A typical list of illnesses and disabilities covered by critical illness cover insurance

Alzheimer's disease before retirement age

Angioplasty

Aorta graft surgery

Benign brain tumour

Blindness

Cancer (most malignant types)

Coma

Coronary artery bypass surgery

Deafness

Heart attack

Heart valve replacement or repair

HIV/AIDS cover for medical staff and other specified groups

Kidney failure

Loss of limbs

Loss of speech

Major organ transplant

Motor neurone disease before retirement age

Multiple sclerosis

Paralysis/paraplegia

Parkinson's disease before retirement age

Permanent and total disability before retirement age

Pre-senile dementia before retirement age

Stroke

Third degree burns

The Association of British Insurers sets out minimum standards for these policies. For further details phone 020 7600 3333 or go to www.abi.org.uk

Income protection insurance

Also known as permanent health insurance or PHI, income protection insurance provides a similar service to critical illness cover, in that you are paid money if you cannot work as a result of illness or injury. You can also buy policies that pay you if you become unemployed. The major difference is that the money is paid in regular monthly amounts, as your pay would have been, and not in a single lump sum. The amount of cover available is up to you, but it is usually capped at a percentage of your current annual pay, typically between 50 and 60 per cent of gross salary.

The other major difference with income protection policies is that you can choose how long you wish to defer the payouts from the moment you stop working. Clearly the longer you can defer the payments, the cheaper the insurance premiums will be. Different deferment options are useful because of the differing lengths of time for which people are paid statutory or non-statutory sick pay, and the differing levels of redundancy payments. Those entitled to the full six months of SSP or a generous redundancy payment might choose to defer their insurance payout until this is exhausted. The self-employed or people ineligible for the full benefit will need payments to start sooner. The deferment period is also known as the exclusion period or excess period (as it is similar to the excess on motor and contents insurance).

The other time period to consider is the benefit period, which is the length of time for which the benefits will be paid once they have started. Conversely, the shorter this is, the cheaper your premiums will be.

Two other types of insurance that you may also come across are considered to be general insurance products rather than long-term products.

Payment protection insurance

This is a policy that will pay the repayments on a specified loan or loans in the event of accident, sickness and sometimes unemployment. It will not provide any extra income. These policies tend to only continue paying for 12 or 24 months, unlike full income protection policies. They are most often offered with mortgages and larger personal loans. Note that credit card companies also offer payment protection policies, adding a small premium charge to your bill each month. These are widely regarded as being bad value for money in most cases.

Accident and sickness insurance

These policies are most frequently found as part of travel and comprehensive car insurance policies, but can be purchased as stand-alone insurance if you wish. You will be paid a guaranteed sum in the event of specific injuries such as loss of a finger or an eye, or if you contract an illness that prevents you from working. These policies generally are only sold in single-year contracts, with the policyholder being reassessed each year. It is unlikely that most people will need such a policy on an ongoing basis unless their lifestyle is particularly risky or their occupation relies on (for example) their fingers or legs (such as a pianist or dancer), in which cases more specific personal policies should be sought from a specialized insurer.

What types of insurance you require and how much it will cost

Life insurance is really only necessary for couples and those with dependants: children, but also elderly or disabled relatives. If you are single without dependants then there is no one who will need the extra money should you die. Life insurance premiums vary hugely according to your sex, age, health and lifestyle. As a very rough rule of thumb they can start from around £10 per month for £100,000 of cover for a 20-year term.

Illness cover, both terminal and critical, is of relevance to both single and married people, and those with and without dependants. We all need to continue paying the bills and feeding ourselves even when we are ill –

in fact especially when we are ill. The added stress of no income if you are ill for a prolonged period of time can only slow your recovery.

Income protection for unemployment is more of a luxury for single people, as they have more flexibility in accommodating any new straitened circumstances. For people with dependants, however, this flexibility is severely restricted, and unemployment insurance must become a more serious possibility.

The decision as to what types of cover you need is relatively straightforward. Imagine the worst of circumstances, and work out the consequences for yourself and your family. Could you cope without extra financial help once your income has stopped? This should be reasonably clear to you.

Trying to work out how much extra financial help you require is much more difficult. As in Chapter 2 it will be necessary to understand what your living costs are. You might be able to minimize some of them, but you will also have to add in any extra costs arising from new circumstances (extra childcare expenses, modifications to your home, inheritance tax liabilities, funeral costs and so on). Only when you have broken down all your requirements and set them against any savings or remaining income sources will you be able to establish an idea of the amount of extra income you will need. Every person will have different needs and provisions. The box lists some of the additional things you should consider.

Potential extra expenses when the worst happens

In addition to your normal monthly expenses as outlined in Chapter 2, you might also need to consider funding new or one-off costs if a partner or main income earner should die or become ill.

In case of death

Any inheritance tax (IHT) obligations. If the deceased's total estate is less than £255,000, including a house, or all the estate is passed to the surviving spouse, no IHT is payable. Otherwise the excess over £255,000 is charged at 40 per cent. (See Chapter 19.)

Funeral expenses – currently averaging around £1,500 for a cremation and over £2,000 for a burial, this cost hits you at a time when you are already distressed and cutting costs seems inappropriate. Only 2 per cent of the population make any provision for their funeral expenses, which leaves the rest of us having to take out loans at a time when money may already be tight. It is definitely worth adding this expense into your calculations. (See Chapter 9.)

Accessible cash. Bank accounts and investments are frozen once someone dies, except for joint accounts. Should the holder of the family savings account be the one to die, the remaining family might not have access to it for some months, while lawyers ascertain that the money is not needed for paying off any loans or inheritance tax liabilities. It is therefore advisable to make sure that each partner has access to enough money to tide over such a period.

If the deceased was not the main earner but the main carer, you will also need to find *money for a carer* to fill in for their role.

In case of illness

The list here is much more difficult to define, as illness can come in many forms and levels of disablement. Think about:

- care staff;
- transport;
- changes to bathing, cooking and access facilities in your home;
- new equipment (wheelchairs, hearing aids, prosthetics and so on) – while the state will provide basic levels of support for these, you might want to obtain particular equipment that is not state-provided.

In either case

If you are no longer fully employed you might also lose other benefits that you have not included in your normal monthly expenditure, but that you would wish to retain in order to maintain a certain living standard. Amongst these might be:

- pension contributions;
- private medical insurance;
- compan car.

Once you have listed your likely needs you will be able to get a rough idea of how much extra income you require. When you go to take out an insurance policy the adviser will be obliged to go through these expenses with you again. This is useful as it could highlight areas you overlooked. However, it is also useful for you to already have an idea of the figure required, so you can assure yourself that the adviser is being realistic, so it is advisable to do this costing exercise prior to visiting your adviser.

Other sources of help

It is possible that you would be entitled to financial assistance from schemes your employer has created in the event of accident or illness. Before purchasing any insurance of your own, check what assistance your employer may be able to provide.

The state will also provide some benefits for people with disabilities – see Chapter 11 for some of these. Finally, your own level of savings will clearly make a difference to the level of insurance you require.

Part 2

Financial Competence: Level 2

In the long term we are all dead.

The celebrated economist J M Keynes

In this second section of the book we focus on the events in your life that require specific financial management. These are the events that will cost you a large amount of money (and stress), such as buying a house, getting married, having children, paying for education and healthcare. Most of these events are positive occasions, but they will be more enjoyable and easier if they are planned for in advance. This is not always possible, but the more you can plan, the easier it will be to deal with unexpected events when and if they occur. Much of the advice follows a similar pattern, is straightforward and can overlap, so the chapters in this section are not as long or as complex as those in Level One.

The chapters cover:

- Mortgages.
- Education.
- Healthcare.
- Long-term care.
- Relationship finance (weddings, marriage and divorce).
- One-off loans.
- Benefits.
- Tax planning.
- Charitable giving.

6

Mortgages

Everyone needs a roof over their head, and it has long been a British obsession to own that roof rather than just rent it. Nor are we alone in that – the other English-speaking developed countries and the Mediterranean countries are similarly keen on owning rather than renting, as Table 6.1 shows.

Table 6.1   Housing ownership in different countries (by percentage)

Country	Rented	Owner occupied	Other
Australia*	29	71	0
Belgium	23	74	3
Denmark	45	51	4
Germany	57	43	0
Greece	20	74	6
Holland	48	52	0
France	38	54	8
Ireland	18	79	3
Italy**	25	68	6
Japan***	39	60	1
Spain	11	83	6
Sweden**	44	39	17
United Kingdom	32	68	0
United States ^	33	67	0

Source: EU Housing Statistics 1999
* Australian government statistics 1998; ** latest figures 1997; *** Japanese Statistics Bureau 1998; ^ US *Building Magazine* 2000

In the UK we are much shorter on space than Australia, the United States, Greece and Spain. Added to that, the UK population likes to cram itself into the south-east corner of the country. And in recent years we have tended to prefer living alone rather than in large families, so the number of households is increasing even though the average size of them is falling. More households mean more houses are needed – and with demand outstripping supply, house prices, as everyone knows, have now risen in value at above the long-term trend level for eight years. This makes buying a house in the UK a very expensive task, far and away the largest single purchase most of us are likely to make in our lives. With the average UK house price at over £160,000, and the average first house now over £100,000, very few people can afford to buy their first house without having to borrow money from somewhere.

Housing trends

Luckily borrowing money to fund a house purchase is not only relatively easy, it is also sensible. Unfortunately it is only easy for those on a regular income who have some savings available for a deposit, and it is only sensible if you monitor your loan repayments carefully *and* the housing market does not fall in value for a sustained period. If you look at Figure 2.10 (page 33) you will see that UK average house prices have only fallen four times in the last 30 years; and that if you had purchased your house in the year either side of the last housing peak (1988–90) and held on to it for five or six years, on average you would still have seen an increase in its value. Had you purchased your property in any other year in the last 30 you would have seen an increase in your property's value in less than half that time. At the time of writing the graph looks as if it is approaching another peak. However, economic conditions are very different now from those of the late 1980s, with much lower interest rates and a more stable economy, so a property bust to follow the recent property boom is in no way assured, but a period of slow house price growth should be expected.

The importance of house price inflation – an example

The importance of house price growth to taking out a mortgage is that it makes your loan much more efficient.

First let us look at an example of what steady growth does. If you buy a house for £100,000 with £20,000 of personal savings and £80,000 of loan, in practical terms you immediately get to enjoy using a property worth five times what you personally have paid for it. The cost of this enjoyment is the regular loan expense. If your loan is charged at 5 per cent a year you will be paying £4,000 a year (£80,000 × 5 per cent) or £333 a month in interest. At this level you are not paying off any of the loan, just the interest cost.

If house prices are increasing by 15 per cent a year (as they have been in the recent property boom), and you own the house for five years, when you sell it five years later the house will be worth £201,137 (£100,000 at 15 per cent over five years). You will have paid five years of interest payments totalling £20,000 (5 × £4,000). This means that you will have made over £100,000 profit on an investment of £20,000 (your initial deposit) in only five years (the sale price of £201,137 less the loan of £80,000 and less the interest payments of £20,000 = £101,137).

However, had the average house price increase only been 7.5 per cent (the average long-term rate in the last 30 years), your house would only have been worth £143,562 after five years, giving you an increase of only £43,562 after paying off the loan with interest.

If there had been no increase in prices over the five-year period, such as happened between 1989 and 1994, your accommodation would have cost you the interest charge. And had there been a price fall in the five-year period, you would have lost money on the capital cost of the property as well. But as we have seen, this has happened infrequently.

So not only does house price inflation make you money, but if you take out a loan it makes your investment more efficient. In the middle example, with growth at 7.5 per cent, you get a 115 per cent return on your money over five years. Had you paid for the house entirely out of personal savings and not borrowed any money, you would not have paid any interest charges but you would still have made a smaller return. You would have paid out an initial amount of £100,000 and received back £143,562 five years later: an increase of £43,562 on an investment of £100,000. That is an increase of only 43.5 per cent, less than half the increase you would have gained if you had taken out a loan. Of course the extravagant returns are due to historically low interest rates. If interest rates increase to nearer the rate of house price growth, this efficiency gain is severely reduced.

We see from this simple example that successful house purchasing (from a financial point of view) relies on a number of factors. The two principal ones are the rate of interest on your loan and the rate of growth in value of your house. Following that, the relative size of your loan makes a big difference – it is more efficient to borrow as much as possible in relation to the initial property value, as long as you can afford the payments and house prices continue to increase steadily. But it is also riskier, as you become more exposed to the possibility that a fall in house prices will leave you owing more than the property is worth. This is known as negative equity.

The real world

In reality for most of us buying a house is not a purely financial process. It is much more than that. It determines where you are going to live, so factors such as your work, your friends and family and local schools all influence your decision on location, and the property's size, age, decoration and atmosphere all play their part in shaping which home you end up buying. Inevitably the house you end up wanting will be the one at the top of or just beyond your budget – it will be that much nicer and therefore that much more expensive. Take a look at any one of the hundreds of property programmes on television to see how many (or rather, few) people find that the house they want is well within their budget!

Mortgages

Hopefully we have established the big picture, that loans on property are generally both wise financially and inevitable, as there is no other way to buy a house that you would like to live in. So what about the details? Mortgages are specifically loans that have a property secured against them. That is, if you cannot pay back the loan, your lender has a right to sell the specific property to redeem the loan. Interestingly the word 'mortgage' first appeared in the 14th century, and originates from the French words *mort* and *gage*, meaning dead and pledge, the implication being that if you have not repaid the loan by your death, the lender is pledged the property. In effect little has changed in the intervening 700 years, as all mortgage documents must tell you 'your home is at risk if you do not keep up repayments'.

Decision tree – two basic questions to answer

When selecting a mortgage there are some important choices you have to make. The first two decisions are how much money you can afford to put down as the initial payment, and how much you can afford to make in monthly payments thereafter.

These two decisions have nothing to do with the cost of property in your area, or even the type of house you want to live in. The answers to these two questions are entirely based on your current savings and current income. You should work out the answers to these questions before even picking up a property brochure!

Answering the first question should be straightforward. How much savings do you (or you and a co-purchaser) have? How much do you need to keep for emergencies? How much does that leave?

Answering the second question takes you back to the monthly expenditure tables in Chapter 2. Once you have worked out your current monthly expenditure, including all other loan repayments and regular savings payments, you can see if there is any part that you can cut back on. (See the box on page 43.) Make sure you are being realistic in how much you can afford to spend, allowing room for unexpected cash demands. Remember that when you buy a house you will find there are a mass of things you want to do to improve it, either structurally, decoratively or with furniture – and all will cost you more than the television makeover programmes suggest!

House buying choices

This chapter is not a guide to house buying, only to mortgage management. But one thing you should consider when taking out a mortgage, and therefore when buying a house, is how easy it will be to pay off the mortgage quickly if you need to. Essentially this means how quickly you could sell the house in the future if you had to. This is often down to location. For example, if you find two similar houses but one is on a busy road or by a railway line, it will almost always be cheaper than the one that is situated more quietly.

You will have to weigh up whether the price difference is large enough to make up for the location, but you should also think about whether the poorer location might make that house difficult to sell in the future, especially if traffic gets heavier.

If you can afford to save a few more pounds from your normal expenses and invest them in your monthly mortgage payments so that you can buy the more desirably located house, this could well be money well spent. Each situation will be different, and you may find that no one can make that decision other than yourself, as it crosses different professional boundaries. The estate agent generally acts for the seller, not the purchaser, so is bound to paint you a rosy picture. The mortgage broker can only tell you the difference in the numbers and not express an opinion on the property.

The flip side of this is that you should not be tempted to buy a house just because it is at the top of your price range. Being costlier does not mean that it is more saleable – it might be just 'expensive'. There is no substitute for exploring your local property market carefully and understanding how much different styles and locations of houses are being sold for.

You must also budget for the other costs incurred when buying a house, primarily the stamp duty. (See the box on page 143.)

Other house purchase costs

Sadly it is not just the cost of the house that is expensive when buying property. There are a host of other expenses you need to budget for as well.

Stamp duty

The major additional cost when buying a house is stamp duty, a purchase tax payable to the government. In recent years it has increased significantly. The rates for the tax year 2004/05 are:

- Properties up to £60,000 pay no duty.
- Properties over £60,000 to £250,000 pay 1 per cent of the house price (from £600 to £2,500 on top of the purchase price).
- Properties over £250,000 to £500,000 pay 3 per cent of the entire house price (from £7,500 to £15,000).
- Properties over £500,000 pay 4 per cent of the entire house price (from £20,000 upwards).

Solicitors' costs

Again these generally depend on the cost of the house. There is usually a regulated fee related to the purchase price, plus expenses the solicitors have incurred (for searches, couriers, duty stamps and so on). Solicitors refer to these costs as disbursements. Make sure any quotation you get includes both the fee and likely disbursements.

For a £100,000 house expect to pay from £300, and from around £1,000 for a £500,000 property.

Survey costs

If you take out a mortgage the lender will want to have a chartered surveyor value the house and assure themselves that there is no significant structural problem with it. It is also a good idea for you to know this. At the end of the day these surveys will only flag up the most obvious defects, as surveyors are not at liberty to lift up carpets and floorboards or bury into walls looking for damp and so on. As such most surveyors are not liable for any problems that appear subsequently that were not highlighted in the report.

These reports come in three different levels of inspection and costs:

- Basic or Level 1 – the minimum level of inspection, usually all a lender will require. As a rough guide this will cost you 0.1 per cent of the value the lender puts on the house. So a survey of a £100,000 home will cost £100, and that of a £500,000 home will cost £500.
- Homebuyers or Level 2 – the recommended level of an inspection for a normal purchase, where information is provided on heating, subsidence, root damage and electrics. Statistics suggest that only 20 per cent of buyers actually have such a survey, relying on the mortgage lender's survey. This is unwise as the mortgage lender's survey does not highlight any further work that might be needed. This is probably because the surveys are quite expensive. Houses up to £100,000 cost around £300 to survey, houses up to £250,000 around £500, and houses up to £500,000 might cost around £800.
- Building/full structural or Level 3. If you are buying a very old or dilapidated building it is often advisable to have a full structural survey, which does look under the floorboards and into the walls. It will, however, take longer to arrange than a simpler survey, and will be considerably more expensive. If you are arranging the survey yourself, make sure the surveying company is approved by your lender, otherwise it might not accept the valuation.

Mortgage arrangement fees

Your lender might charge an administration or arrangement fee for setting up the mortgage, although sometimes lenders try to attract customers by waiving the fee. Usually the fee is incorporated in the final borrowed amount (which means you will pay interest on it). Check your mortgage proposal documents carefully, or ask your mortgage adviser directly what the fee, if any, will be. A typical fee could be up to £500, but you should be able to find an arrangement that costs less.

Removal costs

If you are not going to move your furniture yourself you will have to budget for a removals firm. The charges vary on the amount of furniture to move, although long-distance and special items will also change the price. Generally it does not cost a great deal more to have the removers do the packing as well. Check that the firm has proper insurance against breakages and other damage.

Once you have established how much you can afford to spend, and what the associated costs will be, you can then find out what the current mortgage market will offer you. Sooner or later you will have to visit a mortgage lender or broker, either physically or online. It will pay you to check out a few now to see what they think the market will be able to offer you, given your deposit amount and your maximum monthly payments. (See the box below.)

How much you can borrow

The amount you can borrow for a mortgage is typically 'subject to status and property valuation'. Status refers to your personal circumstances: critically whether you are single, married or divorced; whether you have any other repayment obligations; and finally how much you earn and how secure your job is.

Property valuation unsurprisingly is how much the lender deems the property to be worth. This is a figure calculated by a qualified chartered surveyor and not an estate agent however, and is often below the price paid. It is used as a guide so the lender knows how much it would be likely to get for the property should it have to sell it quickly.

Presuming that you have a stable job as an employee (the self-employed have a more difficult time), typically a lender will offer you a mortgage based on your salary plus any guaranteed bonus and half the amount of any other bonus or overtime you have regularly earned. This figure is known as your 'multiple'. In most cases the lender will offer you up to three times your multiple, or for joint applicants two and a half times both salaries.

If you can afford to put down a larger initial deposit (say nearer 40 per cent than the standard 10 to 20 per cent), you might be offered a higher multiple on your salary.

Beware

Just because the lender is prepared to offer you a higher multiple does not mean that it is wise to agree to it. While lenders are obliged to assure themselves that you can afford the repayments, if interest rates do increase substantially some five to six years after your mortgage starts (and after any fixed rate term is likely to have finished), you could well find yourself unable to make the repayments.

If you find repayments difficult to make because of recently increased interest rates, you will not be alone. If many people are struggling to make repayments there could be many people wanting to sell their properties and few looking to buy, a classic scenario for a fall in house prices. You do not want to have to sell your house when prices are falling because interest rates are too high. It is much better to assure yourself at the outset that you can absorb several increases in monthly repayment charges over the term of the mortgage.

You must remember that your monthly payments will change over the life of the mortgage. Even if you get a fixed-rate mortgage that rate will only be fixed for a limited period (except for long-term fixed rates: see below). So you must calculate for potential increase in your monthly payments.

Remember too that as recently as the early 1990s mortgage interest rates were in the high teens, nearly four times as much as the lowest rates today. If you can only just afford your monthly payments at today's low rates, what would happen if rates doubled in the next five years, let alone quadrupled? Most mortgages last for 25 years, so it is perfectly possible that these rates will be seen again. Let us hope it does not happen, but we cannot disregard it altogether.

The government is keen on people taking up long-term fixed-rate mortgages, so their monthly payments are guaranteed for the whole of the mortgage term. These types of mortgage are popular in the United States and France, and go some way to making the housing market more stable, but they are not popular in the UK yet, as they also prevent borrowers from lowering their payments when interest rates fall.

You should now know how much deposit you will be able to put down and how much you can afford to borrow, thus giving you a total expenditure figure (including additional costs). Only at this stage is it advisable to start searching for properties.

Decision tree – what type of mortgage?

If you have not already decided, you will have to choose what type of mortgage you want once you have found your property. The mortgage market, like that for every other financial product, is full of different varieties and choices. The two main choices, however, are interest only, or capital and interest.

With an interest-only mortgage you only pay the interest charge on the loan, and you either fund the loan repayment by selling the house at the end of the term, or set up a separate savings fund to accumulate capital for the loan. Capital and interest mortgages are also known as capital repayment mortgages, and with these your monthly payment is unevenly split between paying off the interest and the capital.

Interest-only mortgages are cheaper at the outset, but as they do not reduce the capital they could become more expensive as the years go by if interest rates start to rise. With a capital and interest repayment a small percentage of your monthly payment goes towards reducing your outstanding loan, and the rest pays off the interest due. As such the monthly repayment will be higher than with an interest-only payment. Slowly, as the outstanding loan is chipped away each month, the interest payable on it begins to fall. Because the monthly payment is fixed, as the interest payable amount falls, the balance that pays off the capital increases, so eroding the outstanding debt more quickly.

The examples in Figures 6.1 and 6.2 show that at steady interest rates and with the growth rate on a savings fund for an interest-only mortgage at a steady 6 per cent, the interest-only mortgage is about £6,000 cheaper over a 25-year period. However, if interest rates were to double in 10 years' time and remain high for five years before coming down again, you would find that you were paying out £20,000 extra for the interest-only mortgage, but would need only £12,000 extra for the capital and interest mortgage. The further into the 25-year term such a hike in interest rates occurs, the less impact the change makes on the capital and interest repayments, as the capital amount that the interest is charged on becomes smaller and smaller. With interest-only mortgages you are as exposed to interest rate changes in your final year as you are in the first, unless you have paid off any of the loan early. Equally any reductions in interest rates will benefit the interest-only mortgage more than a capital and interest one; but as interest rates are at historically low levels currently, the likelihood of their falling further rather than rising in the next 25 years is small.

Decision tree – interest rate periods

Once you have chosen which style of mortgage you require, you will then need to choose how you would like the interest rate to be applied. There are two elements to this: how regularly the interest is calculated, and for how long the interest rate remains the same.

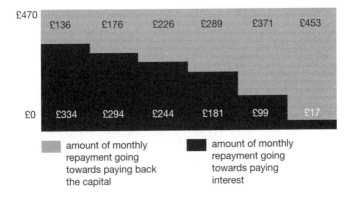

| £470 | | | | | | |
| £0 | | | | | | |

amount of monthly repayment going towards paying back the capital

amount of monthly repayment going towards paying interest

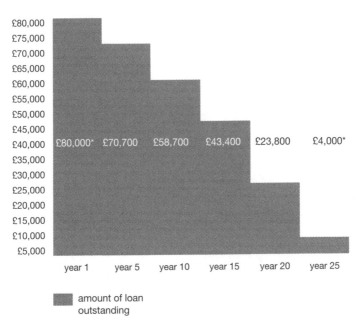

amount of loan outstanding

Notes:
Assumes an £80,000 loan at 5% interest for 25 years (300 months) making payments of £470 a month.
*amount at beginning of year, all other figures show balance at end of year
Total cost: 300 × £470 = £141,000
Total interest charge = £61,000 (£141,000 − £80,000)

Figure 6.1   Capital and interest repayment

Breakdown of monthly repayments at five-year intervals

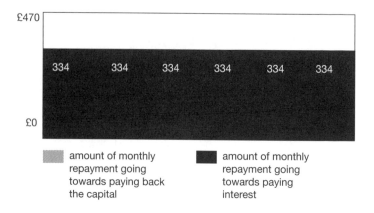

Total outstanding loan at five year intervals

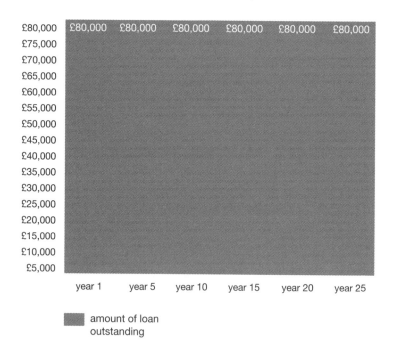

Figure 6.2   Interest only mortgage repayment and savings fund costs

You are best advised to get a mortgage where the interest is calculated on your outstanding balance every day. Traditionally it was calculated on the outstanding balance at the beginning of the year, and any capital repayments you made in the next 12 months would not reduce the interest payments until the next year's calculation was made. Some lenders still use this method – so check.

With interest rates being reviewed by the Bank of England every month these days, it is possible for the rate your lender charges you (which will be based on the Bank of England rate) to alter frequently. When you choose your mortgage you will be offered an array of different options on how the interest is charged for your mortgage. You should bear in mind that to be able to plan your own finances it is useful to have an idea of what your monthly payments are going to be, so having them at a steady rate is helpful.

The main choices are as follows:

- *Standard variable.* This is the basic interest rate. It is likely to change every time the Bank of England changes its rate. It is also the rate to which other rates are usually compared, and to which they revert when any special period comes to an end.
- *Discount.* Here the initial interest rate you are charged is considerably lower than the standard variable rate, so making your first payments much cheaper. The discount period is typically for between two and five years; the longer the period, the smaller the discount.
- *Fixed.* Here your interest rate is set and cannot go up or down for a specified period, usually between one and five years. These are sensible choices for people who like some certainty in what they will be paying but are not desperate for the cheapest deal. The longer your rate is fixed for, the more likely you are to get redemption clauses (see below).
- *Capped.* This is similar to a fixed rate in that it cannot go up beyond a specified level, but it can fall. You are almost certain to get redemption penalties attached to these mortgages. These are sensible choices if interest rates are bouncing around with no clear upward or downward direction. Some capped mortgages also have 'collars' where there is a minimum level below which they cannot fall as well.

- *Cashback.* These are similar to discount mortgages but you receive a single payment of cash based on the amount of your loan in addition to your mortgage payment. This can be very useful when you face the expense of moving house. However, they are usually costly in terms of punitive redemption penalties. Beware.
- *Flexible.* These are the latest development in the mortgage market. Flexible mortgages allow you to pay off your loan in lump sums whenever you are able, make extra monthly payments, take 'payment holidays' and make 'underpayments', and also increase your loan if you need money for something.
- *Current account mortgages.* This is a further improvement on a flexible mortgage, where your salary is paid into the account each month and your loan becomes an enormous overdraft. The effect of this 'offsetting' of your income and your borrowings is that the interest you would have earned on any savings is spent on your borrowings, which is much more efficient, and should result in your paying off your mortgage much earlier, thus saving money. The downside is that the interest rate applied to your mortgage will not be as cheap as the special rates above.

Redemption penalties

Your mortgage lender does not want you to take advantage of its generous special rates and then disappear to another lender when you see a better deal elsewhere, so it will often insert redemption penalties which mean you have to pay a 'fine' if you want to leave a mortgage deal before the term is completed. The fines or penalties are usually multiples of standard variable rate monthly payments, say six months of such payments. The multiple might reduce as you go further into the term. Some mortgages have 'overhanging' penalties where you are penalized if you change lenders or types even after the initial term has finished, so you are forced to accept the lender's standard variable rate for a while, which might be expensive. Redemption penalties are becoming less widely used in today's more flexible market place, but you must check to see if any apply to mortgages you are interested in. Generally, the more attractive a rate and longer the time period it lasts for, the more likely it is to have a penalty attached.

Arrangement fees

Different types of mortgage product attract different administration costs. It is an arguable point whether the difference in these 'arrangement fees' is actually based on how much work goes into setting the mortgage up. You will find that the more attractive offers in terms of interest rate and period length come with the least attractive fees. As the sums saved from the best offers are often considerable, the added costs are usually best put up with – but it always pays to check.

Mortgages for everyone

Mortgages are generally calculated by someone filling your details into a computer and receiving an answer immediately. If you do not fit the computer's preferred model of a typical borrower, the computer might refuse to give you a loan or make it very expensive. This can be hugely irritating for those who do not fit the mould.

The most frequently denied borrowers are the self-employed. Although you might already be risking everything you possess to set up and start a business, lenders still want you to provide more security than average for a mortgage, and will usually charge you a higher rate of interest. You will need to show at least two, probably three, years of certified accounts for your business, or you can apply for a self-certification mortgage if you can afford to put down a minimum of 20 per cent deposit on the house. Self-certification mortgages are a huge leap forward in recognizing the large number of self-employed people. It can often pay to visit a specialist adviser in these cases.

The second group who find mortgages difficult to get are people with poor credit histories. Generally in this case you must go to a lender who specializes in 'adverse credit' mortgages. You must expect to pay a higher rate of interest than average to compensate for the risk of your credit history. Be aware that this area of the mortgage market has more than its fair share of unscrupulous operators, so make sure that you get good advice from a certified financial practitioner.

The elderly also have difficulty in obtaining mortgages. It is now common for older people to supplement their retirement income by mortgaging their homes in return for a lump sum of cash, usually to 30 per cent of its value. Although they do not pay anything for this while alive, on death the property is sold by the lender. Some of the proceeds are used to repay the loan plus a specified percentage of profit, and the remainder goes towards the borrower's estate. These schemes are open to abuse, and anyone considering such a policy should seek professional advice from a certified financial practitioner. This is the original form of equity release: see below.

Savings vehicles for interest-only mortgages

Interest-only mortgages are riskier than capital and interest mortgages as the loan repayment is not guaranteed. In order to build up a sufficient amount of capital to pay off your loan at the end of the term, you need to choose a vehicle to 'grow' your savings in. In the past the government gave generous tax breaks to mortgage savers, but these have now all been removed.

Endowments

Endowment mortgages were very popular in the 1980s but have since run into trouble as they have not performed as well as expected, and many borrowers have discovered that their endowment scheme has not been large enough to pay off the loan at the end of the mortgage. They are a variant of an interest-only mortgage, in that you pay the interest in the same manner, but the savings fund is an endowment policy (a savings vehicle backed by a life assurance policy), either 'with profits' or 'unit linked'. See Chapter 16 for an explanation of 'with profits' schemes and important information on what to do if you still have one.

ISAs

As with a unit-linked endowment policy, you purchase units or shares in a unit or investment trust that can invest in a range of assets (shares, bonds or property). Your hope is that the investment fund will grow at a faster rate than a cash-only fund, so that your savings grow to cover your loan amount. The advantage of doing this with an ISA is that all growth is tax-free. The disadvantage is that you are limited to how much you can invest each year (currently a maximum of £7,000 a year, falling to £5,000 a year after April 2006), but this should be more than sufficient for most people (sufficient to cover a £400,000 loan over 40 years at 6 per cent growth). The other disadvantage with this type of savings fund is that while a shares-based fund should perform well over a 25-year period, you cannot know whether the market will be at a peak or in a trough when you need to repay your loan. For this reason it is considered riskier than a capital and interest mortgage.

Pension

Pension mortgages are where your savings fund is actually a pension fund. Pension funds are very tax-efficient, so your fund benefits from this. If you are a higher rate tax payer you get the equivalent of 67 pence added to every pound you put in (see page 97). The drawbacks are that you can only put a limited amount of your earnings into a pension fund; you can only have this type of arrangement if the mortgage term ends at a point when you can draw down your pension (that is, once you are 50 or over); and only a quarter of the fund can be taken as a tax-free lump sum to be used to pay back the loan, while the rest must go to buying an annuity for your retirement. Again the investment is not guaranteed to cover the loan; and finally, do you really want to spend your pension lump sum on paying off your mortgage? Pension mortgages are potentially very rewarding but also high risk. The industry's 'Mortgage Code for Lenders' does not permit lenders to advertise these types of mortgages.

Life cover

Twenty or more years ago when most mortgages were endowment mort-gages, life assurance cover was built into the policies. Today interest-only and capital and interest mortgages require you to take out separate life insurance to cover the amount of the loan should you die early. This will be cheaper for a capital and interest mortgage as you can buy a decreasing term policy (see Chapter 5), but for interest-only mortgages you will need level term life insurance.

Remortgaging

Nearly half of all mortgage borrowers are on the standard variable rate in the UK – which is almost certainly not the most efficient way of paying for their mortgages. Remortgaging is when you change either your mortgage type or lender to get a better deal. It is increasingly easy to do, as redemption penalties are becoming rarer and less onerous. It is also highly advisable in many cases, especially if the alternative is just putting up with the standard variable rate. That said, make sure that the sums work, that there are no heavy penalties that you might incur; that the benefits of the new mortgage are long term and not just a pretty initial rate followed by an ugly later one with redemption penalties; and that you are not losing out on any other special benefits your current mortgage offers (such as life insurance).

Equity release

With house values having spiralled in recent years, one of the cheapest ways of borrowing money is to add to your mortgage and release some of the extra value in your house. This is a useful thing to be able to do, as these loans are probably the cheapest way you will find to raise cash, and it is efficient in financial terms to be 'leveraging' the value of your home. But there are pitfalls, so it must be thought about carefully.

There are two approaches to equity release. The first is like that outlined above for the elderly, where the money supplements retirement income. The newer approach is where you use the cash for anything you like, but it is advisable to use the money raised for a specific purpose (home improvements; a new car; a special holiday) and not treat the money as an ever-present source of extra funds, as then you know exactly how much you need to borrow. The principal decision, as with taking out any mortgage, is whether you can afford the monthly payments. If you are already struggling to make the payments, taking out another loan is not the answer.

Table 6.2 CAT standard criteria for mortgages

Charges	Access	Terms
On all mortgages • Interest must be calculated daily. • Full credit for all payments when made. • No separate charge for mortgage indemnity guarantee (MIG). • All other fees disclosed in cash up-front. • Borrowers pay no fees to brokers. **Variable rates only** • No arrangement fee. • Interest rate no more than 2% above Bank of England base rate. • When the base rate falls, the interest rate must adjust within a calendar month. • No redemption charges at any time. **Fixed and capped rates only** • Maximum booking fee is £150. • Maximum redemption charge is 1% of the amount you owe for each remaining year of the fixed period, reducing monthly. • No redemption charge after the end of the fixed or capped period. • No redemption charge if you stay with the same mortgage lender when you move home.	• If there is a minimum you must borrow to get a CAT-standard mortgage, it has to be £10,000 or less. • Any customer may apply. • The lender's normal lending criteria apply. • Provided your lender is happy to lend on the new property, you can continue with your CAT-standard mortgage when you move home. • If you make regular payments, you can choose which day of the month to pay. • You can make early repayments at any time.	• All advertising and paperwork must be straightforward and clear. • You do not have to buy any other products to get a CAT-standard mortgage. • Your lender must give at least 6 months notice if it can no longer offer your mortgage on CAT-standard terms. • If you are in arrears you should pay interest only on the outstanding debt at the normal rate.

Regulatory bodies and financial advisers

From October 2004 the FSA (www.fsa.gov.uk) will become the statutory regulator for the mortgage industry, taking over many of the responsibilities previously handled by the industry run Mortgage Code Compliance Board (www.mortgagecode.org.uk). The FSA also has responsibility for many of the investment vehicles that mortgages employ. Currently there are over 150 lenders and 12,000 intermediaries registered with the Mortgage Board. Check that your adviser and lender are registered with the board, and make sure you read its leaflet *You and Your Mortgage* to satisfy yourself that you are being dealt with properly. For more information contact the Mortgage Code on 01785 218200 or at www.mortgagecode.org.uk.

7

Education

'Free at the point of delivery' was the traditional government maxim for both healthcare and education in the second half of the 20th century. As we move into the 21st century it appears that the cost of providing these services has increased so much faster than inflation that central government is no longer able to keep up in all directions.

Critical healthcare is still supplied 'free at the point of delivery', but the edges are blurring with education. University students have had to pay towards the privilege of gaining a degree for some years now, and the funding burden is likely to increase as the government rolls out its plan to replenish university coffers through the controversial introduction of 'top-up' fees. We look at student funding later in this chapter.

The possession of a degree from a good university is so desirable in today's qualification-driven world that the government feels it can charge people for gaining one. In the same manner many parents are prepared to sacrifice a great deal of their wealth, time and comfort to ensure that their children gain a first-class school education so as to enable them to get to a university in the first place.

Independent schools

With the huge variety in standards of education at different state schools, many parents feel their only viable option is to send their children to an independent school (also known as a private or fee-paying school).

Traditionally, independent schools have been seen as the preserve of the privileged upper classes; however, this is not the real situation. There are around 2,400 independent schools in the UK and they educate nearly 600,000 of the UK's 8.2 million school children. More than half those children come from families where neither parent went to a fee-paying school. The percentage of independently educated children in the UK has been steadily increasing to its current level of 7.1 per cent for some years now. While bad independent schools do exist, and undoubtedly there are plenty of excellent state schools, the attraction of paying for your child's education is no doubt linked to the comments made by the Chief Inspector of Schools in his Annual Report published in 2002 on independent schools. 'In the sector as a whole, standards are rarely less than satisfactory, often good and sometimes excellent', while on state secondary schools his opening remarks are 'Some aspects of secondary education have improved, but there remains a wide variation in the attainment of pupils in different schools, and there is significant under-achievement in seven per cent of schools.'

Table 7.1 Typical fees for independent school in the UK

Age	Type	Range (£ per term)
Pre-prep (2 to 7 years old)	Day	900–1,400
Prep (7 to 13 years old)	Day	1,600–3,200
	Boarding	3,100–4,800
Senior (11/13 to 18 years old)	Boys – day	2,300–4,100
	Boys – boarding	4,000–6,500
	Girls – day	2,200–3,300
	Girls – boarding	3,700–6,200

Source: Independent Schools Council information service

Even if you do not have any ideological barriers against sending your child to an independent school, you are likely to encounter some funding barriers. Typical fees are shown in Table 7.1.

A mid-range boys' day school will therefore be charging around £3,000 a term or £9,000 a year, and there are always 'extras' to be added in, for which you should expect to budget a further 10 per cent. Thus one year at the cheaper end of the independent school fees range for one child will cost around £10,000. You will probably only be able to afford this if you are in the upper taxable income bracket (earning over £29,900 a year), and you must earn nearly £17,000 gross income to cover this amount after tax at 40 per cent. Should you have more than one child at school, the figures start to mount up very quickly. So how exactly can anyone afford to send their children to a fee-paying school? As was noted at the outset, there are nearly 600,000 pupils being paid for and the number is growing – so it clearly is not impossible.

Everyone has different situations and priorities, so there is no single definitive solution to funding school fees. The most likely solution will be a combination of paying some of the annual fees from a specific fees product, either a savings fund or a loan, and making up the balance from your income.

Again, the best approach will sound all too familiar: it is to start saving for school fees as far in advance as possible, to begin creating a sinking fund that will go towards the future expenses. This advice is of no help to those who find themselves needing funds now, but as ever there are plenty of ways for immediate funding to be raised. However, they will tend to be more expensive than using an existing savings fund.

Planning ahead

If you are in the fortunate position of being able to plan ahead for fee-paying education you will be looking at investing a regular amount or a lump sum into an investment product that will hopefully grow at a rate significantly above inflation. This could be:

- a savings account or National Savings Certificates (low risk);
- an investment or unit trust (medium to high risk);
- a bond fund (low to medium risk);
- a fixed term annuity (low risk);
- zero preference shares (see below).

Zero preference shares were often suggested as suitable products for saving for costs such as school fees. They are shares from an investment trust that has split itself into two types of share. One produces capital growth but zero income (hence the name 'zeros') and the other just takes the income. The term 'preference share' means that should the trust go bankrupt (normally considered highly unlikely) these shares get repaid before the other shares on the creditors' lists – they are 'preferred'. After the stock market crash of 2001/2 many of these split-capital trusts did indeed get into financial difficulties, and many people lost money, regardless of the 'preferred' tag. With this history they must be deemed high risk, but the problems of a few years ago have led to better management, and many such trusts are now well run. But make sure you get sound independent professional advice before acquiring shares in one.

Your savings should be invested in as tax-efficient a manner as possible, such as in an ISA or children's bonds. You should also be aware that gifts directly to the child from anyone other than his or her parent (usually a grandparent or maybe uncle, aunt or godparent) can be tax-efficient, as children have their own income tax thresholds, so can potentially earn up to the basic rate threshold (£4,745 a year in 2004/5) without incurring any tax liability. (If a parent gifts the money, any income earned on the investment above £100 a year is liable to tax on the parent's tax return: see Chapter 18 for more information.) Remember also that as husbands and wives are taxed separately, allocating savings income to the one with the lower income may be more tax-efficient when it comes to investing for education (as well as for any other reason).

Your savings fund should grow, but how fast it grows will be related to the riskiness of its investments. The further away you are from having to use the fund for education purposes, the more risk you can afford to accept, and conversely the closer you are to needing the money, the more you should be moving your investments to less risky products. The amount the fund grows will also depend on how long you have to invest before you need it. It is unlikely that you will start investing for children's education before you have any children, but you may want to start building up a fund as soon as they arrive. As pre-school and prep school fees are smaller than secondary fees, it may be possible to pay for them out of income and continue putting something into a savings fund and allowing it to grow for longer, until your child reaches senior school or starts to board perhaps.

Flexibility is also important when choosing a savings product for education. Many schools offer composition fee schemes, where you start paying to the school before your child starts going there. This forward paying entitles you to significant price discounts, but these will only be useful if your child attends that school! If your circumstances change and your child does not attend the school, you are unlikely to get all your payments back, let alone earn any interest from them. You should approach each school about these schemes, and assess each one on its own merits, as well as be very certain you will be sending your child there, before committing to a composition fee scheme. Another factor to be aware of with these schemes is that your money must be held in trust and accounted for separately from the rest of the school's finances, to ensure that it is safe from the school's creditors.

When advance planning for school fees there are a number of points to consider:

- Perhaps the most important is that it can be very disruptive to children's education to remove them from a school they like and are doing well at, so you do not want to find that you can no longer afford the fees after they have started. It is therefore vital that you are sure you will be able to afford the fees right through to when your child leaves.
- School fees tend to increase faster than the rate of inflation, so make your calculations allowing for an increase of at least 5 per cent a year.
- You will need to plan for all your children. This can be tricky if you do not know how many you will have, so make a reasonable assumption and build your calculations around it.
- Be aware of your own likely income growth.

Immediate need

If you find yourself in the position of needing extra funds to pay school fees immediately, because you have no suitable savings plan, your savings plan is not sufficient, or for any other reason, you effectively need to take out a loan.

As with all loans, if you can secure your borrowings it will be cheaper for you, although you risk losing the asset the loan is secured against. The most obvious asset to use is your house. Since house prices have increased above trend for the last few years, it is likely that any mortgage on your house will represent a smaller percentage of its value now than when you bought it (assuming you have not bought it within the last couple of years). If this is the case you might find that your lender is happy to increase your mortgage through an equity release mortgage, from which you can draw down money as you need it to cover any fees shortfall. This is a riskier process than paying through a savings product, and should be discussed carefully with an independent financial adviser.

If you cannot release any more equity from your house there are other options. Taking a loan against the value of other financial products you own is a possibility. These are again riskier than the above suggestions and more expensive – and you will need expert advice to suit your particular circumstances.

Bursaries, scholarships and other help

Most independent schools have schemes that can help with paying the fees. They are often for small amounts, several hundred pounds or less, but this might make a considerable difference if you are already stretching to pay the fees. Each such bursary will come with its own rules and conditions – ask the school's bursar or admissions officer for details of any available. Scholarships are usually for more generous amounts, and are awarded to children who have a specific talent the school deems deserving of support. This will usually be academic, artistic, musical or sporting. Many geographical areas – perhaps your village, town or region – have both public and private education trusts that offer funding help. You should ask the schools if they know of any that might be appropriate, and also approach your local council and local libraries for information.

Payment protection insurance

On the basis that breaking your child's education can be very disruptive for him or her, it is well worth considering taking out insurance that will cover any school fees in the event of your being unable to work or becoming unemployed. See Chapter 5 for further details.

Advisers

Most IFAs will be happy to advise you on schemes that will help you to fund school fees. It is a complicated area incorporating both your financial future and your child's educational one, so great care must be taken to ensure that any scheme devised is realistic and long term. There are a handful of specialist education financial advisers. The Independent Schools Council's information service (ISCis) can give you names of suitable firms. They can be found at www.iscis.uk.net, and the ISC London and South-East office on 020 7798 1561.

University education

This is a very contentious subject these days. The costs associated with going to university are changing all the time, and generally only in an upward direction. Whereas most parents of children who are now of university-going age paid nothing for their own university education (if they had one), their children will be expected to contribute towards not only their education costs but also their maintenance. For better or worse, gone are the halcyon, carefree and frivolous student days of Evelyn Waugh's *Brideshead Revisited* and perhaps also the more radical but still closeted academic life of Malcolm Bradbury's characters. Today's students often have to work for money as well as at their studies, with less time and less funds to spare for more 'traditional' student pastimes!

The cynically 'good news' for parents is that the burden of university costs is being swung to paying back loans, so they only need to be addressed after university, although their size is determined while the student is at university. The advantage of this for parents is that it is the student, their child, who is responsible for repaying the loans and not the parent. However, few parents will be happy to see their children leave university and set off on their own into the real world of jobs and mortgages already saddled with many thousands of pounds of debt. So what can be done to reduce this burden at the outset?

Current costs of university

Although the current furore in the press is about 'top-up' fees (more properly the 'graduate tax'), it is actually daily living costs that really stack up the debt for students. It has been calculated that a student in a hall of residence will typically have to spend over £5,000 a year just to exist (rent: £2,000; food and essentials: £1,200; utilities and insurance: £450; travel: £500; books, computer and so on: £450; clothing and cleaning: £400), and this is before the current tuition fees of £1,100 or any leisure expenditure, say £1,500. Private rented accommodation is likely to be more expensive still, especially at universities in large cities. This minimum expenditure totals £7,600 per year. University degrees are a minimum of three years and some last considerably longer. At current levels the cost of a university degree for a student is almost £23,000 – and that is before any inflation or the university vacations are included.

Future costs

The government is proposing to introduce a graduate tax from 2006, where universities will be allowed to 'top up' the current tuition fee of £1,100 by up to a further £1,900, giving a ceiling of £3,000 for tuition fees per student per year. It is expected that all the more famous universities will charge the full top-up amount. In an attempt to quell backbench dissent the government stated that any change to the ceiling will have to get parliamentary approval (rather than just a ministerial announcement). This will presumably delay the moment when the ceiling is raised, but not put off any increase indefinitely. The effect of these topped-up fees is to add a further £6,000 of debt to a three-year course, taking the basic cost of a degree to nearly £30,000.

Student Loan Company

The government has operated its student loan scheme through the Student Loan Company (SLC) since 1990. For loans taken out by students prior to the academic year starting in September 1998, the loans were applied for directly through the SLC and collected by the SLC following graduation, once the graduate was earning over £1,752 gross per month. Since 1998 the situation has been more complex. Students must apply for support (it is no longer referred to as a loan) assessments from their local education authority (in England and Wales), the Students Award Agency for Scotland or the Education and Library Boards (in Northern Ireland), depending on where their home is, not where they choose to study. These bodies make an assessment of their support requirements, including assessing their parents' income. Collection of the support is now done by employers through the Inland Revenue. Repayment is at 9 per cent of the graduate's salary once he or she earns over £10,000 gross per year. The Student Loan Company still makes the payments and administers the paperwork for all loans.

The loans process

Loans are allocated on a year to year basis, not for the duration of entire courses. Applications to the assessment bodies should be made ideally in January for the next academic year. The local assessment body assesses applications and advises students how much, if anything, they must pay towards tuition fees and the maximum amount of help with living costs they can apply for. Students can then apply to the Student Loan Company for anything up to this amount. The SLC then administers the loan, setting up a loan account for the student, and paying the loan to the student (usually electronically to his or her nominated bank account) at the start of each term. Applications to the SLC should be made by June for payment at the beginning of the academic year.

In Scotland, Scottish (and non-UK EU) domiciled students studying in Scotland do not have to pay tuition fees. The Scottish Executive has a different system, where graduates have to pay a fixed amount at the end of their degrees in recognition of higher education benefits. It is called the Graduate Endowment Scheme, and started in the academic year of 2001/2, with students who started their courses in that year liable to pay a single contribution of £2,000 on completion. The figure is £2,030 for students starting in 2002/3 and £2,092 in 2003/4 – it is increased by the rate of inflation each year. The scheme is administered through the SLC. It is not paid by all students. For further details contact the Students Award Agency for Scotland on 0845 111 1711 or at www.student-support-saas.gov.uk

Table 7.2 Maximum loan amounts under the student support scheme

	Students living away from home – in London		Students living away from home – elsewhere		Students living at home	
	Full year	Final year	Full year	Final year	Full year	Final year
2001/02	£4,700	£4,075	£3,815	£3,310	£3,020	£2,635
2002/03	£4,815	£4,175	£3,905	£3,390	£3,090	£2,700
2003/04	£4,930	£4,275	£4,000	£3,470	£3,165	£2,765

Source: Student Loan Company

Table 7.3 Tuition fees payable

Parent's income*	Tuition fees payable
Less than £20,970 pa	Nil
Between £20,970 pa and £31,230 pa	Part of £1,125 pa
£31,231 pa or more	The full £1,125 pa

* calculated on gross income less specific deductions

Helping to fund the cost

Unlike independent school fees, university fees do not have to be funded immediately. If you do not put in place a university funding plan, there is plenty of help available from the government, as outlined above. However, the accumulation of so much debt at such an early stage in a person's life with nothing tangible to secure against it is a frightening prospect, and trying to reduce that debt burden can only be wise.

The solutions to helping fund your child through university are very similar to those suggested in the first half of this chapter for funding independent school fees. Forward planning will make an enormous difference, and the further in advance that you can start putting away a regular amount of money each month, the better. Saving up a sum for university is no different in practice than saving for anything else, except that you may be able to persuade grandparents, and your children as well, to make use of their tax-free allowances and make donations to a fund. The major advantage of saving for university over school fees is that you have considerably longer to invest before the funds are needed. Thus in addition to the products mentioned above, less glamorous products like tax-free child savings plans from friendly societies and baby bonds can be accumulated over a long period of time to help build up a cushion of funds to set against the loan. Of course your child might choose not to go to university, but the accumulated savings will no doubt be of use in any case.

Borrowing to help reduce your child's debt is a more serious decision, as you will be unable to better the interest-free rate your child is offered from the Student Loan Company. However, if you feel the stress of the student loan is not reasonable for your child to have, you can obtain a loan in the same manner as outlined for school fees above. If your reason for reducing the loan burden is to enable your child to get on the housing ladder, you will be better advised helping with the purchase of a house than the repayment of the loan.

8

Healthcare

Far more important than having your finances in perfect shape is making sure that you and your family are in perfect shape. It will be of great comfort and hugely important to know that your mortgage is well managed, your pension growing nicely and that there are some savings tucked away in a tax-efficient ISA if you are ill – but it will always be more important to know that you or your family are fit and well in the first place.

Managing your health is not the obvious subject for this book, but if you are not in good health you are less likely to have time or energy to look after your finances, nor are you likely to be able to enjoy the rewards that good financial management can bring you. So it is as important to look after you and your family's well-being as it is to look after their finances. The box gives some very basic tips for a healthy lifestyle.

Living a healthy lifestyle

As with managing your finances, managing your health is three-quarters common sense and good discipline. The basic rules are the same as well:

- Do not allow yourself to get into debt by constant over-spending or overweight by excessive eating or drinking.

- Keep your savings in shape with regular and manageable contributions to a savings fund – and keep yourself in shape with regular and manageable exercise.
- If you do occasionally spend too much, take some corrective action immediately rather than giving in – clearly the same applies to your health.
- Finally, monitor your finances at least yearly and preferably more often. As you get older and your financial responsibilities become more complex, get your finances checked by an experienced professional, an IFA. Likewise, monitor your health regularly, and as you get older get these regular check-ups from a doctor.

As a quick check list:

Calories: according to the British Heart Foundation, this is the average recommended daily intake (RDI) for an average person.

To maintain weight:

Men:	2,500 calories
Women:	2,000 calories

To lose weight:

Men:	1,800 calories
Women:	1,500 calories

Alcohol: according to the Department of Health, the average acceptable units of alcohol consumed per day is:

Men:	3–4 units
Women:	2–3 units

A unit equals a half pint of beer, lager or cider, a pub measure of spirits or a small glass of wine.

The acceptable quantity of alcohol if you are driving is none at all, and the legal limit is only slightly higher.

Studies suggest that drinking in moderation (a glass of red wine a day) can help reduce stress and heart disease.

Smoking: there are no known health benefits to smoking; therefore the acceptable level is not to smoke at all.

Eating and drinking: a balanced diet for most of us means cutting down on red meat and fried food, and increasing our intake of vegetables and fresh fruit. The government promotes the eating of five pieces of fresh fruit a day – the vast majority of the country is some way short of doing that. We should also drink more water than we do to keep ourselves hydrated and flush out toxins. Tap water is very cheap compared with all other drinks, and in most respects better for us. Two litres a day is suggested as a reasonable amount, although some of this can be taken as watered down fruit juices, herbal teas (try to reduce your caffeine intake) or in fresh fruit.

Exercise: little and often is the solution, at first anyway. Too many of us have expensive gym memberships which we never use. Financially and bodily it will be better to walk a little further every day, use the local pool for half an hour's swimming each week or cycle to work, than to spend each January pumping the exercise machines at the gym and then forget about them for another 11 months.

Health checks: as you get older your checks should get more sophisticated, but keeping an eye out for any lumps or skin lesions that appear, and smear tests for women, should be done from your twenties onwards. In your thirties your blood pressure and cholesterol starts to become a more possible problem area. In your forties you should add bowel cancer checks to the list, and prostate checks for men. In your fifties some supplements may be required to keep the joints working and bones strong, and for women HRT may be advisable. Into your sixties and beyond regular check-ups with a doctor to discuss any new conditions should be arranged.

Stress: throughout your life as your responsibilities to your family and work increase it is likely that your stress levels will increase as well. It is therefore good practice to make time to alleviate stress, through setting aside periods of time just for yourself to relax; through regular exercise and healthy eating and drinking. Make sure you recognize your own body's particular signals in reaction to stress, and act on them early. This is much easier said than done, but is valuable both to you and those who rely on you.

These are just some basic tips. For more complete advice consult your doctor or a recognized health expert.

The government tries to provide healthcare 'free at the point of delivery', and to an amazingly large extent it achieves this. However, as we are living for longer we are also incurring more diseases and incapacities than we ever have before. This means the NHS has to treat more people for longer than ever before. Added to this, medical science is advancing quicker than ever before, and that brings more diagnoses and solutions than ever before, which requires the health service to offer more medicines, procedures and equipment than ever before. This inevitably all adds up to more pressure both financially and physically on the NHS, and it is none too surprising that in some areas it does not cope as well as we would like it to.

Private medical care and insurance

There are still few places in the world better to be than the UK should you have a critical health problem. The state will look after you pretty well. The major complaint with the NHS is with non-critical procedures: acute conditions such as hip replacements, eye surgery or heart surgery even. It is here that, if you can afford it, private medical care can make a significant difference, allowing you to choose the time, the place and who will give you treatment.

Obviously the drawback with private healthcare is that it costs you money, whereas the same treatment on the NHS would be free. Despite that nearly 7 million people in the UK have private medical insurance (PMI) – although the vast majority of these have their insurance premiums paid by their employer as a taxable benefit in kind, rather than paying for it themselves.

The Association of British Insurers describes PMI as being:

…designed to cover the costs of private medical treatment for what are commonly known as acute conditions. Most insurers define an acute condition as a disease, illness or injury that is likely to respond quickly to treatment that aims to return you to the state of health you were in immediately before suffering the disease, illness or injury, or which leads to your full recovery.

Do you need PMI?

This is a question of your priorities and attitude to risk. There is a body of opinion that suggests for most people under the age of 40, PMI is poor value for money. As medical procedures become more expensive PMI premiums have risen steadily above the rate of inflation. A typical premium for a young man or woman for a standard PMI policy could be around £500 a year. It is estimated that on average people in their twenties and thirties only have an in-patient treatment once every 10 years. So if your treatment costs less than £5,000 in that period, which is likely, and the typical treatment cost is around £2,000, you will have a poor return on your premiums invested. Of course, treatment might cost much more: you never know, and some complicated modern procedures can cost up to £100,000. However, if you have taken the gamble not to buy PMI there is always the NHS to look after you should you require such expensive treatment.

Over the age of 40 your premiums start increasing steadily as you become more likely to require treatment of one sort or another. Depending on your state of general health and your family's health history you might decide that PMI is more valuable later on.

The flipside of this argument is that by buying PMI for you and your family you are also buying peace of mind: that should a treatable complaint develop, you can take advantage of the ease and comfort provided by private medical care and funded by your insurance company regardless of cost. (Note that some policies have no maximum cost limit, while others impose a ceiling.)

It is up to you to decide whether you want to take on the risk of not having PMI and maybe requiring treatment, or take on the risk of having PMI and not requiring treatment.

Things to consider in purchasing PMI

If you decide that you would prefer to have PMI then there are some decisions you need to make. First you should discover if your employer is able to offer you PMI through a company or group scheme. If this option exists it is usually the cheapest way to have cover, as the insurance companies will discount the policies as they save money on the administration costs. Remember that any PMI received through your work will be taxable at your highest rate of tax. Company PMI schemes are available for even the smallest, single-person companies.

If company or group schemes are not available to you, you will need to shop around for the best individual or family PMI offers available. These can be sourced directly from the insurance companies themselves (most large insurers now offer PMI policies – although 80 per cent of UK PMI cover is provided through non-profit making 'provident associations', such as BUPA and PPP); through IFAs or through insurance agents (banks, building societies and supermarkets).

When selecting which level of cover is appropriate for you, you will be offered a wide range of options. The three standard areas of cover are:

- in-patient treatment (where you stay in hospital overnight or longer);
- day-patient treatment (where you require some supervised recovery time, probably in a private room with bed and en-suite facilities, but do not stay overnight);

- out-patient treatment (where you get treatment at a consulting room or surgery).

Generally most policies will cover in- and day-patient treatment, but you may have to pay more for out-patient treatment. Other choices you will have to make are:

- whether you wish to have unlimited care available or have a ceiling of cover for each calendar year;
- whether you wish to be able to go to any private hospital of your choosing; one from a selection offered by the insurance company; or let the company choose where you are to be treated;
- whether cover is only offered if the NHS cannot provide treatment within a certain period of time (typically 6–12 weeks);
- the size of excess you are willing to pay;
- the opportunity to pay for a certain part of the treatment yourself, such as consultations.

When applying for PMI you will be required to make a statement about your current health and any previous conditions you may have had. As with all insurance policies, failure to disclose all the relevant facts can void your policy. The insurer is unlikely to cover you for any existing or previous conditions. A consequence of this is that if you choose to change insurers at a later date, any condition that has developed during your time with your current insurer is unlikely to be covered by a new insurer.

There is a standard list of medical conditions that insurers tend not to cover. The Association of British Insurers list the following as likely non-covered conditions: pre-existing conditions, GP services, long-term (chronic) illnesses, accident and emergency admissions, drug abuse, self inflicted injuries, out-patient drugs and dressings, HIV/AIDS, infertility, normal pregnancy, cosmetic surgery, gender reassignment (also known as sex change), preventive treatment, kidney dialysis, mobility aids, experimental treatment, experimental drugs, organ transplant, war risks, and injuries arising from dangerous hobbies (often called 'hazardous pursuits').

Making a claim

If you need treatment you should keep your insurer informed from the very beginning, generally notifying it of any likely treatment before it happens. The insurer will probably require confirmation of treatment and its necessity from your GP or specialist. Following treatment the hospital might claim the payment direct from your insurer, or you might have to pay and your insurer will reimburse you.

Regulatory structure

Almost all PMI providers in the UK are members of the Association of British Insurers (ABI) and registered with the General Insurance Standards Council (GISC) – check that your provider is, before signing up to any scheme. The GISC has a Code of Practice that regulates how PMI should be marketed, sold and administered. If you have any complaint you should take it up with your insurance provider in the first instance. If it does not satisfy you, you can then go to the GISC (tel 0845 601 2857 or www.gisc.co.uk).

The FSA will take over general insurance regulation from 14th January 2005.

9

Long-term care

The issue of long-term care (LTC) is a relatively new one for the personal finance industry, and is consequently little understood by most of the public. The structure of the industry and provision from the state are complex, and there are still too many firms, both providing care and providing finance for care, that fail to reach good standards.

Until relatively recently the different generations of families typically lived close by each other and depended on each other at different stages of their lives. Grandmothers helped out with their grandchildren, and adult children cared for their parents in their failing years. Today people's mobility and the pressures of work have disrupted this pattern for many families, with adult children living far from their parents, or having full-time jobs that prevent them being able to offer care to their parents should they require it.

While this pattern is set to continue, the issue of LTC is further exacerbated by the fact that as our total life expectancy is creeping up all the time (see Table 8.1), so is the number of years that we are expected to live in less than full health. Current government statistics suggest that the average UK male can expect to have around seven years of less than full health, and the average female as much as 10 years.

Table 9.1 UK life expectancy (in years)

Year	1911	1961	2000	2021 est
Male at birth	50.4	67.8	75.2	78.6
Male at 60	74	75	79	82
Female at birth	53.9	73.7	80.1	82.7
Female at 60	75	80	82	85

Source: ONS

Types of long-term care

All these facts suggest that many of us will need some extra care in our old age. LTC comes in two basic forms, sometimes confusingly called home care (where individuals are looked after in their own houses) and care homes (where they go to a residential or nursing home for their care).

Home care services range from meals-on-wheels, through home alterations, to community nursing and day care and respite centres. Your local authority will provide the majority of these, but the NHS is responsible for certain areas. The NHS aid is free, but typically only available when it is considered that it can improve the patient's medical condition. If no improvement is thought possible, responsibility reverts to local authorities. While local authorities can provide some services free of charge, others may be charged for, and grants are allocated for certain one-off costs, such as home alterations for access. This leads to a complicated structure that will vary from local authority to local authority, so you should contact your council to see what is available in your area. As a general rule the majority of state aid is spent on the most elderly and disabled. The less in need you are, the less likely that any help will be available at all.

The state has been encouraging care homes to be 'contracted out' for nearly 20 years. This means that the number of local authority care home places is much smaller today, the vast majority being run as private businesses. The standards of these homes can vary enormously, as can their price. Over half a million people are resident in UK care homes, but less than 20 per cent of these are funded by local authorities.

Where care comes from

The first source of care is still best sought close to home. It is estimated that over three-quarters of care for the elderly is provided unpaid by family or friends. If you have family or friends who are willing and able to help you or an elderly dependant, this is likely to be the least complicated approach. However, this is not an option for everyone. If you do require to get professional help you might be eligible for some state aid, but most probably the bulk of the financial burden will have to be borne privately.

The general rule, for those in England and Wales, is that you are only eligible for aid if you have assets worth less than £19,500. This figure includes all savings and investments, and in most cases also your home. If you continue living at home and receive home care, or go to a care home while your partner or a dependant relative remains in your home, your house value is removed from the asset calculation. The value of your home is calculated on the portion you own outright, so it excludes any mortgage on the property. Still, if you own any more than 10 per cent of the average-value UK house you are likely to already be approaching the £19,500 limit. The lesson here is that if you own a house you are unlikely to receive any aid for paying for a care home residency. Note that the system is different in Scotland, where the local authority should fund personal and nursing care for everyone regardless of assets.

You may be eligible for other benefits from the state. Your eligibility will depend on your personal circumstances. Some benefits are means tested but by no means all. Attendance allowance is a non-means tested and tax-free benefit, payable to people over 65 who have difficulty with three out of the five basic daily functions (known as activities of daily living (or ADLs): they are mobility, dressing, eating, continence and washing/bathing). There are two levels of help: the lower for those who need help either during the day or at night, and the higher for those who require help during both the day and night.

Disability living allowance is similar but is awarded to people who start requiring help before they are 65. There are two parts to this benefit: a care component for personal care needs and a mobility component for those who require assistance in getting around. Depending on the requirements, the benefit is paid out at lower, medium and higher rates. Carer's allowance (formerly known as invalid care allowance) is paid to the carer rather than the patient. To be eligible for the benefit the carer must care for someone who receives one of the above two benefits, do over 35 hours a week of caring for that person, and be under 65. Finally, the benefit is also dependent on the carer's total earnings. You might also be eligible for income support (see Chapter 11 for further information). Contact your local benefits office for more advice.

Private funding for LTC

The above benefits will not cover everybody, and in any case are often not intended to provide full cover for all living and care expenses. Many people will therefore have to fund any LTC requirements privately. The range of costs for LTC obviously vary with the level of care that is required. Meals-on-wheels and the addition of special handles and rails to a bath are clearly cheaper than full-time residential or nursing care, which can cost up to and beyond £1,000 a week. Typically residential care costs around £350 per week or £18,000 a year, and nursing £500 per week or £24,000 a year.

Approaches to funding LTC

There are two approaches to providing funding for LTC. Either you purchase insurance while you are fit and healthy, which guarantees to cover some or all future LTC costs, or you decide to wait and see if you need LTC, and purchase an 'immediate need' policy if and when the moment arises.

LTC insurance

These are 'pre-funded' policies, where you purchase the insurance cover through the payment of regular premiums or with a one-off lump sum payment. You can start the policy at any age, although some insurers only offer policies to people over 40 or 50. If you have enough spare cash younger than this to invest in an LTC scheme, and you have no special medical reason to expect that you will need it soon, you may be better advised to invest the money in other ways, but where you can access it easily if you need it.

You decide at the outset whether the policy is to cover all your LTC expenses or just up to a specified amount, and whether it will be a fixed level of insurance or will increase with inflation. Note that LTC is labour-intensive and so its cost increases with the rate of earnings rather than inflation, so you should try to link the cover to earnings and not the standard inflation rate.

Most policies are straightforward insurance only, but you could apply for an investment-based policy which will repay some capital at the end of the term or when you die should you not have used it all in claims. These policies tend to be more expensive, and are riskier as the value of the cover will be affected by the performance of the investments.

There are certain risks with LTC insurance (LTCI):

- The primary risk is that you might never need it. LTCI is relatively expensive, and if you die without requiring LTC all the premiums will have been for nothing (unless you have an investment-based policy).
- Other risks are that as you are purchasing cover for (hopefully) some years in the future, it is quite possible that the level of cover purchased will be insufficient for your LTC needs. Your insurance company should review the cover every five years, and advise you if you need to either increase your premiums or add to the lump sum invested.
- The provision of LTCI can affect any means testing from the state in respect of potential benefits.
- Certain illnesses and disabilities might not be covered (some mental illnesses such as depression or schizophrenia are often excluded).
- Some policies only pay out for a limited time period, but most should pay for as long as is required. Check the small print.

The cost of LTCI will depend on your sex, age and state of health at the time you take out the policy.

Immediate-need policies

The downside of LTCI is that you might never need to claim, in which case the insurance company will make a nice profit out of you. An alternative strategy to funding any LTC costs is to wait and see, and if the moment arises where you require LTC you can then purchase an immediate-need policy.

Immediate-need policies are really a variant of impaired life annuities. Life annuities are financial policies where in return for your paying a lump sum now, an insurance company guarantees to pay you a regular income each month for the rest of your life, however long that is. With impaired life annuities you tend to get a better rate of return from the insurance company because they reckon you are likely to live for less than the average remaining lifespan of someone your age. Thus the older you are and the more ill you are, the more 'generous' the company will be.

There are two usual ways to pay for immediate-need policies: with a cash lump sum, which obviously requires you to have the cash available, or popularly these days through equity release. The benefits should be the same, as they are determined by the annuity. The annuity amount will depend on the same factors as for a pre-funded policy above: the amount of income required; whether there are fixed or inflation-linked payments; your age, and your sex and health.

These policies are less risky than pre-funded policies as you only purchase one when you know you need it (they are not available until you have a care need), but they are more expensive as the insurance company is certain to have to pay you something, even if it does not know for how long. In most cases once you have purchased the annuity you do not get any money back other than the regular payments. If you die unexpectedly early your estate could lose out as a result. Some policies also offer death benefits, and others offer guaranteed periods, where regardless of when the policyholder dies, regular payments are made for the guaranteed period, usually around five years.

The methods of payment for annuities, cash lump sum or equity release are covered in Chapter 4. It is important to consider how much of your assets you wish to leave to your inheritors. Equity release can eat in to the value of your home unless it is properly contracted for. Definitely seek professional advice.

Regulators, advisers and providers

At the beginning of this chapter we noted that LTCI is a relatively new financial product. The industry has been through the first phase of development, where many providers jumped in and offered advice and policies. As these policies came to fruition many discovered that they were inadequate for what they were supposed to achieve, in terms of both cover provided and cost charged. The Financial Services Authority published a consultation paper in September 2003 examining the weaknesses and needs of LTCI provision, following the government's decision to bring LTCI under its responsibility. The industry will be regulated by the FSA from November 2004. For further information on this contact the FSA or visit its Web site.

The FSA's involvement is good news for this sector. LTC funding is a complicated decision to make, involving many different variables and assumptions. Proper financial advice should be sought. A recent survey of financial advisers discovered that many, including some from the largest firms, do not really understand the LTC market and all its variables, and that advice given was often incomplete or worse, inaccurate. If you are seriously considering LTCI, make sure you use an adviser that specializes in this field. From November 2004 the FSA's new rules come into effect. This means that all new advisers must undergo training on LTC issues. However, existing advisers do not have to retrain. It will be a long time before all IFAs are fully qualified in LTC intricacies.

Funeral costs and pre-paid plans

There are three things that must be done when someone dies:

- The death has to be certified by a doctor or coroner.
- The death has to be registered with the Register of Births, Deaths and Marriages.
- The body must be buried or cremated.

It is not obligatory to have a funeral ceremony at all, let alone one conducted by a religious minister in a place of worship, and nor is it essential to use a funeral director. However, the vast majority of people do use funeral directors and choose a traditional funeral, and these can be costly.

With the average cremation costing around £1,500 and a burial over £2,000, some planning for this cost can be worthwhile. Funerals are treated in very different ways by different people. Some would not dream of anything less than a 'no expense spared' occasion with hundreds of mourners, flower arrangements, limousines, and a fully catered gathering or 'wake' afterwards. Others prefer a solemn and discreet ceremony with only a handful of close relatives. Others wish for a 'woodland' or even sea burial. All are appropriate, if they fit the wishes of the deceased. Regardless of which style of funeral you desire, it will always be appreciated if you set out your wishes on paper, preferably with your will (see Chapter 19).

Having established what type of funeral you would like, it may be necessary to consider how it will be paid for. Given that most funerals cost into four figures, and some cost several thousand pounds, burdening a grieving family with finding this money can add extra trauma to an already upsetting time. Pre-paid funeral plans generally all operate on the same basis. You pay for your own funeral at today's prices, either in a lump sum or with an instalment plan spread over a number of years. The money is then invested by the plan provider, and is paid out at the time of death. Most pre-paid funeral plans are sold through firms of funeral directors.

The advantage of a pre-paid funeral plan is that you have the time to shop around to look for the best deal and choose exactly what you want, which your grieving family might not feel able to do at the time of death. The problem is that the plans have not always paid out as expected. Typically there are two parts to a funeral's cost: the funeral director's charges, and then extra charges from doctors' fees to payment of all the charges associated with the burial or cremation (grave diggers, headstones, burial plot, flowers, cremation fee, minister's fee and church fees).

A pre-paid plan will almost certainly cover the cost of the funeral directors but might fall short on the extras.

Do not confuse pre-paid funeral plans with funeral expense insurance. The latter is a form of life insurance that pays out on death, but you pay the premiums until you die, otherwise the policy is cancelled. Funeral expense insurance is usually a bad investment as the premiums tend to be high, as it is usually the elderly who take them out, and if you do live for a long time after you start paying, you might pay out more in premiums than you would have for the funeral itself.

To ensure that you get what you expect, check the following:

- Critically, check that your pre-payment goes into a trust fund that is accounted for separately from the funeral planning company.
- Check that your plan will cover everything you need to be covered. This includes funeral director's fees plus the other expenses outlined above. Note that some local authorities charge double the normal rate for people from outside their area to be buried in their cemeteries. If you wish to be buried in a different local authority area, check whether there are any surcharges.
- Does the plan cover the cost of a specified funeral director's charges, regardless of cost increases? Or will it cover any funeral director?
- If you are paying by instalment, what happens if you die before all instalments are paid?
- Can you change the plan to another funeral director or get a refund if you move to a different part of the country?
- Does the plan include removal of a body 'out of hours', that is, at night or on holidays?
- Does the plan include removal of the body from anywhere in the UK?
- Is the funeral planning company a member of a recognized trade organization with an enforceable code of conduct, such as the National Association of Pre-paid Funeral Plans (NAPFP)?

The FSA now covers the pre-paid funeral plan sector.

10

Relationship finance

Life is never easy, and just when you think you have got yourself sorted out, something comes along to upset the balance. This is as true with personal finance as anything else. Any change in your lifestyle, marital or family status is only going to cause upheaval to any plans you have carefully put in place.

Marriage

Getting married has some financial consequences. First, if you want a traditional 'white wedding' you will have to find the money for it, and they are not cheap. Second, once you are married different sets of benefits and tax regimes affect you, and may affect how efficiently your savings and investments can work.

Wedding costs

The average cost of a wedding in the UK is around £12,000. This includes the price of the honeymoon. The honeymoon, reception catering and the dress in fact make up around half the total costs. Obviously you can tailor your (or your child's) wedding to fit your own budget, and it can be cheaper or infinitely more expensive. Posh and Becks reputedly spent £800,000 on theirs – although the £1 million they received from *OK* magazine presumably made it money well spent.

As with all financial decisions, unless money is no object (in which case why read this book?) you must decide before you start booking venues, honeymoons and caterers and choosing engagement rings and dresses who is going to pay for what, and how much each can afford. There are traditional divisions of expenditure (the bride's parents pay for the reception and dress; the groom for the ceremony and honeymoon); but clearly these need not be stuck to, and if one party is willing and able to pay for more, then in the interests of the day running smoothly perhaps they should. All wedding organization is set to a background of tension, and anything that can be done to ease that, either financially or emotionally, should be eagerly embraced.

It is worth setting out on a piece of paper exactly what figures each can afford. If some of the participants do not want to answer such a blunt question (perhaps so as not to appear tight-fisted or unable to pay), you should suggest that they indicate a realistic figure. Once these general amounts are known it is up to the bride and groom to decide whether it is sufficient or whether they would like to add some extras of their own. This will always be a delicate decision, and the management of your family's sensitivities will often be more complicated than the management of the finances!

Once you have decided what you want and tried to fit it to your budget, you might discover that you still do not have enough – in which case you may be tempted to borrow. This luckily is an easy decision – financially. If you work out how much you require to borrow, you can then work out how much it will cost you and whether you can afford it. Chapter 3 discusses this in greater detail. If you can afford it, fine; if not you should carefully explain the calculations to your partner and work out where you can cut costs. It is probably foolish to start married life working all hours to cover the cost of the wedding!

Above all remember that your wedding is supposed to be a day of celebration and enjoyment. Setting up an occasion where you are forever worrying whether Uncle Bob is drinking too much champagne or you can really afford the 10-piece band is not going to make it any more fun; so arrange the day so as to reduce your anxiety as much as possible.

Finally, having committed all this money to the big day it would be disastrous if for whatever reason you have to cancel the wedding. The bride or groom or another integrally close member of the family could be taken ill; perhaps there will be a transport strike which prevents people from turning up, or some other unforeseeable problem. For a small percentage (usually under £200) of the total amount you are spending on the wedding you can get specific insurance cover for cancellation and reorganization of your wedding, plus cover for wedding gifts and any liability you might incur on the day itself. This is almost certainly worth acquiring.

If all this seems like an enormous amount to pay for your friends and relations to party at your expense, a registry office can offer you the same outcome – that is, marriage – for under £100.

Married couples, tax and savings

Until recently there was a different tax threshold for married couples than for singles – the married couple's tax allowance – but it was abolished in 2000. However, couples where one spouse was born before 6 April 1935 receive married couple's age allowance, where the tax threshold is raised for those aged between 67 and 74 to £5,725, and for those over 75 to £5,795. However, if your income is over £18,900 a year, the threshold is reduced by £1 for every £2 extra you earn, until a minimum threshold of £2,210 is reached. The married couple's age allowance is only advantageous if one spouse earns less than the individual tax threshold.

The main tax benefits for being married are applicable to all married people regardless of age, but they are only beneficial on specific occasions. The principal one is that there is no inheritance tax payable between spouses. This is only of interest if your estate is worth more than the inheritance tax threshold (see Chapter 13), currently £263,000. Any amount over this normally incurs tax at 40 per cent, but not if it is inherited by a surviving spouse. Nor is there any capital gains tax (CGT) payable for gifts between spouses. This has a real benefit in that if one partner in the marriage is not using up his or her full tax-free allowances for income or capital gains, the other partner can gift the income-bearing or capital-gaining asset to him or her, to maximize the use of the allowances.

The downside of marriage is that you can become liable for your spouse's debts if you have a joint account or debt, such as a joint loan or mortgage. You can be forced to use assets kept in your own name to pay off any such joint debts. However, you are not liable for any debts a spouse runs up solely in his or her own name, unless he or she moves money into your name to avoid having to repay debts on bankruptcy, in which case the money can be reclaimed.

Away from the tax and legal financial implications, life can be cheaper for couples, married or not. The obvious situation is that buying a house (or renting one) is cheaper when the cost is divided between two salaries rather than just one. This arithmetic also works for other large purchases such as buying a car and going on holiday. Finally, although keeping your savings accounts separate might be a good idea for the reasons outlined above, there is a benefit from pooling your savings, as you often get a better rate of interest for higher sums in your accounts. One way of having your cake and eating it is to use a bank that allows savers to pool their savings in 'schemes', which are made up of individuals' separate accounts, but the interest rate applied is that relating to the total amount in all the accounts in the scheme. As the accounts are separate and hidden from the other members of the scheme, you do not have to limit the scheme membership just to your spouse!

Divorce and money

The division of funds becomes much more complicated when trying to untie the knot than when tying it. After deciding on residence and contact with children, divorce negotiations are principally financially based ones of dividing up money and other assets. There are certain basic procedures to make this process as uncontroversial as possible, but inevitably everyone has a unique situation which might make this process more or less straightforward. In summary, if either party in a divorce feels that a negotiated agreement is unfair, he or she can ask for a court to decide. It is therefore sensible to agree in mediation to decisions that a court will deem fair.

A court is obliged to consider:

- the needs of the children;
- the length of the marriage;
- the age of the couple;
- contributions during marriage;
- the financial resources of each spouse;
- the needs of each spouse;
- pensions and any loss of widow's benefits.

The less third parties are involved, the cheaper the divorce process will be. Therefore, if couples can agree the details directly between themselves, so much the better (as long as they both understand what they are agreeing to). Failing that mediation is advisable, after which the lawyers will negotiate and then the courts intervene.

Whatever approach you take, both parties need to provide all relevant financial details. This is called financial disclosure. Typically this will include:

- recent valuation of any property/ies owned by either party;
- a redemption statement on any mortgage;
- valuation of any other assets held, such as a share portfolio or premium bond holdings;
- statements for any other liabilities held;
- the last three pay slips plus the most recent P60 income tax form;
- notification of surrender values of life assurance policies;
- notification of the value of any pensions;
- bank account statements (for both current and savings accounts);
- details of any business accounts.

Both parties are also required to show what their financial needs are, so a breakdown of where you spend money, as in the budget lists in

Chapter 2, will be required. The more information and detail you can present here, the better.

At this stage it might become clear that the type of lifestyle you had when both living in the same house and sharing many costs cannot be sustained when you are living separately. If so, cutbacks will have to be made, and this is when inequalities may be perceived and difficulties arise. At this stage negotiations begin with trade-offs being offered. Trade-offs can make the whole process much simpler and the break cleaner, but clearly you need to be happy that broadly both sides are benefiting equally. One typical trade-off is that one partner gets to keep the house but the other does not have to pay maintenance.

This book cannot hope to cover the details necessary in dealing with the financial implications of a divorce, beyond noting that in most circumstances, after a divorce both parties find themselves with less money and in less comfort. It is always advisable to disclose, through your legal adviser, all relevant financial information. There are plenty of Web sites that can give more detailed information on the different aspects of divorce, and if you do not have access to the Internet your local library, Citizens' Advice Bureau or Relate might be able to provide you with information.

Note that the law regarding divorce is different in Scotland from that in England and Wales.

Children

The arrival of children into a relationship is so exciting as well as transforming a moment that the financing aspects of having an extra small person to care for can often be forgotten. When set out in a single figure, the expense of caring for a baby and bringing up a child can seem astronomical, but in practice it should not be hugely burdensome. For those people already having difficulty making ends meet there are resources to help fund the extra costs, and even for those who have enough money the government still rewards parents with child benefit.

Work done by academics at the University of Loughborough ('Small fortunes' by Sue Middleton *et al*) suggest that in 2001 the extra cost of having a first child was around £67 per week, and of subsequent children £56 per week, or £3,500 a year for the first child and £3,000 a year for each subsequent child. Obviously this is a very approximate figure, and it does not include the costs of having to buy a bigger house, larger car and so on, only day-to-day expenses in keeping children fed, clothed, entertained and so on.

The government gives child benefit to the main carer of any child under the age of 16 (or 19 if still in full-time education). The main carer does not have to be a parent. The current rate of child benefit is £16.50 a week for the first child and £11.05 a week for each subsequent child. That is £834.50 a year for the first child and £559 for each subsequent child, and represents approximately 25 per cent and 20 per cent respectively of the total extra costs of children outlined in the research mentioned above. Lone parents get higher rates. Child benefit is not affected by the income or savings of the carer claiming the benefit. You should claim child benefit immediately your child is born: contact the Child Benefit Office (0845 302 1444 or www.inlandrevenue.gov.uk/childbenefit).

Separate from child benefit is child tax credit. This is part of what replaced working families tax credit in April 2003. The current system splits the tax credits into two parts, child tax credit and working tax credit. Child tax credit is paid to carers of children (in the same way as is child benefit) regardless of whether either of the parents work. It is payable to couples with a joint income of £58,000 or less, although it pays out less as you near this ceiling. There are two available parts to the tax credit. The first is a families element payable to all families with less than the ceiling income. Currently this is £10.45 per week (£543.40 per year), although it is doubled in the first year of a child's birth. Second, any family earning less than £13,480 a year can claim £1,625 or £31.15 per child a week from the 'per child' element of the tax credit. As your income increases above this level, the amount you receive in tax credit reduces, until you are no longer eligible for the credit at the income ceiling. The government has pledged to increase the 'per child' element in line with earnings inflation for the life of this parliament. The working tax credit element of the tax credits system is explained in the next chapter. It does have one child-related benefit, however, in that in-work parents can claim child care benefit through the working tax credit system. For more information contact 0845 300 3900, www.taxcredits.inlandrevenue.gov.uk/

Child care

One of the most difficult decisions parents, particularly mothers, face today is trying to balance a working life with bringing up children. For many families, for both parents to work is a necessity rather than a choice, so that a desired standard of living can be achieved. For the better off, plenty of mothers feel they would like to continue working, at least after the arrival of the first child if not subsequent ones.

Child care options include childminders, out-of-school services, nurseries, pre-school playgroups and nannies. Generally they increase in expense through that list. As mentioned above, people eligible for the working tax credit can apply for the child care element, which pays out a maximum of 70p for every £1 cost of child care, up to £135 a week of costs for one child or £200 of costs for two or more. See the Inland Revenue for more information: details as above.

Child maintenance

Child maintenance is paid for children who live away from one or both of their parents. It is an amount of money paid regularly by the non-resident parent for the child. For parents who do not live with their children, most usually divorced or separated fathers but others as well, there is help available with the payment of maintenance for those on low incomes, receiving income support or jobseekers allowance. This is administered by the Child Support Agency (CSA), which has had a poor press since its inception in 1993, but is less controversial today. More information on child maintenance rules and benefits can be found by contacting the CSA on its National Helpline, 08457 133 133, or at www.csa.gov.uk . Note that different rules and maintenance calculations apply to those who were initially assessed by the agency before April 2003 and those who have been assessed since.

Maternity and paternity rights

From April 2003 there has been a new regime regarding maternity and paternity rights. All new mothers can now take 26 weeks maternity leave regardless of how long they have worked with their company. Those eligible for statutory maternity pay (SMP) (maternity leave only guarantees that you can return to your job, it does not pay you anything), will receive 90 per cent of their average earnings for the first six weeks of maternity leave, and then £100 or 90 per cent of earnings whichever is less, from the government for the next 20 weeks. Those mothers who have worked for a company for more than 26 weeks can continue on maternity leave unpaid for a further 26 weeks if they so choose.

Since April 2003 fathers have been allowed two weeks' paternity leave, and can get £100 a week statutory paternity pay. They must have worked with their employer for at least 26 weeks by the fifteenth week before the baby is due, must take the leave within eight weeks of the baby's birth, and must be earning more than the minimum earnings level. For further information contact the Maternity Alliance on 020 7490 7638 or at www.maternityalliance.org.uk

11

Benefits

It is estimated that up to £3.5 billion of state benefits goes unclaimed each year, the equivalent of around £70 for every adult in the UK, or substantially more for those people actually entitled to the benefits. As benefits are provided to help those in most need of extra financial help, this is a ridiculous situation.

State benefits are losing the stigma that was once attributed to them. This stigma arose from the depression era of the 1930s when 'means test' inspectors, who oversaw unemployment payments, were empowered to enter homes and pry into the circumstances of the unemployed to ensure that their dependence upon relief was absolutely necessary. This memory of the means test has become a great national folk myth, and in some respects continues today – but it is an outmoded fear as many benefits are no longer means tested, and many of those benefits that are still related to income are also based on other factors.

If you are entitled to a benefit, you should take it. The problem is that because of the lingering associations of benefits and total poverty, few people seek out their entitlements, and many benefits are poorly advertised. In this chapter we outline some of the most widely available benefits, and explain who can claim them and who provides them. For simplicity's sake we list them in alphabetical order:

- **Access to work (AtW)**: advice and practical support provided by Jobcentre Plus to disabled people and their employers to help overcome work-related obstacles related to disability.

- **Attendance allowance (AA)** is paid to those who need help looking after themselves; become ill or disabled over the age of 65, and need help for at least six months. See Chapter 9 for more information.
- **Back to work bonus** is payable to those who have been on income support or jobseekers allowance but stop getting these payments because they have found employment. It is a lump sum payment administered by Jobcentre Plus, and must be claimed within 12 weeks of the other benefits ending.
- **Bereavement allowance** (formerly widow's pension) paid to widows or widowers who do not have sufficient pension contributions, assuming their late spouse did. A regular payment administered by Jobcentre Plus.
- **Bereavement payment** (formerly widow's payment) is paid to widows or widowers whose late spouse had made sufficient NICs to make them eligible. It is a one-off lump sum of up to £2,000, administered by Jobcentre Plus.
- **Carer's allowance (CA)** is paid to full-time carers over the age of 16. It is means tested. See Chapter 9 for more information, or call the Carer's Allowance Unit on 01253 856 123.
- **Child benefit**: see Chapter 10. Administered by the Child Benefits Office.
- **Child maintenance bonus** is paid to people leaving the child support maintenance scheme. It is a one-off payment of up to £1,000.
- **Child support maintenance** is paid to help finance bringing up a child where a parent is living away from home or is on income support or jobseekers allowance. Administered by the Child Support Agency.
- **Child tax credit**: see Chapter 10. Administered by the Inland Revenue.
- **Christmas bonus** is a tax-free payment made to those already receiving one or more of the main benefits.
- **Council tax benefit** is paid by local authorities (councils) and can help pay council tax if you have a low income – regardless of whether you are working or not.

- **Disability living allowance (DLA)** is paid to anyone between the ages of 3 and 65 who has a severe mental illness or physical disability. It is paid at three different rates depending on the level of disability.
- **Free milk for disabled children:** for mentally or physically disabled children between the ages of 5 and 16 who cannot attend school, free milk is available. No other benefits are required to receive this. Administered by Jobcentre Plus.
- **Free prescriptions and dental treatment:** all expectant mothers receive these, as do the elderly. Call the NHS on the Freephone Advice Line on 0845 850 1166.
- **Free television licence for the over 75s:** contact TV Licensing Over 75s helpline on 0845 603 6999.
- **Guardian's allowance** is payable to someone looking after a child where one or both of that child's parents have died. The recipient must be receiving child benefit for the child. Contact the Guardian's Allowance Unit, part of the Child Benefit Office on 0845 302 1464.
- **Help with health costs:** Jobcentre Plus will award payments to cover certain health-related payments to people on the main benefits.
- **Home responsibilities payment (HRP)** is paid to mothers and carers to recompense them for lost pension rights. It is automatically applied with child benefit. Administered by the Pension Service.
- **Housing benefit** is paid by local authorities (councils) and can help pay your rent if you have a low income – regardless of whether you are working or not.
- **Incapacity benefit (IB)** is payable to those who have paid sufficient National Insurance contributions (NICs) and been unable to work for four days in a row including weekends and holidays. If you have not paid sufficient NICs you will only be eligible if you are between 16 and 20 (25 if recently in full-time education) and have been unable to work for 28 weeks. This benefit is administered through Jobcentre Plus.
- **Income support** is available to people on a low income, who do not have to look for work to receive benefit. These include carers, pensioners, lone parents and people with a health problem. For pensioners this is often described as the minimum income guarantee.

Income support is means tested, so applicants have to provide information on all their other sources of income and savings.

- **Industrial injuries disablement benefit** is paid to employees (not the self-employed) who are unable to work due to an accident at work. In some circumstances those with a work-related disease or deafness are also eligible. You do not have to prove your employer was negligent to receive this benefit. This benefit is administered by Jobcentre Plus.

- **Job grant** is paid to people who have been receiving one of the main benefits for over a year and are now starting full-time work. It is a £100 one-off payment made by Jobcentre Plus.

- **Jobseekers allowance** is paid to people who are not eligible for income support (see above) and who must look for work to qualify for benefit. Like income support it is means tested. Those on low incomes receive the income-based jobseekers allowance. You must prove that you are both available for work and actively seeking work. (If you are on a course it must be for less than 16 hours a week for you to remain eligible.) You apply for both yourself and your family.

- **Minimum income guarantee** is paid to pensioners in place of income support. It is administered by the Pension Service.

- **Mortgage interest costs** can be paid if you qualify for income support or jobseekers allowance, are buying a house, and someone in the house is disabled. These will normally be paid direct to your mortgage company, but may not cover all of your mortgage interest.

- **Mortgage interest run-on** is payable to eligible people leaving income support or jobseekers allowance who have been having help with their mortgage payments. It is administered by Jobcentre Plus.

- **New Deal** is a government programme designed to help and support people to get into work. It is administered by the Department of Work and Pensions (DWP). It is split into various areas of help:
  - for young people (18 to 25);
  - for those aged 25 plus;
  - for those aged 50 plus;
  - for disabled people;
  - for lone parents;
  - for partners (of someone claiming a benefit);

- for the self-employed;
- for musicians.

- **Rapid reclaim** is for people who have returned to jobseekers allowance or income support within 12 weeks of the benefit stopping previously. Administered by Jobcentre Plus.
- **Reduced earnings allowance** is payable to those who cannot earn as much as they normally would through illness or disability. Administered by Jobcentre Plus.
- **Severe disablement allowance (SDA)** is paid to people between the ages of 16 and 65 who cannot work through illness or disablement and are not eligible for incapacity benefit.
- The **Social Fund** is a system of loans and grants to help cover unexpected costs or payments for certain events. For more detailed information on eligibility and how to claim contact the DWP or your local Benefits Agency, or read leaflet SB16 (Oct 2003), *A Guide to the Social Fund*. The main benefits are set out below:
  - Budgeting loans are available to people on income support, income-based jobseekers allowance, pension credit or payment on account for one of these benefits or entitlements. It is made to help meet occasional expenses they otherwise might have problems funding.
  - Budget Boost 2004: the government will pay all households with someone aged 70 or over £100 in addition to any other entitlement they are already receiving. The payment is initially only for the tax year 2004/5 and is to compensate pensioners for the rise in council tax bills.
  - Cold weather payments are made to some people on income support or income-based jobseekers allowance and to all people receiving pension credit. They are made specifically to go towards heating expenses when there is cold weather in a particular area. They are paid regardless of savings.
  - Community care grants are non-repayable payments made to people leaving residential accommodation, to help people to continue living in a community or on a resettlement programme.

In exceptional cases grants can be offered to families in extreme need, with people on release from prison and the like, and to help with certain travel costs. They are only available to people on income support, income-related jobseekers allowance, pension credit or similar entitlement.

- Crisis loans are available to anyone, to meet unexpected expenses in the event of an emergency or as the consequences of a disaster.

- Funeral payments are what they say: help to cover the expenses of organizing a respectful funeral. Any money left by the deceased is reclaimed, to the amount of the payment. They are available to the same groups as can receive Sure Start maternity grants, plus those on housing or council tax benefits.

- Sure Start maternity grants are one-off lump sums to people with a baby, their own or officially adopted, under 12 months. It is available to those receiving income support, income-based jobseekers allowance, pension credit, working tax credit (if a disability element is included), and child tax credit (above the family element rate).

- Winter fuel payments are made to most people over 60 (people over 80 get more). They are paid regardless of savings.

Statutory adoption pay (SAP) is the same as statutory maternity pay but for adopted babies.

Statutory maternity pay (SMP): see Chapter 10.

Statutory paternity pay (SPP): see Chapter 10.

Statutory sick pay (SSP) is paid by your employer for up to 28 weeks after you have been unable to work through illness for four days or more. To be eligible you must have paid the relevant minimum NICs.

Vaccine damage payment: a one-off payment to those severely disabled as a result of receiving a vaccine. Administered by the Vaccine Damage Payment Unit.

War disablement pension is payable to those disabled while working for the armed forces, as a Civil Defence Volunteer, or as a civilian disabled through enemy action in the Second World War; also for merchant seamen and some other special groups. It is administered by the Veterans Agency.

- **War widow's pension** is payable to widows of those grouped above. It is administered by the Veterans Agency.
- **Widowed parents allowance** is a regular benefit for widowed parents still bringing up children, based on the late spouse's NICs. It is administered by Jobcentre Plus.
- **Working tax credit** is to help top up low earnings. To be eligible you must work for at least 30 hours a week and be over 25. If you have either a child or are disabled you only have to work for 16 hours or more a week.

Special rules

For most of the benefits mentioned here, special rules apply to certain groups of people such as hospital in-patients, people from abroad, students, prisoners and those who live in special accommodation. You should get further advice if you are in any of these groups.

Who to contact

The vast majority of these benefits are paid by central government, although a few (housing and council tax benefit) are paid by local government. Of the central government benefits, most come from the Department for Work and Pensions (DWP).

The DWP (formerly the Department for Social Security, DSS) is split into numerous different departments. This can make it a little complicated trying to find the correct person to give you advice on particular benefits. The DWP prefers you to try to contact the correct department or agency directly; however, if you are unsure which is the relevant one you can contact the DWP Public Enquiry Office: 020 7712 2171 (9.00 am–5.00 pm Monday–Friday) or write to Department for Work and Pensions, Correspondence Unit, Room 540, The Adelphi, 1–11 John Adam Street, London WC2N 6HT.

Within the DWP the main agencies are:

- **Pension Service:** 0845 6060265 or at www.thepensionservice.gov.uk.
- **Jobcentre Plus:** contact your local Jobcentre Plus office, which will be listed in the telephone book, or visit www.jobcentreplus.gov.uk. (These are replacing existing Jobcentres. If you do not have a Jobcentre Plus in your area yet, contact the Jobcentre or local Social Security Office.)
- **Child Support Agency:** 08457 133 133 or at www.csa.gov.uk.
- For the disabled and carers go to the government agency **Disability**. It has a benefits enquiry line 0800 882200 (and textphone service 0800 243355) or visit www.disability.gov.uk. Also the **Disability Rights Commission**, www.drc-gb.org. You can also call the **Carer's Allowance Unit** on 01253 856 123.
- For further information on the **New Deal** you can get leaflets from 0845 606 26 26 and at www.newdeal.gov.uk.

Other useful government guides can be obtained from the DWP Public Enquiry Office, or visit www.dwp.gov.uk/resourcecentre/leaflets_guides.asp. Guides include the following.

Guides for families and children

Babies and Children (BC1)
Expecting a Baby (BC2)
Bringing Up Children? (BC3)
Prisoners and their Families (GL32)
Separated or Divorced? (GL13)
Service Families (GL26)
Sure Start Maternity Grant

Guides for sick, injured or disabled people and their carers

A Guide to Incapacity Benefit (IB1)
A Guide to Industrial Injuries Schemes Benefits (DB1)

A Guide to Non-Contributory Benefits for Disabled People and their Carers (HB5)
Caring for Someone? (SD4)
Disabled because of an Accident at Work? (SD7)
Disability and Carers Service: Customer Charter
Going into Hospital? (GL12)
Help if you Live in a Residential Care or Nursing Home (GL15)
Ill or Disabled because of a Disease or Deafness Caused by Work? (SD6)
Ill or Disabled because of Working with Asbestos in your Job? (SD8)
Incapacity Benefit (IB203)
Long-Term Ill or Disabled? (SD3)
Permitted Work Rules
Personal Capability Assessment (IB214)
Sick or Disabled (SD1)
Sick and Unable to Work? (SD2)
Vaccine Damage Payments (HB3)

Guides for people in work and looking for work

Financial Help if you are In Work or Looking for Work (WK1)
Financial Help if you are Looking for Work (WK2)
Need Help Starting Work or Getting Back to Work? (WK3)
Financial Help if you Work or do Voluntary Work (WK4)
Help to Move to Work and Independence (WFL5)

Guides for people aged 60 and over

Minimum Income Guarantee for People aged 60 and Over (MIG1L)
Pensioner's Guide – England and Wales (PG1)
Pensioner's Guide – Scotland (PG3)
Pension Credit – Pick It Up, It's Yours (PG1L)
Are You Over 50? – England and Wales
Are You Over 50? – Scotland
Your Guide to Winter Fuel Payments

Guides for school leavers and students

School Leavers and Students (GL19)

Guides to benefits and services following death

What to Do after a Death – England and Wales (D49)
What to Do after a Death – Scotland (D49S)
Widowed? (GL14)

General guides to benefits, services and the Social Fund

A Guide to the Social Fund (SB16)
A Helping Hand for Benefits (GL21)
Coming from Abroad and Social Security Benefits (GL28)
Going Abroad and Social Security Benefits (GL29)
Help from the Social Fund (GL18)
Help with your Council Tax (GL17)
Help with your Rent (GL16)
How to Prove your Identity for Social Security (GL25)
If you Think our Decision is Wrong (GL24)
Social Security Benefit Rates (GL23)

Non-state benefits

It is not only the state that provides benefits. Many companies have schemes for the disabled, elderly and disadvantaged, as of course do charities. It is not possible to list them all here, but some include:

- The Warm Front Scheme run by Powergen and Eaga Partnership provides help with heating and insulation improvements to those on pension credit or council tax benefit. Freefone 0800 952 1555 or visit www.powergen-warmfront.co.uk.
- Free or half-price bus travel is often available. Contact your local council.

- The Senior Railcard can give substantial discounts on rail travel. Contact a main line station, call your local rail operator (GNER tele-sales 08457 225 225), or visit www.senior-railcard.co.uk.
- Finally, the Community Legal Service (an organization funded by the Legal Services Commission and the Department for Constitutional Affairs) can provide further advice on many of these areas. The Community Legal Service directory line, on 0845 608 1122, or text-phone on 0845 606677 (local rates) gives people information about lawyers and advice centres local to them, and with the right expertise to help with their problems. It can also be found at www.justask.org.uk.

12

One-off purchases and loans

Throughout this guide we are keen to stress that the foundation of good personal finance is a set of simple, if boring, rules. The principal pair are to start saving as soon as possible, and to save a little money regularly. This builds up funds from which you can, and should, draw from when you need to. Typically this will be in emergencies and when you want to buy a substantial item. Underpinning this rule is the fact that you should first pay off any expensive, unsecured debts you have, as they will cost you more than any savings will earn you. And built on top of the main savings rule is that when you need more money than you have saved, you should only borrow as much as you can afford.

In Chapter 6 we looked at mortgages and the positive reasons for buying a house. The core of the argument was that housing is an investment-type asset. Over time it should increase in value, making your loan more efficient as it does so. Also mortgages are secured loans, which are much cheaper than unsecured loans. So you benefit on two counts from taking out a loan.

Sadly not all the things we want in life are investment-type assets that we can borrow against (that is, give as security to guarantee a loan) as well as borrow for (that is, when we need extra money to buy them). In fact the huge majority of purchases are strictly not of this kind. Depending on your weekly or monthly pay and the level of your savings, there will be an approximate amount you can spend from your assets, and if you wish to buy something more expensive than this amount you will have to borrow some money. That amount will vary from person to person. It could be for items over £100, say – so any consumer electronics or electrical item, perhaps a hi-fi or a new fridge, will require you to borrow some money to make the purchase. It could be for items over £1,000, perhaps – so a new three-piece suite or a family holiday requires you to take out a loan. For some it may be over £5,000 or even £10,000 – so they only need to borrow money if they are buying a new car or doing some major home improvements. Whatever the level, you should be aware of where your need to borrow money kicks in, so you can mentally prepare for how you will manage any purchases above this level.

When making the calculations you should have a good idea of your regular income and basic weekly or monthly expenditure, as discussed in Chapter 2. You should also try to continue making your regular savings if possible, although you will need to make a judgement whether it is worth taking out an extra loan so as to enable you to continue making savings. Often it will not be sensible to do this. Having a good understanding of income, expenditure and your savings amount, you will then be able to calculate how much you can afford to borrow. This sum should be based on how much you can afford to repay each month, and not how much you need to buy the item you want! Once you know how much you can afford to repay each month (or put another way, how much you can afford to spend on repayments each month, as repayments are expenditure), you can look around for the best type of loan you can get: that is, one that will provide the most amount of money, for a balance between the least monthly expenditure and the shortest repayment time. The main types of loans and their benefits and drawbacks are covered in Chapter 3.

In this chapter we look briefly at purchasing five different items, and ways to cover the cost if you cannot meet it out of savings. The items are a digital camera costing £215; a new computer costing £750; a Mediterranean holiday for two adults and two children costing £1,750; some improvements to your kitchen costing £6,000; and a new car costing £18,000.

Digital camera: £215

Buying consumer electronics is a complicated business, largely because there is a baffling and enticing array of options available to you – and frequently today's extras are tomorrow's basic equipment. As with all expensive items, the best approach is to do as much research into the product as possible rather than buy on impulse. Discover first what the cheapest available models are (with consumer electronics the Internet offers an easy way to compare prices, either through specialist price-comparison sites or by visiting particular retailer sites), and from there see what extras you get by going up in price and quality. The important thing is to be as clinical as possible in choosing what extras you require. How often will you use the product? How many extra 'bells and whistles' will you actually use, rather than just find nice to know you have? How compatible will the item be with new technologies appearing at the top end of the scale? You do not want to buy something that will be obsolete within 12 months because technology has moved on quickly.

Having done your research and satisfied yourself that you are getting the best price available without sacrificing reliability, warranties and the like, you will then know what sort of prices you are looking at and whether they fit your purse.

For this example we have chosen a mid-priced digital camera. It is a consumer electronic item and therefore has little investment-type asset value, although you should be able to sell the camera for something, if you need to, in the months after you purchased it. Financial organizations will not be interested in repossessing the camera should you be unable to make the repayments, so any loan from them will be unsecured.

To the list of loan types mentioned in Chapter 2 (unarranged overdraft, arranged overdraft, credit card or store card, unsecured bank loan, secured bank loan, and mortgage) we can add a seventh option: a loan from the retailer. All these options are available to you, although for a loan amount of this small size a secured bank loan and a mortgage are wholly unrealistic, as you would have to pay for surveys and other administration costs in raising a secured loan against your house or other asset, and these costs alone would be greater than the cost of the camera. The unarranged overdraft is always so foolish a choice as not to be a logical option either. That leaves an arranged overdraft, credit card or store card, unsecured bank loan, or retailer's loan.

The overdraft should really be avoided, as overdrafts are very expensive ways of borrowing money. If you just need the money for a couple of days or so before you get paid, it is best to wait until you get paid. If you need the camera for a special event before you get paid, perhaps this option is worth considering.

If you have a credit card or store card, this is a better route to borrowing the money, if you are sure you can pay the balance off in the next few weeks. Depending on the interest rate applicable for new purchases on your credit card, it might be the best compromise between ease and cheapness.

If you know you can only pay off the minimum amount on your credit card (in which case you should probably not be buying the camera in the first place), you could look at getting a small bank loan. However, there are not many banks that lend amounts less than £500, and those that do tend to charge as high rates as credit card companies. This is because of the administration costs involved and the relatively little profit they can make from lending small sums. That said, many banks offer better rates of interest on small loans to students (see www.support4learning.org.uk) and other special groups, so it is always worth asking your bank if any special deals are available to you.

This leaves the retailer's loan, which can be the best way to borrow money if you can find a retailer that offers incentivized initial interest rates. Many of the larger retailers offer loans that have a six-month, or sometimes longer, interest-free period. This is a real opportunity if you use it wisely. Most such arrangements change quickly from interest-free to quite high rates of interest once the initial period ends. This is where the company makes its money, hoping that you will not be able to pay off the loan within the interest-free period. Purchasers must make sure they do not fall into this trap – and must start putting money aside immediately to cover the cost of the loan, so they can pay it all off at the end of the initial low-interest or interest-free period. If you just forget about the payments until the end of the period, you will pay heavily for it. Again 'little and often and starting now' is the way to better personal finance solutions.

Beware that at this level of borrowing there are many 'finance' companies willing to lend small sums but at outrageous prices. Be very careful about the small print and the interest rates charged when taking out any loan, no matter how small.

Computer: £750

A computer is another non-investment type asset: its value starts falling from the moment you buy it. All the same advice applies for buying a computer as for the example above. The only difference is that the computer is sufficiently expensive to allow you to consider bank loans more realistically. You will still probably pay an interest rate from the mid- to high-teens, which could add up to half as much again to the total cost if payments are spread over two years or more.

It is worth noting that computers are considered such important pieces of equipment for both education and everyday living purposes these days that there are often grants from local organizations to help cover the cost of purchase for students and others.

Holiday: £1,750

This is a real consumable product; once you have 'used' it there is nothing left of financial value. Bank loans are the most obvious method of paying for such expenditure, although you may find that package holiday companies offer interest-free deals to give you space to save up for paying for your holiday. In addition, if you tend to book holidays quite far in advance you should not have to pay out all the costs until shortly before you actually go on holiday. This can give you several months to save up for the final payment.

There is often a gamble in when to book holidays. If you can book them many months in advance, say 10 months to a year, you will often be able to negotiate a cheaper rate. However, buying at the last minute can also be very much cheaper. The most expensive time to book a holiday is usually between one and five months from when you want to go – the period in which most of us normally do it. The further in advance you book your holiday, the more imperative it is that you take out insurance to cover the possibility of cancellation.

Home improvement: £6,000

There are, of course libraries of books, not to mention hours of television programmes, on this subject. Home improvement can cover a wide range of activities and expenses, from putting in a new cooker to building a new wing on your house. For this example we focus on kitchen improvements at around £6,000.

Most home improvements can be relatively cheaply funded as they should, if done properly, increase the value of your home over time. They are an investment-type asset, meeting both the criteria set out above: their value should increase with time, and you should be able to borrow against them. This means that you ought to be able to find a loan that is much cheaper, percentage-wise, than for the smaller amounts discussed above.

As the loan is considerably larger than for the previous examples, you will be looking to pay not from credit cards or overdrafts as they will be too expensive, but from an unsecured or secured bank loan or a mortgage. Since this is an investment-type asset you should be looking for a secured loan. However, in certain circumstances (particularly if you already have a mortgage of 90 per cent or more of the house's value) this will not be available. If this is the case, you should be careful to make sure that you can cover the cost of any extra borrowings, and first of all consider whether you would not be better advised to pay off more of your mortgage and so reduce the mortgage liability before embarking on an expensive improvement project. If you feel the improvements are essential, you will need to approach your bank to discuss an unsecured loan. If it refuses to advance one, you might need to search out a different lender. With each step further away from secured loans you can be sure that the rate of interest will increase, making the whole project more expensive.

If you are able to take out a secured loan you have two main options: a straightforward secured loan or a variant of your mortgage, which is a type of secured loan anyway. The mortgage variants are usually the cheapest in terms of monthly repayments. The most normal variant is an 'advance on mortgage', which is just a further loan on top of your existing mortgage amount. No revaluations, searches or lawyers are likely to be involved, as the repossession element of the contract remains the same; the financial side is likely to have different terms, however. That is, the new or extra mortgage amount may well have a different interest rate from the original mortgage. It could also have a different repayment period if you wish. It might also be more (or less) flexible in terms of payment holidays, lump sum payments and so on. There will be an arrangement fee for taking out an advance on your mortgage, usually around £100–200.

A second mortgage variant is to pay off your existing mortgage and take out a completely new and slightly larger mortgage (known as remortgaging). This is only advisable if you can find a substantially cheaper mortgage elsewhere, and you will not be losing out on any special terms or incurring any extra penalties by so doing. All this is covered in greater detail in Chapter 6.

A non-mortgage secured loan will be more expensive but have fewer administration costs and hassles than a mortgage-based loan.

Finally, it is worth noting that not all home improvements do add value to your property. This is especially the case if you are just redecorating or interior-designing your house, when you might discover that your taste is not that of potential purchasers or will become dated in a few years' time. More significant building projects tend to be more profitable, but you might not see the value immediately. Home improvement projects are generally only worthwhile if you intend to benefit from them by continuing to live in the house for some while afterwards.

Car purchase: £18,000

After buying a house, a car is likely to be the most expensive single purchase you ever make. If you take into account that, unlike a house, your car will start losing value the moment you get inside it, perhaps it is actually the most expensive purchase you will ever make, in terms of money spent, never to be seen again.

Many organizations, from banks to supermarkets to motoring organizations, and plenty of specialist firms, have realized that buying a car is expensive, and all have come up with ways to make the financing easier. At the end of the day it will be your decision which type of car finance you choose, for they all have elements that might appeal to different people. The bottom line as ever is the rate of interest you will pay on your loan, and how long you take to repay it.

Purchasing a car is made more complicated because most specialist car loan companies are aimed at the company car market, where factors affect the cost of loans that do not work for the private customer. If you are a private buyer your three main choices for car loans are:

- A personal loan – a straightforward unsecured loan as described above.
- A car loan. You take out a loan in the normal way, but repayment of part of the loan is then deferred for a specified period, usually between one and four years. This deferred element is paid back in a lump sum plus interest at the end of the period. The expectation is that you pay off the lump sum with proceeds from selling the car. You then take out a new car loan for your next car. This type of loan means that you can purchase a more expensive car than you would otherwise be able to do, yet your monthly repayments should remain low in comparison to the size of the loan (because some 30 per cent or more of the loan is only paid at the end of the period). Obviously the bank or loaning organization will have a claim to the car as long as the loan exists.
- A private lease arrangement – this is becoming more popular, and is similar to many company lease arrangements. You choose the car you wish to buy – this will normally be a new car, but sometimes nearly new cars are available under these schemes – and let the leasing company know what it is. It pays for the car, and you then pay it a monthly amount, which is fixed at the outset. (This often covers

maintenance costs as well.) The payment agreement is for a fixed period, typically one to four years. At the end of the period you usually have the choices of paying the lease company a final lump sum (known as a 'balloon payment') and keeping the car, or giving the car back to the company and paying nothing more. A third option of upgrading the car to a more modern version is usually available too. In these contracts you do not own the car; the lease company does. Often it can negotiate low prices from dealers as it will be buying in bulk from them. Also, you can usually put down an initial deposit for the car, which will lower your monthly repayments. You will be penalized if you wish to break the contract early. Often insurance is offered to protect against this, but it can be expensive.

Generally loan repayments are more expensive each month than lease payments. However, depending on the depreciation of your vehicle a loan may be cheaper overall. With leases the leasing company will most likely sell on the car when you have finished with it (if you have not bought it yourself). If the car has lost much of its value, the final 'balloon payment' will be large to cover the initial cost of the car. With some prestige cars, where depreciation is slower, this payment might be relatively small. If you have a large balloon payment to make at the end of the contract period, you may find that it outweighs the savings of the cheaper monthly payment amounts – and you will therefore be better off with a loan. As a general rule leasing is better for more expensive models of cars, and loans for more standard cars.

With all these different types of loans for purchases it is important that you understand how much you can afford to repay each month before you enter any contract. It always pays to have thought through your options and spending limits before you find yourself in front of an aggressive salesperson, whether he or she is trying to get you to buy a hi-fi or a supercar. Choosing the most appropriate form of borrowing is dependent on knowing what are the most likely 'best products' available to you, then researching that area to find the best rates at that particular time.

13

Inheritance issues and wills

This is an area of personal finance that many of us find difficult to get on and deal with – we have a natural preference for not thinking strategically about the reality of our own death. However, it is worth looking at the situation from the point of view of your survivors rather than yourself. Your passing will be a traumatic occasion for your family, and you will not want to make an upsetting situation worse for them by leaving your financial affairs in a state of disarray and confusion. For this reason it is critical that everyone who has any assets or savings writes and maintains a will.

Wills

Dying intestate (without a will)

The law regarding wills and inheritance is quite different in Scotland, and different again in Northern Ireland, from that in England and Wales. The following is a brief guide to how the law deals with the assets of someone who dies without a will. It is here only to serve as an indication of what might happen, and it would be unsafe to assume that it states the law as it will apply in any particular case. One aim is to encourage you to get a will drawn up to prevent your heirs having to go through this process, which will be done through the courts and incur expenses, and may take many months, if not years, to be resolved. With a will the process is much swifter and clearer.

In England and Wales, after debts and liabilities the division of your assets depends first on whether you were still married at the time of your death. If your spouse survives you by at least 28 days, he or she will receive the first £125,000 of your assets (this includes the value of your home). If you have left more than £125,000 and have children, your spouse still inherits the first £125,000, plus certain belongings to enable him or her to survive, plus the income from half of what remains above the £125,000 figure. Your children receive the rest divided equally amongst them. If you have no children, the above applies except that the figure given to your spouse increases to £200,000 and the remainder goes to your parents, or if they do not survive you any brothers or sisters, or if there are no brothers and sisters, any nieces or nephews. If none of these people are alive, your spouse inherits everything.

If you are not married, all your assets go to your children. If there are none they go to your parents (if alive), failing which the following receive your assets if they survive you: your brothers and sisters, failing which any nieces or nephews, failing which your grandparents, failing which your aunts, uncles or other cousins. If none of these people exist, the state (usually the government, but the Duchy of Lancaster if you were resident in Lancashire, or the Duchy of Cornwall if you were resident in Cornwall!) takes it all. And remember that the government will tax any assets over £263,000 at 40 per cent.

There are special rules that apply to half-brothers and half-sisters, adopted children and so on.

In Scotland, after debts and liabilities have been met your spouse has 'prior rights'. This entitles your spouse to your dwelling home up to a value of £130,000, plus £22,000 of furnishings and the like, plus the first £35,000 of the remainder of the estate if you have children, or £58,000 if you do not.

Your spouse and children then have 'legal rights' to your 'moveable property' (money, investments, cars, jewellery, furniture, as opposed to 'heritable property', which is land and buildings). Your spouse has legal right to one-third of your moveable property, and all your children to equal shares of one-third of your moveable property. Should you have no children or no spouse, that one-third share becomes one-half.

After the prior rights and legal rights claims, all the remainder of the intestate estate (both heritable and moveable) goes to whoever appears first in the following list: all to your children, half to parents and half to siblings, all to siblings, all to parents, all to your spouse, uncles and aunts and their children, grandparents, great aunts and great uncles and their children, further ancestors and their children, and finally the state.

In Northern Ireland if there are no children, parents or siblings the spouse inherits everything. If there are children, the spouse gets the furnishings plus £75,000 plus half or one-third of the remainder depending on whether there are one or more children. If there are no children but parents or siblings, the spouse gets the furnishings plus £125,000 plus half of the remainder.

Children get what is left after the spouse has taken his or her rightful claim. Failing a spouse or children, the inheritance is subject to the same list as in the rest of the UK.

The main problems with dying intestate

The main problem with dying without a will is that if your house is worth more than the figure your spouse is allowed, he or she might have to sell the house so as to be able to free up money to distribute to the other legitimate inheritors. The amount spouses can claim solely is now substantially less than the average UK house value, so in many cases this situation will arise.

If you have investments, pension funds, life policies, a business or other income-producing assets there are strict and complicated rules for dealing with these in all three jurisdictions. If you are not married but living with a partner, writing a will is even more important, as your partner might not be recognized as having any rights to your estate unless you put it in a will.

Making a will

The intestatacy process is long, slow, clumsy and complicated to administer. How much easier it is if you can set out simply a will instructing how you would like your belongings and assets divided after you die. The important thing to remember with wills is that you can change them whenever you wish, but having made one you need not do any more with it unless your circumstances change (principally on marriage, arrival of children or divorce).

The main things you will need to consider when drawing up your will are:

- Are there any special bequests or legacies you would like to leave to specific individuals or charities?
- Who will be your executors? This will usually be a close and trusted relative or friend, and also possibly your solicitor or accountant. The number of executors is up to you, but it is normally one or two. You should, of course, ask them first although this is not a legal requirement.
- If you have children, you should set out who is to be their guardian if both you and your spouse (or the other parent) should die. If both parents die and no guardian is named, the courts decide who will be the guardian for the child, and this might not be the person you would have chosen. Again this could be a hugely distressing and painful experience for all involved, at what would undoubtedly already be a difficult time.
- You may also wish to set out whether you wish to be buried or cremated, and where, if that is important to you.
- When considering your will it may be useful to also consider what would happen to your affairs should you have a stroke or other accident that makes you unable to make your own decisions. When writing a will it is also useful to discuss power of attorney options with your solicitor.

The simplest way to make a will is to visit a local solicitor who should be able to draw up one for you (and often a mirror will for your spouse if he or she so wishes). This should cost somewhere between £75 and £150. You can also 'build your own' from will writing Web sites online, or buy a standard will form from a large stationer. This is only really advisable if your assets are less than the inheritance tax (IHT) threshold and your affairs are uncomplicated (no children from an earlier marriage, no dependants other than your spouse, no foreign property or business interests, and so on).

The greater the size of your assets, the more important a will will be, and the more essential, as you can use some simple procedures to lessen the burden of IHT on your survivors. One of the problems of writing a will without the right professional help is that you are likely to miss out on simple but effective ways of protecting your heirs from inheritance tax.

Inheritance tax

Lord Jenkins described IHT as 'a voluntary levy paid by those who distrust their heirs more than they dislike the Inland Revenue'. This sums it up fairly well. Much of it can be avoided – if you are willing to gift your assets early to your heirs.

However, for many of us gifting large amounts of money to our heirs seems a damaging thing to do, for both us and them. Giving too much money to people too young can be a disincentive for them to build their own wealth and careers, and there is a risk that they might spend it poorly on 'wine, women and song'. Furthermore, there is the chance that they might decide that, although you gifted them your money so that they would benefit from not having to incur IHT, once it is theirs they do not need to sustain you in the manner to which you have become accustomed. Finally, your heirs might have IHT issues of their own, so gifting them large sums early might not be an ideal solution for them anyway.

IHT is only paid on any inheritance over a certain threshold. Currently that threshold is £263,000. This may seem a lot of money, but if you consider that the value of your house is included, it will probably not leave much spare to cover the car, the furnishings, jewellery, and savings and investments including pensions and life assurance policies. The chances are that it will not cover even the house for many people.

At this point it is worth noting that the value of your house is only the part that you own. So if you own a house jointly with your spouse or another person, it is only your share that is valued. In addition, any mortgage that is held on the house is deducted from the value, even though you might well have a life policy to pay off the mortgage on your death.

How to reduce your IHT exposure

The largest IHT reduction opportunity is that anything you leave to your spouse is free of IHT regardless of how much it is. However, if you gift everything to your spouse, you are not maximizing the use of your £263,000 IHT allowance.

If you die before your spouse and give him or her everything, when he or she dies only £263,000 (at 2004/05 levels) will be IHT-free. However, if you die and give £263,000 (or a part of that) to your children or grandchildren or anyone else, and the rest to your spouse so that she or he has enough to continue living happily on, when he or she dies he/she can also leave a further £263,000 tax free to children, grandchildren or whoever. In this way up to £526,000 has been passed on tax free, rather than just one parent's allowance.

Trusts

A popular way to administer leaving sums to children (or others), which also enables you to control to some extent how and when the money is used, is to arrange for trusts to be created on your death, and sometimes before.

Trust law is complex, and is constantly changing and being modified as the loopholes are closed by the government, and tax lawyers and accountants seek out and find new routes to avoid tax. Many of the newer schemes professionals put in place are not challenged in courts for some years, and it is only then that they find out whether the scheme actually works or not. For these reasons expert professional advice is imperative (this means trust experts rather than a general solicitor) when considering setting up trusts and other avoidance schemes. The professional body, the Society of Trust and Estate Practitioners, STEP, is worth contacting. For more information and to find a local representative contact 0207 763 7152 or visit www.step.org.

(Note: tax avoidance is legal. Indeed, the Scottish judge Lord Clyde stated in 1929 that 'no man in this country is under the smallest obligation, moral or other, so to arrange his legal relations to his business... as to enable the Inland Revenue to put the largest possible shovel into his stores.... The taxpayer is... entitled to be astute to prevent, so far as he honestly can, the depletion of his means by the Inland Revenue' – and that still stands. Tax evasion, however, is illegal.)

There are a huge variety of different types and styles of trusts that can be adapted and altered to fit numerous different situations. All trusts will have a settlor, the person who is giving the money or asset into the trust; one or more trustees, the people who look after the trust while it is in existence and are legally responsible for managing it on behalf of the beneficiaries and paying any taxes due; and beneficiaries, the people who will eventually benefit from the trust, through receiving income, capital or both. The four most common types are set out below.

Absolute or bare trust

An absolute or bare trust is the simplest and therefore the least sophisticated of trusts. You will normally set it up while you are still alive. You put an asset or selection of assets in to it (money, investments, property and so on) and they immediately become the property of the trust. The trust will have to pay IHT on these assets if you should die within seven years of making the gift (see PETs below), but after that no IHT is payable.

These trusts are usually used to gift assets to children. However, they have two great weaknesses. The first is that the beneficiary or beneficiaries get absolute rights to the assets when they reach the age of 18. This age cannot be altered. The second is that once you have set up the trust you cannot change it, even if your circumstances change or if you feel the beneficiary is no longer deserving.

Accumulation and maintenance trust

An accumulation and maintenance trust (also known as a children's trust) is a more flexible version of a bare trust. It has to be used for your children (or grandchildren), and the income from it can only be used for 'education, maintenance or benefit' of the beneficiaries. However, the age at which the beneficiaries can get hold of the capital is flexible, and the trustees have the ability to choose which beneficiaries get what and when throughout the life of the trust. The beneficiaries must gain access to the income from the trust within 25 years of the trust's creation, but not necessarily the capital. Again it will be liable to IHT for up to seven years after creation.

Interest in possession trust

An interest in possession trust is similar to an accumulation and mainte-nance trust, except that anyone can be named as a beneficiary. However, while the income must be paid out to the beneficiaries according to the rules of the trust, the capital can be distributed at the discretion of the trustees. This type of trust has a version known as a 'life interest trust', which can be used in certain circumstances to provide income to a spouse, say, but keep the capital ring-fenced for the children. When the spouse dies the children get access to both the capital and income. This can sometimes also be used so that a widow can continue having use of a house although it is actually held in trust for her children.

Discretionary trust

A discretionary trust is the most flexible of trusts. It can be set up in favour of any beneficiaries, and the trustees have complete discretion which beneficiaries get what and when, both for capital and income. Its drawbacks are that should you put more into the trust than the IHT threshold, the excess will be taxed, and once the trust has been set up the Inland Revenue can tax it every 10 years for the life of the trust.

Will trust

You might also see reference to will trusts. These are any trusts set up on the instructions of a will, at the settlor's death.

Costs associated with trusts

When setting up a trust there will be some expenses to pay, which might be significant. First, you will need to pay for expert advice about what sort of trust you need, and also for drafting of the trust deeds. Other set-up costs might include valuation fees, transfer fees (from one owner to the new owner, the trust) for any shares or property, stamp duty, taxes (capital gains, inheritance) and accountancy fees. Once the trust is up and running, there will be annual accounting fees, occasional legal fees, and brokers' fees and commissions. Income, capital gains and dividend tax until April 2004 were levied at a special trust rate of 34 per cent (and 25 per cent for dividends). However, this has now been scrapped and they are now taxed at the individual higher rate of 40 per cent and 32.5 per cent respectively. If income is paid out of the trust to someone not liable for the higher rate, he or she should be able to reclaim the difference. All this means that trusts are quite expensive to set up and run, and therefore only really suitable if you are to put a considerable amount of assets in to them. Careful advice needs to be taken before proceeding.

Deeds of variation

An option to avoid setting up trusts before you die is to allow for your executors to write a deed of variation, where your will can be changed to accommodate the most tax-advantageous decisions at the time of your death. The problem with this is that the government has been eyeing the use of deeds of variation for some time, and may well make them illegal at some point in the future.

Potentially exempt transfers

You can make gifts to anyone at any time for any amount. However, they will all be subject to IHT should you die within seven years of making the gift. 'Potentially exempt transfers', or PETs, can be applied to any gift if it is liable for IHT. Any gift made will be IHT-free if you survive for seven years after making the gift. If you die within seven years there will be IHT to pay, but it is on a sliding scale, reducing the longer you live. This is known as 'taper relief'. (See Table 13.1.)

Table 13.1 Taper relief on potentially exempt transfers

Years before death in which gift made	Percentage of IHT payable
0–3	100
3–4	80
4–5	60
5–6	40
6–7	20

Smaller gift allowances

The government does allow you to make certain small gifts which are also free from IHT. Each person can give away £3,000 each year and it will be IHT-free. Say you have three children. You can give them each an annual gift of £1,000; as long as it is noted down it will not be liable for IHT. Further, you can give gifts of up to £250 to any number of people without their having to notify the gifts for IHT should you die.

Marriage gifts also exist, where you can give your child a one-off gift of up to £5,000 at the time of their marriage. Other relatives can give £2,500 each. All these are IHT-free.

Gifts from income are also IHT-free. These are described as 'modest amounts that do not affect the donor's standard of living'.

Life assurance

If you are reasonably sure what your likely IHT bill comes to, you can take out life assurance that will pay out that amount on your death, so covering your liability. Life assurance is IHT-liable, so the policy would have to be written in trust for your beneficiaries so as not to add to your estate. This also means it will pay out more quickly as it will bypass probate. Depending on the size of IHT bill you are facing, this may be a costly way to proceed. It also will reduce your disposable income while alive. Versions of this are to just cover certain assets that you do not want to be sold, such as a family home, and also having 'seven-year policies' to cover IHT in the event that you die before a PET becomes IHT-exempt. Again you will need to discuss the details with a qualified adviser.

Your home and equity release

The main burden when considering IHT is how to deal with your home. You will want to use it until your death in most circumstances, so you cannot give it away, but it will also represent the largest part of your estate (assets on death). One option increasingly being used is an equity release scheme, where you mortgage part of your house and give away the money so released to your heirs. If you live for seven years after this time there will be no IHT to pay, and on your death the value of your house will be reduced because it will be mortgaged. It will be further reduced as the mortgage company will require some more of its value in interest payments, and so more of the tax-free allowance may be available for the rest of your estate.

Avoiding long-term care charges

Another consideration with the value of your home is that should you need long-term care (see Chapter 9) you will be liable to pay for it unless you have limited assets. It is possible that your heritable and moveable wealth will be severely diminished by this unless you have already passed it on in some way or another.

Jargon

Inheritance planning is a specialist area which is littered with jargon. Some phrases you may come across that have not already been explained here are:

- Nil-rate band: this refers to the IHT threshold allowance, currently £263,000. It is referred to as the 'nil-rate band' in legal documents so that when the Chancellor raises it (as he does from time to time, usually each budget in line with inflation) the document does not become out of date.

- Estate: this term refers to all your assets after your death.
- Probate: the court order authorizing a person to deal with the assets of the deceased.
- *Per stirpes*: this phrase means the estate is divided by the number of original heirs rather than the current inherited heirs. That is, if you have three children who in turn have two children, one child and five children respectively, and you leave your estate to your grandchildren *per stirpes*, then your first child's two children will get one-sixth each (that is one-third divided by two), your second child's child will get one-third (one-third divided by one), and your third child's five children will get one-fifteenth each (one-third divided by five).

14

Charitable giving

Individuals give a total of over £7 billion in charitable donations each year in the UK. A recent survey showed that the Scots, contrary to their popular image, were the most willing to donate while Londoners were the least forthcoming. Whatever your personal preference, if you do give to charity and you are a tax payer then you are likely not to be maximizing your donation if you are not using a tax-efficient donation method. It is calculated that only 20 per cent of individual donations are made tax-efficiently – which means that nearly £1 billion of money is going to the Chancellor that could otherwise be going to deserving charities.

Depending on your circumstances you could find that tax-efficient giving will not only benefit the charity but also reduce your own tax bill. There are few truly win–win situations in personal finance, but this could be one!

Until the last decade the main tax-efficient means of giving to charity was by way of a deed of covenant, whereby you signed a document pledging to give a specific sum of money to a charity for a specific period of time, normally several years. The annual sum you gave was deducted from your income before tax, and so reduced the total income figure that you were taxed on, and your tax charge. This was a method that charities liked because it secured them reliable income streams over several years. The tax advantage of deeds of covenant were removed in 2000, however, and a new regime now exists.

Tax-efficient donations to charity

There are three main methods of making donations to charity that will benefit you as well as the charity.

Gift Aid

Gift Aid was introduced some years ago, and has largely replaced the deed of covenant. In 2000 the minimum donation limit of £250 was removed, and now you can use Gift Aid for any donation, no matter how small.

With most donations you make to charities these days, the charity will ask you if you wish to use Gift Aid. If you choose to do so, you have to make a declaration that you agree to let the charity claim tax back on your donation – and that is it. You should always ask if the charity is using a Gift Aid scheme. It should be, but for some small charities the administration may be too expensive.

The charity can claim only basic rate tax back on your donation, currently 22 per cent. However, this will add 28.2p to your donation for every £1 you give.

> To calculate how much tax the charity will receive, do the following sum:
>
> $$\frac{\text{Basic rate of income tax}}{1 - \text{Basic rate of income tax}} = \frac{22}{78} = 28.2\%$$

Higher rate tax payers reclaim the difference

If you are a higher rate tax payer the charity cannot claim 40 per cent back on your donation, as this would involve too much in administration costs checking whether people really were higher rate payers or not. You, however, may claim the difference of 18 per cent back from the Inland Revenue on a self-assessment return at the end of the year. It is therefore worthwhile keeping a note of all your Gift Aid donations throughout the year, so that you can claim back the difference. This is clearly more critical, the larger the Gift Aided donations you make.

Gift Aid rules

- If you are not a UK tax payer, you cannot use Gift Aid.
- You can only use Gift Aid to the amount that you pay tax. That is, the extra amount that charities claim, as per the calculation above, must be less than the amount you pay in income tax.
- You can include income tax from dividends and (non-reclaimed) tax on savings interest.
- You can make as many Gift Aid donations as you like, for as much as you like, as long as they total less than your income tax liability.
- Gift Aid can only be used with donations. You cannot apply it to products or services bought from a charity.

Payroll giving

Payroll giving is the second easy way to make your donations more tax-efficient. This is a system where you get your employer to deduct your donation from your pay. Your employer pays the donation over to a payroll giving agency approved by the Inland Revenue, and the agency then distributes the money to the charity or charities of your choice. Your employer is not obliged to operate a payroll giving scheme, but most will if asked.

Note that the payroll giving agency will deduct a small amount (currently 4 per cent or 35p, whichever is the smaller) for doing this each month.

As your donation is removed from your income before your income tax is applied, you save your higher rate of tax by using this method. The government, however, only adds back 10 per cent of the donation to the charity. So the charity does less well from this type of donation – but in fact the government is being more generous, as with Gift Aid it is only repaying tax already paid, whereas with payroll giving it is adding money when tax is not being paid at all.

You can change who your donation goes to at any time by notifying the payroll giving agency, and you can cancel your donations at any time the same way. Any donations made cannot be refunded. You can give as much as you wish through payroll giving, and it does not affect your ability to make donations through Gift Aid or any other scheme.

Gifts of shares and securities

Gifts of shares and securities are the third tax-advantageous method of giving money to charities. Although the gift is a capital asset, the tax relief to the donor is from his or her income. The value of the share donation plus the incidental transaction costs, less any payment, product or service given in return, can be deducted from your annual income before tax.

To qualify, the share or security has to be quoted on a UK or recognized foreign exchange, or be an authorized unit trust or OEIC.

Other tax issues with donations

Outright gifts and bequests to UK charities are completely free of inheritance tax. No capital gains tax (CGT) is payable on gifts of assets, either property or financial, to UK charities even if they would otherwise incur CGT liability.

Other forms of giving

There are a number of other organizations that try to make the process of giving to charities easier. Perhaps the best known is the Charities Aid Foundation (CAF), which offers a number of straightforward ways to make donations simply and regularly. The main two are by opening a CAF Charity Account, which you can manage online like a normal online bank account, and charity gift vouchers. For more information contact CAF at 01732 520 050 or visit www.allaboutgiving.org.

For further information on gifts to charities you can contact:

In England and Wales:

Inland Revenue (Charities)   for Gift Aid telephone:
St Johns House   0151 472 6056/6038/6055
Merton Road   for Payroll Giving telephone:
Bootle   0151 472 6029/6053
Merseyside L69 9BB   for gifts of shares and securities:
     0151 472 6043/6046

In Scotland:

Inland Revenue (Charities)   all enquiries:
Meldrum House   0131 777 4040
15 Drumsheugh Gardens
Edinburgh EH3 7UL

Part 3

Financial Competence: Level 3

There are two types of forecasters, those 'who don't know' and those 'who don't know they don't know'.

The economist J K Galbraith

This third section of the book deals with the areas of savings and investment. The preceding two levels were about building your financial foundations and creating some comfort from your existing financial situation. This section is about improving that situation by growing and managing your assets effectively. It involves dealing with the concepts of risk and reward.

It includes chapters on:

- Saving.
- Investments.
- Buy-to-let.
- Saving for children.
- Tax planning.

15

Saving

When people refer to personal finance they often just mean saving and investing. They are partly right. If you flick through the chapter headings of this book, after the introductory chapters nearly all of them can be boiled down to being a particular type of saving or investment. Pensions, mortgages, education, healthcare, long-term care, the relationship finance chapter – all are based on the need to save or invest. Of course we often do not consider these actions to be saving or investment processes, and nor should we. Buying a house should principally be about finding a safe, comfortable and convenient place to live rather than a way of getting rich. Pensions are for making your old age safe, comfortable and convenient and not about getting rich. Education is often considered an investment, but not necessarily in a purely financial sense. And so on.

This is an important lesson – saving and investment is not primarily about becoming rich in the having 'pots of gold' sense, although if it goes some way to achieving that, you will not complain. The foremost reason to save is to protect your current way of living, and allow you the occasional one-off purchase: a new fridge, new car, new house, holiday, wedding or whatever.

Managing your personal finances is just that – management. It is a constant balancing act between having enough to live comfortably on now, and also putting enough away to enable you to live happily in the future. It is this 'putting enough away' part that saving is concerned with. All individuals will have their own priorities as to which things are most important to them that require saving for, but as a first approach you should consider saving for the following:

- Emergency fund. It is reassuring to know that if the roof leaks or your car breaks down, you have some money easily accessible to repair it quickly and efficiently. Some people recommend keeping several months' worth of income in an easily accessible account, so that if you find yourself without pay unexpectedly you will always have a 'back-up' supply of emergency cash.
- Pension – as discussed in Chapter 4, this is now an essential.
- Housing – whether your 'saving' is in fact capital repayments on a mortgage or saving for a deposit on a house.
- Education – whether your saving is paying off your student loan or really saving for future education expenses for yourself or your family.

No saving is going to be really effective if you still have any expensive debts or loans. These must always be attended to first. Note that with mortgages and education you are in fact paying off debt and loans in any case, and these are the cheapest forms of debt you will ever have.

Only when you have got these 'savings' under control is it worth considering your 'pot of gold' savings and investments. The first step in this savings management is to check that you have built a solid foundation for your financial future, with regular amounts going to the above areas. The emergency fund may not need regular payments if you are happy with the level it is at, but your pension and mortgage are likely to take regular sums from your monthly income for most of your working life. Luckily the pension is normally deducted before you see your pay, so its cost is relatively painless!

Definitions of savings and investments

A definition of 'savings' is 'a fund of money put by as a reserve'. This is a good way of differentiating savings from investments, which are defined as 'the laying out of money with the expectation of profit'. With savings you are not risking your money; with investments you are. That is why your emergency fund goes into a savings account or some form of financial product where you do not risk losing any of the money that you put into it.

Capital and income: 'trees and apples' or 'cows and milk'

A basic rule for managing your savings and investments is to keep a clear distinction between capital and income. A popular comparison for showing the difference is to think of an apple tree as your capital and the apples as the income. If you look after the tree well, make sure it gets enough sunlight and water and protect it from frosts, it should bring you a regular supply of apples for many years. In the same way if you look after your capital sensibly, investing it in the right places, it should bring you a steady supply of income in the form of interest payments or dividends.

However, if you chop down some of the tree's branches to build yourself a nice bench to sit on, you will have less tree to provide apples next year. Similarly if you use your capital to buy a car (or a bench!) it means there will be less income available next year. New branches will grow as, hopefully, will the capital, but it will take some years before they produce as much in apples or income as they did before you chopped down the branch.

A more drastic comparison is with a cow. It is not as accurate, but it does highlight the perils of spending capital. If you have a nice Friesian cow that produces a healthy supply of milk, you can milk it and have the milk as income for many years. Alternatively you could indulge yourself and live a brief high life by slaughtering it and eating prime steak for a week or two – but after that you are left with nothing. The cow was obviously the capital, the milk the income. The lesson is that it is your choice how you look after it.

How safe are your savings?

Ultimately we can dream up circumstances where your money could always be lost. The safest place to save your money is with the government through a National Savings and Investment (NSI) product. The government guarantees that it will be able to repay your money – and the circumstances you have to dream up where they would not be able to repay you are so extreme that your money will probably be the least of your problems by that stage anyway!

After NSI your money is safest with a bank, building society or credit union that is a member of the Financial Services Compensation Scheme (FSCS). The FSCS was created in 2001 to replace a number of other compensation bodies, and covers all financial companies that are regulated by the FSA. To find out if a firm is regulated by the FSA you can call its Firm Check Service on 0845 606 1234 or visit www.fsa.gov.uk/consumer. The FSCS guarantees deposits in savings accounts for 100 per cent of the first £2,000 and 90 per cent of the next £33,000 per individual (not account). It will pay out if the firm cannot. (There are different rules for investments and insurance.)

If you keep your money under your mattress it is not safe at all!

Where to save your savings

There is a wide range of different savings options. Where you choose to put your savings will depend primarily on:

- how easily you want to access your money;
- how frequently you want to add to your savings;
- how much you want to/have to save;
- how long you expect to be saving for;
- what level of return (interest) you want to receive;
- whether you want to benefit from tax-free opportunities.

In order to make comparisons of different products easier, we shall look at different products using a fixed set of criteria. These are:

- Risk rating: can you lose capital on them?
- Income rating: is the return on the capital high, medium or low?

- Amount: is there a minimum (or maximum) amount you can save with the product?
- Time period: is there a minimum, maximum or fixed period of time you have to save with the product?
- Tax status: does the product exempt you from tax, on either the income or the capital (or both)?
- Costs: is money deducted to cover the provider's expenses (and profits)?

NSI has a range of products, all backed by the government, that suit different purposes.

Premium bonds

For a long time considered an out-of-date anachronism only used by great aunts, premium bonds have become increasingly popular since the stock market crash and also since the shine went off the National Lottery.

How they work

Like with the National Lottery you buy £1 bonds. Unlike the National Lottery these are entered into a prize draw each month and every month until you sell them. There is a range of prizes, from a single monthly jackpot winner of £1 million to nearly 1 million £50 prizes. Anyone over 16 can buy premium bonds, and parents, grandparents and guardians can purchase them for children under 16.

Risk rating

Premium bonds are a gamble, but unlike the National Lottery where once you have spent your £1 a go, it is gone forever, with premium bonds you never lose your capital. Even if you win, the bond goes back into the next month's draw. And if you want the money for something else, you can always sell your bonds and get your money back.

Income rating

It is possible that you will not earn any income at all from your investment. The more bonds you have, the better your chances of winning, obviously. If you are fully subscribed (see below) you can expect to earn 3 per cent (one £50 prize per month: as it is tax free it is equivalent to 3.75 per cent for a basic rate taxpayer or 5 per cent for a higher rate taxpayer), but this is not guaranteed – it could easily be less, or could be more if you win a big prize.

Amount

You have to buy at least £100 of £1 bonds, and can then buy further bundles of £10 of bonds to a maximum amount of £30,000.

Time

Your bonds usually do not go into a draw until the month after you have bought them. You can sell them at any time, although the money takes up to a couple of weeks to be repaid.

Tax

You pay no income or capital gains tax on the prizes.

Costs

There are no charges applied to your saving with premium bonds. Note, however, that if you do not win sufficient prizes your capital may be reduced by the effects of inflation.

Fixed interest savings certificates

These are lump sum savings that earn a guaranteed rate of interest over fixed periods. The certificates are issued periodically by the government. There are only limited amounts of certificates for each issue, so when they are all sold you cannot get any more.

How they work

You buy the certificate for a specific period, usually for two or five years, and the return (interest earned) is paid at the end of the period. Anyone over the age of seven can buy them, and the under-sevens can have them bought for them.

Risk rating

There is no risk. You get your capital back at the end of the period, and you know exactly what interest rate you will be earning.

Income rating

The level of interest you earn on your certificates varies with each issue – contact NSI for details of the latest issue available and interest rates.

Amount

The minimum amount is £100, the maximum £15,000, although if you are reinvesting you can reinvest an amount over £15,000 if you have it.

Time

As stated on the certificate, usually two or five years. You can cash them in earlier if you need to, but you will earn a smaller interest rate than if you hold them full term.

Tax

There is no income or capital gains tax payable.

Costs

There are no costs applied. If inflation rises while you hold the certificates, you could find that they earn less than the rate of inflation.

Index-linked savings certificates

These are similar to the fixed-interest certificates above except that the interest rate you earn is variable.

How they work

You buy a certificate for a specific period, usually for three or five years, and the return (interest earned) is paid at the end of the period. The interest earned is calculated by the rate of inflation (as calculated by the Treasury) during the period of time you have held the certificates, plus a fixed amount on top of that (for example, inflation plus 1.25 per cent).

Anyone over the age of seven can buy them, and under-sevens can have them bought for them.

Risk rating

There is no risk. You get your capital back at the end of the period and you know that you will be earning a set amount over the current rate of inflation.

Income rating

The level of interest you earn on your certificates varies with each issue – contact NSI for details of the latest issue available and interest rates.

Amount

The minimum amount is £100, the maximum £15,000, although if you are reinvesting you can reinvest an amount over £15,000 if you have it.

Time

As stated on the certificate, usually three or five years. You can cash them in earlier if you need to, but you will earn a smaller interest rate than if you hold them full term.

Tax

There is no income or capital gains tax payable.

Costs

There are no costs applied and you know you will always be earning over the rate of inflation.

Income bonds

These are different from savings certificates in that the income is paid out monthly and not at the end of the term.

How they work

These work in much the same way as savings accounts. You put money into them by buying bonds, and hold them indefinitely, being paid the interest each month.

Risk rating

There is no risk. You get your capital back when you decide to sell your bonds.

Income rating

The level of interest you earn on your bonds will vary as with a savings bank account; you will earn higher rates of interest if you invest over £25,000. Contact NSI for details of the latest issue available and interest rates.

Amount

The minimum amount is £500, the maximum £1,000,000.

Time

There is no stated limit to the bonds. They are guaranteed to exist for 10 years, after which the government can withdraw them at six months' notice. You can cash in your bonds without penalty if you give three months notice, or immediately with a penalty.

Tax

Interest on income bonds is taxable, but the interest is paid gross, so they are simple to operate for people not paying tax as they will not have to reclaim any tax.

Costs

There are no costs applied.

Capital bonds

In contrast to income bonds, this is a way of building up your lump sum rather than taking income from it. Unlike savings certificates, capital bonds are taxable, but you can hold much more in them.

How they work

You buy your bonds for a specific period as available at the time of issue. At the end of the period you get the money back plus a fixed rate of interest.

Risk rating

There is no risk. You get your capital back at the end of the period and you know how much interest you will have earned.

Income rating

The level of interest you earn on your certificates is fixed at the time of issue, but varies from issue to issue. If you do not hold your bonds for the full term you will receive a reduced rate of interest. Contact NSI for details of the latest issue available and interest rates.

Amount

The minimum amount is £100, the maximum £1,000,000.

Time

As stated on the certificate, usually five years. You can cash them in earlier if you need to, but you will earn a smaller interest rate than if you hold them full term.

Tax

The interest on the bonds is subject to income tax, but is paid gross – this makes it easier for non-tax payers.

Costs

There are no costs applied.

Fixed-rate savings bonds

These are similar to the other two bonds above, in that you can choose whether you receive income or get all the return added on at the end of the term as with capital bonds. The difference is that the return is applied net of tax – the only NSI product to do this.

How they work

You buy your bonds for a specific period, usually for one, three or five years, and you choose at the outset whether the return (interest earned) is paid monthly or at the end of the period. The interest earned is fixed at issue. Anyone over the age of seven can buy them, and under-sevens can have them bought for them.

Risk rating

There is no risk of capital loss. You get your capital back at the end of the period, and you know that you will be earning a set amount over the term of the bond. As with all fixed-rate products, if interest rates rise or inflation increases you could find that they are uncompetitive.

Income rating

The level of interest you earn on your certificates varies with each issue, but also by the term you choose (the longer the term the higher the rate), and by how much you invest (the more you invest, the higher the rate). Contact NSI for details of the latest issue available and interest rates.

Amount

The minimum amount is £500, the maximum £1,000,000.

Time

As stated on the certificate, usually one, three or five years. You can cash them in earlier if you need to but you will lose 90 days' interest.

Tax

The interest is taxable at the rate applicable to savings (currently 20 per cent). Non-tax payers can reclaim the tax, higher rate tax payers must declare the interest in their annual tax returns.

Costs

There are no costs applied.

Pensioner guaranteed income bonds

These are the same as standard income bonds but only available to people over 60 years of age. They pay marginally better rates of interest.

Children's bonus bonds

See Chapter 18.

Guaranteed equity bond

This is not currently available. It is only issued from time to time. It offers you a 'no loss' way of benefiting from the stock market. You put your money in on a certain day and it is held there for a fixed period of time, during which you cannot get it out. At the end of the period (five years with the last issue) you get your capital back plus the amount the FTSE 100 has grown during that period, between 1 per cent and 65 per cent. If the FTSE 100 has fallen, you get back your original investment. If it has grown more that 65 per cent you still only get back 65 per cent! You are taxed on your gains. Essentially you get some of the benefits of the stock market without risking a loss.

National Savings accounts

There are two National Savings accounts. The first is the Investment Account, which is a passbook-based account. You can open an account with just £20 and put in anything up to £100,000. The interest rate paid on your account balance is variable and tiered. That is, the rates paid will vary from time to time as the underlying interest rate changes, but the more money you have in the account, the better rates of interest are available to you. You can withdraw money from the account with no penalty with one month's notice, or immediately and lose 30 days' interest on the amount you have withdrawn.

The second account is the Easy Access account. This was only created in January 2004 and replaced the old Ordinary Account from July 2004. You must have at least £100 in the account (to a maximum of £2 million!) and you can make payments and withdrawals by phone or with a card. Again the interest paid is variable and tiered, and is paid gross (so if you pay tax you must declare this to the Inland Revenue). You must be at least 11 years old to have this account. Note that the card on this account is not a debit or credit card – you cannot shop with it. This is not a current account, but a savings account. For information regarding this account or the old Ordinary Account call 0845 366 6667.

National Savings products are very safe as you can be certain you will always get your money back. The price you pay for this low level of risk is that the return (the interest paid) you get from them is never going to be the best available.

For more information on NSI products contact it at 0845 964 5000 or visit www.nsandi.com. Alternatively, visit your local post office.

Other savings products

NSI products offer the cast-iron security against default (the bank not being able to repay your money) that they are backed by the state. However, this level of security is unnecessary in most cases, partly because for most people their savings will be covered by the FSCS as explained above should a bank default, but largely because the risk of banks defaulting is very, very small. It could happen and it has happened – but not with a well-known high street bank for a very long time.

Current accounts

Current accounts are not really for saving at all, although they are safer than having piles of cash sitting at home. Current accounts are about convenience, the ability to withdraw money instantly, have cheque books and cash cards, pay direct debits and standing orders, and on many current accounts you can earn a tiny amount of interest. They usually do not have any minimum or maximum amount rules. Current accounts are principally vehicles for managing your money, and not for saving it.

Savings accounts

Many savings accounts today offer many of the same facilities as current accounts, particularly paying of direct debits and standing orders and being able to withdraw money instantly. These are known as instant access accounts or something similar (for example, the NSI Easy Access account). Like current accounts they usually have no minimum or maximum amounts. The rate of interest offered on these accounts will be higher than for current accounts but still will not be particularly generous. Normally you will get better rates of interest the more money you have in the account. This is slightly irrational because you should not really have any large sums of money in these accounts for long periods of time in any case, as that money can earn better interest elsewhere.

For better rates of interest on savings accounts you normally have to sacrifice the ability to withdraw money instantly. Notice accounts, so called because you have to give notice that you want to take money out, usually require you to notify the bank a month or even 90 days before it will release the money to you, unless you are prepared to pay a penalty of that amount of interest for releasing the money instantly.

Term accounts and bonds

These are the least flexible of cash savings products. As with NSI bonds, you buy your savings amount for a fixed period, and withdrawing money is limited to once a month or less. However, in return for this inflexibility you are likely to get a better rate of interest than with more flexible products offered by the same bank.

Table 15.1 Summary of savings products

	Current accounts	Savings accounts	Notice accounts	Term accounts and bonds
Risk rating	Low	Low	Low	Low
Income rating	Lowest	Pretty low	Below average	Average
Amount	Min: £0	Min: £0	Min: often from £500	Min: often from £2500
	Max: unlimited	Max: unlimited	Max: unlimited	Max: unlimited
Time	Unlimited	Unlimited	Unlimited	Specified period
Tax	Interest normally paid net of tax	Interest normally paid net of tax	Interest normally paid net of tax	Interest normally paid net of tax
Cost	Normally none*	None	None	None

* Some premium current accounts do charge monthly amounts in return for 'extras'. Be careful to weigh up whether these are really worth the cost.

Alternative savings accounts

All-in-one accounts

In the last few years a new type of account has appeared that bundles all your cash and borrowings into one account. Each provider calls its offering something different, but they are all variations on 'all-in-one' accounts. The idea behind this type of account is that if you have any borrowings (either a mortgage or other loan) you will be paying more in interest on it than you would be earning in any positive balances in savings accounts. Therefore the interest you are earning in your savings accounts is being more than offset by the interest you are paying on your borrowings. By putting all your savings into the same account as your borrowings are in, you reduce the size of your borrowings and therefore pay less interest on those borrowings. With smaller interest charges you can afford to pay off the borrowing more quickly, so overall you pay less in interest charges. The drawback is that the rate of interest charged on these accounts will not be the best mortgage or loan rate available. But they are probably cheaper in the long run if you do use their overpaying facilities, and they simplify your own personal accounting tasks, as you only have one account to look after.

The prerequisites for this type of account are that you have a significant loan with the bank – almost always a mortgage – and that you pay your earnings into the account. These accounts are tax-advantageous in a sense: as you are not earning interest you cannot be taxed on it, but as you are reducing your interest payments on your borrowing by more than the amount you would have been earning interest were your savings in a saving account, you are making a significant benefit which is not taxed.

Online accounts

Part of the reason that you get low rates of interest on current accounts and instant access accounts is that they involve more administration costs, which the bank has to pay for. It does this by paying you less interest than it would on notice or term accounts.

The 'online account' is a way of automating the banking process and reducing the administration charges. As such, the theory goes, the bank has more money available to offer its customers in the way of interest. This is generally true, and online accounts, of whatever type (current, savings or notice) tend to pay better interest rates than their high street equivalents.

Tax-free savings

Individual savings accounts (ISAs)

ISAs are examined in more detail in the next chapter. One of the ISAs available is a cash ISA, where you have been able to invest up to £3,000 a year in cash in an ISA wrapper, and all the interest that you earn on that amount is tax free. You can do this each year, so building up a significant tax-free cash investment. From April 2005 the maximum amount you will able to put into a cash ISA will be reduced to just £1,000. You can deposit up to the maximum permitted amount (£3,000 until April 2005, £1,000 thereafter). This can be done gradually over the tax year (from 5 April to 4 April the next year). Note that your withdrawals are not relevant to the deposit limits – if you put in £2,999 on 6 April 2004 and then withdrew £2,998 the next day, so leaving a balance of £1 in your cash ISA, you will only be allowed to deposit a further £1 during the rest of that tax year, as you can only make a maximum of £3,000 of deposits. This means that for all practical purposes you should only use a cash ISA if you are not going to want access to the money over the period, or at least not very often.

The tax-free benefits of cash ISAs are even more attractive to higher rate tax payers, as they save 40 per cent on their earned interest rather than just 20 per cent. That said, if you have surplus cash sitting in a bank or building society account it will be more efficiently saved if you can transfer up to the maximum amount into a cash ISA. Most banks and building societies (and NSI) have cash ISAs available.

For more details on ISAs see Chapter 16.

Things to consider with savings

Banks and buildings societies change the rates applicable on their different accounts frequently. While it may not be a good use of your time to keep opening and closing accounts and switching your money every time a new account starts offering a better rate, it will certainly be a wise thing to keep an eye on how your account is doing relative to the best accounts on the market – and if the difference between yours and the best becomes significant, you should consider moving accounts. Remember that it is your money and no one else's – if you do not take action no one else will.

The best rates currently available are usually shown in the newspapers each weekend, or you can compare them at one of the many personal finance Internet sites (see Chapter 21).

When is the interest paid? Most interest-paying savings accounts pay interest monthly, but some pay it annually. It may appear at first glance that the annually paid interest is at a better rate than the monthly paid interest. This is probably not the case, it is just that the effects of compound interest (see Chapter 2) mean that if your interest is paid monthly the capital sum gets larger each month, so the annual rate has to be larger to compensate for this. If you compare the annual equivalent rates (AERs) they should be the same.

16

Investments

The money invested by most individuals has usually been hard-won and slowly accumulated over many years. It is unlikely that you will be willing to risk losing all, or even a large part, of this accumulated capital in any circumstances regardless of the potential return. You may well be prepared to gamble £1 on the National Lottery for untold millions, but you are unlikely to want to invest several thousand pounds in it. For most people a £1 loss is acceptable; several thousand pounds of losses is not, even if the potential reward is enormous.

What you are investing for

At this point it is traditional to ask what level of risk is acceptable to you. This is an awkward question as the answer is hazy and does not really get you anywhere. Rather than have a hazy answer to a concrete question, a better approach perhaps is to have a concrete answer to a hazy question. Peer into the future and see what you would like to have some years down the line. Do you want to have built up a sum of money to pay for your children's university expenses; or to buy yourself a new car; or a retirement flat in Spain; or the deposit on a house for a grown-up child; or just to have accumulated enough cash to enable you go on some exotic holidays and buy some nice clothes when you want to? You will know your wants, desires and priorities better than anyone else, so you make the list.

Once you have identified what you wish to use your investment money for, you will be in a much better position to choose how to achieve the amount required. Say you have decided you need to boost your emergency fund; with the arrival of your first child you also want to start an education fund for future education expenses, including school fees and possibly university fees much further on; with the new family you realize that you will also need a larger car and possibly a larger house in a few years' time. All these 'wants' are sensible and necessary. They each have fairly clear time horizons, and you should be able to estimate the approximate amount of money each will require. You will also know how much money you have at the moment.

How are you going to get there?

All this information means you know your starting point, you know your goal and you know how long you have to get there. With this information you can choose much more effectively whether you can do it by walking, cycling, taking the bus, buying a car, buying a motorbike or buying a plane and flying yourself. That is, you can decide how risky and potentially expensive the investment vehicle you use needs to be to get you to your destination – and whether for some of your goals, the risk and expense necessary are really justifiable.

Investing for a purpose or for fun

The final and in many respects most critical question you should address should be, is the investment process an end in itself? Are you out to enjoy the ride? Since the first privatization issues in 1984 with BT and the British Gas 'Tell Sid' campaign in 1986, the UK has become much more of a share-owning democracy. This reached its peak during the dot.com extravaganza over the millennial years – when, initially, making money from the stock market was dangerously easy. Any fool can make money in a sharply rising market: you buy at the beginning of the week and sell at the end of it.

There is no harm in 'playing the stock market', as long as you are clear that the money you are playing with is money you can afford to lose, and

that what you are doing is not part of your personal financial management. This is not to advise you not to have shares as part of your financial portfolio; it is just that picking shares is a high-risk activity. The large majority of highly paid and very dedicated professionals in the finance industry struggle to achieve average results. It would be bold for a part-time non-professional to think he or she can better that, especially without access to all the information and technology that the City investors have at their disposal.

So chase a few 'hot tips' if you want, and enjoy the rewards if they come, but do not confuse this with being part of a sensible financial plan.

Investment options

There are essentially three core types of investment asset you can invest in: bonds, shares and property. Beyond these there is a vast array of 'other' assets you could invest in, such as the many commodities sold at regulated exchanges (primarily metals: gold, silver, tin, copper and so on, then agricultural goods: coffee, grain, pork bellies... the list is endless). You can also make money investing in collectibles – fine art, furniture, vintage cars, wine and so on. However, all these 'other' investments operate in much smaller and more specialist markets. This makes them less 'liquid' (there are fewer buyers and sellers, so finding someone to buy your 'asset' is not always easy) and more susceptible to 'shocks' and 'fashion' (where a single piece of news or idea can make the market soar or crash suddenly). Clearly these factors make the 'other' assets much more risky investments, and not sensible areas for average individuals to invest their hard-earned wealth in.

This guide will limit itself to focusing on the three core asset types: bonds, shares and property. They are all more risky than the savings options outlined in the previous chapter, but as long as the risk is carefully managed they should all provide a better profit than straight savings would.

Bonds

Of the three types of investment, bonds are probably the most complicated to understand. They can be the least risky or the most risky
depending on who issues them. They can provide huge returns for little
outlay, but often return only moderate amounts for moderate cost. If
bought at issue and held until maturity they are simple to understand,
but if bought and sold between those points their pricing requires
increasingly sophisticated mathematics to understand. Their values can
be as volatile as the other two asset classes, shares and property. Finally, as
this paragraph has started to show, they have their own jargon.

What a bond is

A bond is a share of a loan, where the bond purchaser is providing the
money to the bond issuer in return for the promise of repayment at a
specified date in the future, and with a specified rate of interest being
paid on it until that date.

The simplest (and least risky) forms of bonds are those issued by the
government. The government always needs to raise money, and if it
cannot do that by taxation alone it supplements that by issuing bonds.
Traditionally this was done through the Bank of England, but in 1998
this responsibility was transferred to the Debt Management Office
(www.dmo.gov.uk), which is part of HM Treasury. Bonds issued by the
UK government are known as 'gilts'. (Originally the bond certificates
were gilt-edged.) They are essentially risk-free as far as the promise to
repay is concerned, as they are guaranteed by the government.

In simple terms, the Chancellor says he needs more money and
instructs the DMO to raise money for the government through the issue
of a new gilt or bond (there were 24 new gilt issues in 2003/4, for
instance). The DMO then offers for sale gilts at a certain nominal price:
for example on 28 January, 2004 the DMO offered £2,500 million of
gilts that pay 5 per cent each year until 2025. At issue you can buy any
amount of gilts you wish above £1,000. After issue you can purchase any
amount you like. Prices for gilts are however quoted 'per £100'.

Say you were to purchase £1,000 of the gilt issued on 28 January 2004, the '5 per cent Treasury Stock, 2025'. These will pay you 5 per cent each year. For this particular issue you will receive half the interest payment on 7 March each year and the other half on 7 September (other gilts may have different dates). On your £1,000 holding that means you will receive £25 twice a year (5 per cent of £1,000 divided by two), every year until 2025 when the gilt 'matures' and you are repaid the capital of £1,000. In the jargon used with bonds, the interest payment is known as a 'coupon'.

Bond pricing

Now it starts to get complicated! The actual price you pay for a bond or a gilt will probably not be the amount that will be repaid to you if you hold it to maturity, the so-called 'nominal price'. This is because the main benefit of bonds is the guaranteed income they pay out regularly – the coupon. The value of the bond is really the value that investors place on the interest rate it pays out.

If you buy the gilt described above, the 5 per cent Treasury Stock 2025, you will receive £2.50 every six months for every nominal £100 that you own of the gilt. If the average interest rate you can get elsewhere is, say, only 3.5 per cent, then the 5 per cent the gilt is paying will seem generous, and people will pay more to receive that interest. However, by paying more for the gilt than its nominal or redemption value (also known as 'par' or 'face' value) you will actually be reducing the yield it offers. (The yield is the ratio of price to interest rate. At issue the 5 per cent gilt has a nominal yield of 5 per cent, but if you pay £110 for nominal £100 of the gilt, that is 10 per cent more than its redemption value, the yield will drop to 4.54 per cent, £5/£110 = 4.54 per cent.) Equally, if the current standard interest rate available is above 5 per cent, investors will pay less than £100 for the nominal £100 of the gilt, so that the yield increases. Investors will not just focus on what the current interest rates available are in relation to the gilt's rate, but also factor in what they think interest rates are likely to do in the years that are left until the gilt matures. They will also try to guess what inflation will do in that time. All this makes the pricing of bonds very complex.

Unfortunately this is not the only thing that affects the price. Investors also want to know what their total investment will be worth if they hold the bond to maturity. If they have paid more than the nominal price for the bond, they will lose money when the bond is repaid (or 'redeemed') at maturity, as only the nominal value is repaid. So if you pay £110 for a nominal amount of £100 of a bond or gilt, at redemption you will only receive £100, so losing £10 of capital. There are equations that work out these calculations (see the DMO Web site), although the easiest way to find the resulting 'redemption yield' is to look in the newspapers each day for the current one.

Who issues bonds and how you buy them

UK government bonds

As we have noted, the least risky bonds (because you can be sure they will be repaid on maturity) are government bonds, or gilts. The UK government issues two different types of gilts, conventional gilts and index-linked gilts. Conventional gilts are as described in the section above: they have a fixed 'coupon rate' (the 5 per cent in the example above), and they are sold with maturity dates of various lengths. In early 2004 the longest maturity date for a conventional gilt is 2036.

Index-linked gilts operate in the same way as conventional gilts except that the 'coupon rate' is added to the current rate of inflation, and the capital repayment is also adjusted for inflation. The change in the rate of inflation is calculated by the inflation index figure. (This is as published by the Office of National Statistics, www.statistics.gov.uk. Note that although the HM Treasury now uses the European calculation for the rate of inflation, HICP (also known as CPI), index-linked gilts will still be calculated using the old RPI measure, which is still published.) The rate from eight months before the issue date is given as the base rate, and the current applicable rate is that which occurred eight months previously. The eight-month lag is to allow calculations to be made today with known figures, as the inflation rate is only known several months in arrears. This 'inflation-proofing' makes index-linked gilts very attractive, even though the coupon rate is usually quite low. A further advantage of index-linked gilts is that the growth due to inflation is not included in any capital gains tax calculations for most UK investors.

There are also two other types of gilts traded on the market: undated gilts and 'rumps'. Undated gilts are those that have no maturity date and will go on paying out for an unspecified period. There are only two currently in circulation and they are quite small. 'Rumps' are gilts that do not have fully quoted market availability. They are by definition illiquid and are generally not suitable for the individual, private investor.

You can register as an approved private investor with the DMO and will then be able to purchase gilts as they are issued. If the issue is not over-subscribed you will pay the nominal value; if it is over-subscribed you can either bid competitively or pay an average amount for the competitive prices. Over-subscription is quite normal for new issues, and they often raise more money than their nominal value at issue.

Once the gilt has been issued you can buy and sell gilts on the stock market through a stockbroker or through the Bank of England's Brokerage Service (01452 398333, or visit www.bankofengland.co.uk/registrars/brokeragehome.htm). The brokerage service is being transferred to Computershare (www-uk.computershare.com; tel 0870 702 0000) from December 2004.

Strips

Many but not all gilts are available as 'strips' (separately traded and registered interest and principal securities). With strips, each separate coupon payment (the six-monthly interest payment) is sold separately, as is the capital repayment. The repayment strip therefore has no interest value to it, and becomes a 'zero-coupon' or 'zero'. In order to purchase and sell strips you have to be a member of CREST (see the box on page 267). For more information on strips visit www.dmo.gov.uk.

Conversions

From time to time the government decides to convert one gilt into another. This is usually done because the 'to be converted gilt' is little traded and difficult to sell. Sometimes the DMO will pay a market price for the gilt instead of converting it.

Accepting the conversion is voluntary, but if you do not accept the conversion it is likely that the remaining 'rump' will be even more difficult to sell should you want to do so. It will continue to pay interest and be repaid in full, however.

GEMM

The vast majority of gilts are bought and sold by large institutions. They are traded by gilt-edged market makers (GEMM), large financial institutions that set the market price for gilts. GEMM members will also bid competitively at auction for new issues.

Foreign government bonds

In addition to UK gilts, all other governments issue bonds. Bonds from other countries are riskier as they will be priced in that country's currency, which will fluctuate in price against the pound. If the UK joins the euro this currency risk will disappear for other euro-denominated bonds.

The risk of foreign government bonds will vary with the perceived stability and strength of that country's economy and government.

Local authority stocks and bonds

These are similar to Treasury bonds but are issued by local authorities. In practice they work in the same way as Treasury bonds but there are two major differences. Firstly local authority bonds are much less flexible in that they can only be bought at issue and are not traded thereafter. Local authority stock on the other hand is traded. Stockbrokers will be able to advise you, and some newspapers carry the stock details. Being smaller issues than Treasury stock, they are less liquid. Generally these types of investment are only subscribed to by institutions and professionals – but you can apply as an individual by approaching the local authorities directly. The municipal bond market is much more active in the United States than the UK for private investors.

Corporate bonds

Large companies issue bonds just as governments do. The major difference is that companies can go bankrupt more easily than governments, so the risk of not being repaid your capital (or even your interest) is higher. All companies that issue bonds that are traded on the stock market are rated by the international rating agencies such as Standard & Poor's or Moody's. The different agencies have slightly different ratings methods and grades. The top four grades of bonds are considered 'investment grade'. With Standard & Poor's these are AAA, AA, A and BBB, and with Moody's Aaa, Aa, A and Baa. These ratings can be further modified with pluses and minuses.

Corporate bonds from large international companies with a good rating are usually secure, but they can still be a risk. Enron's bonds were being rated by Standard & Poor's as BBB+ until four weeks before its debt scandal broke.

Corporate bonds tend to offer more attractive rates of interest to reflect their riskier nature. The more risky the better the rate, is the general rule.

Below-investment-grade bonds are classed as 'junk bonds'. With Standard & Poor's these run in worsening risk BB, B, CCC, CC, C and finally D, which is in default. The B ratings can all currently meet their interest and repayment obligations but are considered vulnerable. The C ratings are only meeting their obligations because of currently favourable circumstances; should these change default would appear likely in increasing degrees.

Corporate bonds can be purchased through a stockbroker.

Reasons to purchase bonds and points to consider

There are five main reasons for purchasing bonds. The most significant are to provide the investor with a regular and dependable source of income, and at an attractive rate. These reasons are backed up by the fact that bonds are pretty safe investments (and you generally know how much risk you are accepting by the rating each has been awarded).

Diversification is easy: you can spread your potential risk between different issuers of bonds (UK government bonds, foreign government bonds, AAA corporate bonds and risky corporate bonds – as well as different sectors of industry). Finally, they are liquid investments: most bonds are easily bought and sold on the open market through your stockbroker.

Because bond values change in response to investors' views on future rates of interest and inflation, they react in different ways from shares, which respond to how investors expect companies to perform. Very broadly, this means that they do not always move in the same direction as shares, and thus can also help diversify a share-based portfolio.

Generally, bonds with long maturity dates are more price-volatile than bonds that are nearing redemption, with prices more affected by long-term views of interest rates and inflation. Nearer the redemption date, prices tend towards the nominal value.

Brokers make money not just on their fees but also by charging a different rate to buyers and to sellers. This is known as the 'spread'. The price at which you buy a bond will be slightly higher than the price the person who has sold it to you received for it – the difference is taken by the intermediary, the broker.

Bond risk ratings continue to change after you purchase them – so if you bought a bond with a medium interest rate which was rated AA, if the company's circumstances change the bond might be re-rated to a more risky rating, but the interest it pays will remain the same. Therefore you must keep an eye on the yield and risk of any bond holdings you have. Of course, if you buy gilts you avoid this risk, but you receive less interest generally.

Rising interest rates not only reduce the capital value of your bond but can also have adverse effects on the financial stability of the companies that issue bonds, so increasing their riskiness.

For the average private investor a good way of lowering both your risk and your need to monitor any bond holdings is to invest in a bond fund. See below for more information on 'pooled investments'.

Bonds and tax

Interest payments on gilts are paid gross, so individuals must declare the payments in their annual tax return. Corporate bonds, however, have their interest paid net of savings tax (20 per cent): higher rate tax payers will have to declare the payments and non-tax payers reclaim the interest. Profits or losses on the capital repayment of both gilts and corporate bonds are tax-free for private investors, with no capital gains tax to be paid.

Table 16.1 Bonds: a summary

	UK govt. bonds – gilts	Foreign govt. bonds	Corporate 'investment grade' bonds	Corporate 'junk' bonds
Risk rating	Low	Low–medium	Medium	High
Income rating	Low–medium	Variable (depends on exchange rates, as well)	Medium	High
Amount*	Min: £1,000 Max: unlimited	Min: £1,000 Max: unlimited	Min: £1,000 Max: unlimited	Min: £1,000 Max: unlimited
Time	To maturity or less	To maturity or less	To maturity or less	To maturity or less
Tax	Interest paid gross. No CGT	Varies**	Interest paid net. No CGT**	Interest paid net. No CGT**
Cost	Brokers fees and the spread	Brokers fees and the spread	Brokers fees and the spread	Brokers fees and the spread

* You can usually invest as little as you like, but less than £1,000 is likely to be uneconomic after charges have been levied.
** Foreign-denominated government and corporate bonds will be taxed differently depending on where they originated – seek specialist advice.

Shares

The second of the main three investment types is shares, also known as equities. These are generally less complex than bonds. A share represents a portion of a company's capital value (all its assets). The ownership of a share means that the investor owns an equal proportion of the company. Typically a large company will divide its capital value into many millions of shares, so the ownership of a share or even a few thousand shares will represent only a tiny fraction of a per cent of the ownership of that company.

Shares come in different forms, but the majority of shares give the owner rights to vote at AGMs, elect (or depose) directors, and the right to dividends. Shareholders collectively choose the directors of the company, and it is the directors that make the decisions about the company's direction and administration. Shares therefore come with an implied responsibility that the shareholders oversee the directors – the shareholders are the owners of the company, after all. In practice individual shareholders are unlikely to be able to change anything within a company, and if every shareholder started making suggestions to the directors chaos would ensue. However, recently in the UK the very large institutional shareholders (fund managers and insurance companies that hold large amounts of companies' shares) have been flexing their muscles. In the recent merger between Carlton and Granada television companies to make the new ITV company, the institutional shareholders forced a change of chairman against the wishes of the merging companies' directors. Note that this shareholder power is only available to you if your name is on the company's share register – see the box on page 267.

Share jargon: issues, dilution, splits, buybacks and mergers

The ownership of shares and the tracking of how well they have performed can be made more complicated by the directors of companies altering the value of those shares through some form of share restructuring.

When a company is first created and its shares are issued they have a 'nominal' value. This is typically somewhere between one penny and one pound. In the normal course of events this 'nominal' value (sometimes also called 'par value' or 'face value') is not important. The nominal value bears no relevance to the market value of the shares, which as suggested by its name, is created by the supply and demand in the market. The nominal value is of more importance with unquoted companies, where the market value can be unknown.

If the company issues further shares at a later date this may 'dilute' the value of the existing shares, depending on whether the new shares are paid for at a price above or below the existing share price.

If the directors believe that the price of the company's shares is becoming high in comparison to the share price of similar companies, they may choose to 'split' the shares. Shares can be split in any number of ways, but the simplest is a two-for-one split, where initially you have, say, one share valued at £10. After the two-for-one split you receive two new shares valued at £5 each, and the old share is nullified. Your total holding remains £10 but now you have two shares rather than one. This makes the shares more 'tradable' psychologically, and perhaps more likely to rise in value on that basis. Note: do not confuse a 'share split' with 'split-capital shares'.

Companies sometimes also carry out 'share buybacks', where rather than use all their distributable profit for dividends they choose to spend some of the money purchasing a tranche of their shares on the open market. This reduces the number of shares available to investors, so making them 'less diluted' – and thus increasing their value. This is good for investors looking for capital growth, but not for those looking for income.

When two companies merge many different things can happen to your shares. If your company is taking over another, it may issue new shares in itself to give to the shareholders of the company it is buying. (Depending on the value of the new company this might or might not dilute the value of your shares.) If your company is being bought you might be offered shares in the company buying it, or offered cash, or a mixture of the two. You should get professional advice if you are unsure which option is the best value.

Settlement, CREST, nominee companies and security ownership

Settlement is the process of administering the transfer of money and the updating of certificates of ownership when shares, bonds and other securities are bought and sold. This is now largely done electronically.

CREST is the Central Securities Depository for the UK market and Irish equities. CREST is operated by Crest Co. CREST provides electronic, real-time settlement for a wide range of corporate and government securities. These include:

- UK and Irish equities;
- UK government bonds;
- UK and Irish unit trusts and OEICs and ETFs;
- other financial instruments and international securities.

For a long time you did not need to pay for your share purchases for up to two-weeks after you had bought them. This was to allow clerks time to manually shift the paper certificates from A to B and update them. With new technology and increasing competition from overseas stock exchanges, this length of time became outdated, and in the last 15 years the standard settlement time has reduced to 10 days, to five days to the current three days, or T+3 as it is known.

For T+3 to work both the buyer and seller need to have electronic settlement accounts. For private individuals to have access to the T+3 process they must either have an electronic settlement account of their own or use a nominee account of their stockbroker or bank.

For most investors a nominee account is acceptable. However, it means that the stockbroker or bank's nominee company actually owns the shares and holds them for you on trust. Nominee companies are separate from the actual stockbroker or bank company, so that they cannot become liable for any debts the stockbroker or bank may incur. As it is actually the nominee company that owns your shares, its name will appear on the share register of the shares you have bought, and not your own. You will not automatically be able to vote at company AGMs or benefit from any perks that share ownership affords you, although some nominee companies do pass on these rights.

Alternatively, if you are over 18 and resident in the European Economic Area you can become a Personal Member of CREST. This is usually done through your stockbroker, and it will charge you for the process. Your stockbroker will act as your sponsor to CREST, and when your membership is approved, normally a simple process, you will be able to have access to your personal CREST account, although all access is gained through your sponsor. For more information contact your stockbroker or CREST on 020 7849 000, or visit www.crestco.co.uk. In this way your shares will be registered in your own name and your voting rights and so on will be entirely your own.

You can still own securities without an electronic account, and generally you will be able to use a 10-day settlement period, but you may not be able to access the best prices and can be charged higher dealing costs.

Most people do not buy shares to have a say in running the company, however. We buy shares because we believe that the financial reward for share ownership will make us better off. The financial rewards come in two forms, as with bonds. Shares provide income in the form of dividends (although not all shares do – see below), and the value of the share can increase (and, of course, it can fall).

Types of shares

Ordinary shares

As noted above, shares come in a variety of forms. The basic share type is an 'ordinary' share. This is as described above, a stake in the ownership of the company offering certain rights. The cost of those rights is the potential risk that the company will do badly and the value of the shares will fall, or even disappear entirely. Shares do however provide you with the certainty that you can only lose as much money as you have invested. As the ultimate owners of a company, shareholders are the last people to be given any money if a company goes bankrupt and the assets are sold off. They sit in last place in the queue behind the creditors, bondholders, tax authorities and everyone else.

Preference shares

These types of shares have more similarity to bonds than shares – although they do confer ownership, unlike a bond. Preference shares usually offer the investor a fixed rate of dividend, such as 8.5 per cent per £1 of nominal share value. This means that for every nominal £1 preference share that you own, you receive 8.5p in dividend each year. Preference shareholders are paid their fixed dividend before ordinary shareholders are paid their variable dividend. Preference shareholders are also one step higher up the creditors' ladder than ordinary shareholders in the event of bankruptcy: that is, they will be paid before ordinary shareholders. The cost of being 'preferred' over ordinary shareholders is that preference shares normally do not give the holder the right to vote.

There are some different versions of preference shares. Cumulative preference shares mean that in the event that the company is unable to pay the fixed dividend, the unpaid amount is carried over and accumulated until the company restarts paying dividends. Participating preference shares can have a limited increase in the dividend in the years when the company has done well: they 'participate in the profit'. Convertible preference shares can be converted to ordinary shares at certain times.

Dividends, yields, EPS and P/E

When companies make a profit they distribute all or part of it to the shareholders. The company directors decide how much profit will be distributed as dividends. It is possible that when a company has had a poor year it will distribute more dividend than was earned that year as profit, calling on reserves of cash to do so.

As a result, for most large companies dividends do not tend to vary hugely from year to year, as the dividends are smoothed out over good and bad years. Generally, the directors like to increase the dividends by a small percentage each year to indicate the increasing profitability of their company. But they need not, and dividends can be reduced just as easily.

As a rule of thumb, companies in fast-growing sectors tend to keep most of their profits to reinvest in the company, and distribute very little in the way of dividends. The reward for ownership is the increase in the share price. Microsoft paid its first dividend in 2003, 24 years after it was founded, and even that was only a yield of 0.33 per cent. Equally companies in mature industries, that have little capital growth, tend to pay out more generous dividends. Sainsbury's currently yields around 5.5 per cent.

The yield is the dividend as a percentage of the current share price, so it will change all the time as the share price changes. The average yield for FTSE 100 companies is around 3 per cent. When share prices rise, as during the 'dot.com bubble', yields decrease. US shares tend to have lower yields.

Yield should not be confused with earnings per share (EPS), which is the company's net profit divided by the number of shares. If you compare the EPS with the actual annual dividend you will see how much profit has been distributed as dividend and how much retained. Note that EPS uses last year's reported profit for the calculations; for under-standing the current situation you should look at what City analysts forecast the future EPS might be.

P/E, or the price/earnings ratio, has nothing to do with dividends but focuses on profits earned and the current share price. It is the current share price divided by the EPS. This figure is used to compare the 'cheapness' of shares: the lower the figure, the cheaper the shares. The figure actually shows how many years it would take for the current EPS to pay for the current price of the share. If the figure is high it indicates that the market thinks the company has great growth potential, and is 'pricing in' future growth to the share price. Fast-growing companies will have higher P/Es than mature companies. During the 'dot.com bubble' P/Es for some of the most hyped shares were astronomical. Intel achieved a P/E of over 100. The long-term average P/E for the UK is around 14, although currently it is around 18. In the United States and Japan P/Es are usually higher. Note that a low P/E does not necessarily mean that the company is a bargain. It could have a low price because circumstances have changed since its last earnings were reported, and it could be in decline.

Tax on dividends

Basic rate taxpayers pay only 10 per cent income tax on dividends. Higher rate taxpayers pay 32.5 per cent. This 10 per cent tax is paid 'notionally' at source by the company on the taxpayer's behalf. (The tax is actually a 'tax credit' because for complicated reasons relating to previous tax regimes it was a rebate to prevent double payment of tax on the same piece of money. As such the company does not actually pay the tax at all, so it is only 'notional', but as far as the taxpayer is concerned it has been paid.)

When applying income tax to dividends you need to know the gross amount (dividend plus tax credit).

Working out tax applied to net figures

If you have a net dividend of £90, it means it has had the tax already removed from it. Dividends have a notional tax credit of 10 per cent. To work out the gross amount (net amount + tax credit) you have to apply the following simple calculation.

$$\frac{\text{Tax \%}}{1 - \text{Tax \%}} = \frac{10\%}{1 - 10\%} = \frac{10}{90} \quad 0.11111$$

You then multiply the net figure by 1 + the above figure. So we get from the above example £90 × 1.11111 = £100.

For higher rate taxpayers the additional tax that must be paid is only 22.5 per cent of the gross dividend, as the first 10 per cent has already been paid. All higher rate tax payers must declare their dividends in their annual tax return, so that the additional tax liability can be calculated.

The situation is not so beneficial for non-tax payers as they cannot reclaim the 10 per cent tax credit. Until April 2004 the tax credit was reclaimable by investors who kept their shares in ISAs. The ISA plan manager was able to claw it back, but this has now also been stopped.

Drips, scrips and reinvesting your dividends

Most investors look at their share portfolio as producing two separate types of return, the capital growth that shares hope to make year on year, and the dividend income. All the research that shows how lucrative investing in shares is over the medium to long term as compared with other forms of investment is, however, based on the principle that dividends are reinvested and not consumed. If you do not reinvest your dividends, you will not be able to achieve the long-term average return on investment that you might expect from investing in shares.

Until the abolition of advanced corporation tax many companies offered shareholders scrip dividends. This is where you are offered extra shares, in place of cash, for your dividend. However, the tax advantages of doing this have now diminished, and as scrip shares were created by the company rather than bought from the market they diluted the value of shares already in existence. The increasingly popular way to reinvest dividends is by way of 'drips' or dividend reinvestment plans. If a company offers a 'drip' and an investor chooses to take it up, the

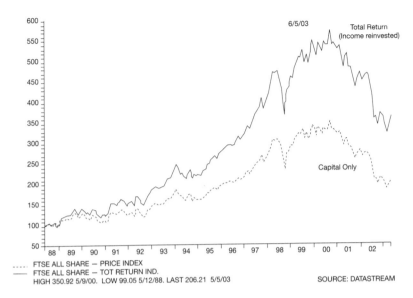

Figure 16.1 The effect of dividend reinvestment

company buys the new shares to the value of the dividend in the stock market. There is a cost to doing this, but as the company is buying a large amount of such shares at one time (for all the shareholders choosing to use drips) the cost becomes minimal, around 1 per cent, when spread amongst the shareholders. There is no tax advantage in accepting drip shares in place of dividends, as they are still considered as income, and a voucher is produced for your tax records.

What changes the price of shares?

This is the holy grail question. If you knew the answer so that you could predict share movements, you could retire tomorrow and would not need to worry about your finances as you would have untold riches!

Simply put, share prices move because of supply and demand – but what drives those is more difficult to pin down. In a simple world the expected future performance of an individual company, based on its management, its product and its sales would tell you all you need to know. Unfortunately it is not a simple world. Competitors affect companies' performance, as does the general economic climate. External factors such as political decisions and 'shocks', which include terrorist attacks, natural disasters and other less dramatic changes such as fuel price increases or transport problems, can all affect individual companies' prices.

All these 'hard' factors could be used in deciding whether a single company's share price will rise or fall, and a clever reading of them could give you a fairly accurate answer. However, the stock market is also subject to the 'soft' factor of 'sentiment'. Investors, both professional and private, have a 'feel' for what they think the market as a whole is going to do.

This leads to two consequences. One is that when shares reach a certain point, usually an arbitrary index figure such as 4,000 points for example, investors feel that shares have risen (or fallen – depending which direction they are travelling) enough, so stop buying and start taking a profit (or if falling, stop selling and start buying now that they think shares are cheap). This 'soft' factor is very hard to second guess, but influences the market hugely – in the short term. Another version of it in the UK stock market is the way the UK prices take a lead from the US stock market. Due to the time difference between London and New York, the US market opens two hours before the London market closes, and closes some 10 hours before the UK market opens the next day. Thus you frequently read of market reports like 'FTSE 100 opened strongly after a strong finish in New York last night', or 'after rebounding this morning the FTSE closed down after downbeat news from the US this afternoon'. Investors are clearly trading not just on their convictions of how particular companies trade, but also on how the rest of the market is doing. This leads to lemming-like following of the pack. It takes a brave investor to ignore what the market is doing and invest in the opposite direction – so called 'contrarian' investing.

A famous example of an investor not following the pack was the investment strategy followed by the fund management arm, Phillips & Drew, of UBS, the Swiss bank. Its chief investment officer, Tony Dye, did not understand where the future profit lay in all the high-tech dot.com companies and so refused to buy them during the dot.com bubble. Phillips & Drew's previously successful funds started to lag behind the market as they did not benefit from the rapid rise of the dot.com stocks. Dye stuck to his guns, predicting doom ahead, but as the months rolled by and 1997's rise was out done by 1998's, and that in turn by 1999's and early 2000's, he started to look very isolated and Phillips & Drew's funds looked very poor in comparison to their dot.com rich competitors. Ironically Dye was forced to leave his job in March 2000, only days before the bubble started to burst – and his opinion was vindicated. It remains arguable, however, whether he was right to ignore the market rise entirely. Even if he did not believe the fundamental reasons beneath it, by doing so he missed out on the largest rise in stock market history.

All this tells us that predicting winners in the stock market is not easy, and is more an art than a science as the 'soft' factors cannot be calculated logically.

A final note on share prices is that there are thousands of professional teams following the progress of individual shares around the clock. They are supported by teams of analysts and massive amounts of real-time computerized information. Publicly quoted companies are required to announce any information that might affect their share price in public announcements to the stock exchange. (Manchester United got into trouble by announcing David Beckham's departure to Real Madrid to the sports news rather than the stock exchange first, for instance.) As a result all these professionals receive important information at the same time and react to it immediately. This leaves private investors at a disadvantage, as they will most likely not have access to these announcements immediately, and even if they did they are likely to be at work or on holiday or otherwise occupied when such announcements are made, so that when they come to react to the news the professionals with their large purchasing power will have already changed the price of the share to factor in the news. This means that private investors will be unlikely to take the profit from such announcements, and so will have to content themselves with general shifts in share prices for average returns. For the part-time investor too much exposure to single stocks can be quite risky.

Pooled funds

For the investor who is not trying to squeeze every last potential drop of profit out of securities (bonds and shares), which is a risky approach in any case, the advantages offered by pooled funds are appealing. A pooled fund is a portfolio with a range of assets in it, created by a financial institution. The private investor can then buy a part of that portfolio, thereby gaining the professional investor's expertise and resources in stock picking, as well as getting a diversified range of assets. As the first investment trust set up by Robert Fleming, a clerk from Dundee who moved to London, stated in its prospectus in 1868, 'we intend to provide the investor of moderate means with the same advantages as large capitalists in diminishing the risks... by spreading investment over a number of stocks'. Pooled funds are available for a wide range of asset types: shares, bonds and life insurance. Within each of these assets you can buy funds that specialize in specific sectors, for example geographically or by industrial sector.

Investment trusts

There are a variety of different types of fund structure. The oldest form is the investment trust. This is a company that is quoted on the stock exchange like other companies, but its business is to buy and sell shares only. The investor buys shares in the investment trust, and so gains the value of its holding of shares in other companies. The particular point to note with investment trusts is that the share you buy will not necessarily equal the net asset value (NAV). (NAV is the current value of the company's assets, so for investment trusts it is all the shares they hold, divided by the number of shares in the company.) Normally investment trusts trade at a 'discount' to their NAV; that is, the share price is less than the NAV. This is because the investment trust share price is dictated by buyers and sellers of its shares and not the underlying value of its assets.

Unit trusts

Unit trusts are not traded on the stock exchange. They are funds set up by financial institutions, and you buy the 'units' (rather than shares) through the financial institutions that manage them (or your stockbroker will). They are what is known as 'open-ended' funds. This means that if you wish to buy units in them your investment cash is added to the invested portfolio, so making it larger (or smaller when you sell). The 'units' are priced according to the average NAV of the fund. Pricing is usually done at midday each day. When you instruct the unit trust manager to buy or sell your shares, you will not know exactly what the price will be, as instructions have to be submitted before the price is fixed each day. Also units have different buy and sell prices – the difference between them or 'spread' being taken by the manager.

OEICs

Because of unit trusts' drawbacks on pricing they were unpopular in Europe, and the UK unit trust industry risked losing market share to European-based funds. In order to stop this, open-ended investment companies (OEICs – known as 'oiks') were invented in the late 1990s. OEICs are hybrids between investment trusts and unit trusts. Like unit trusts they are open-ended so the price is based on their NAV, but they are quoted on the stock exchange and have a single price, with no spread. Since their first appearance in 1997 OEICs have largely taken over from unit trusts.

Because you only get truly good returns from shares if you reinvest your dividends (see Figure 16.1), unit trusts and OEICs often offer you the same fund of investments but with the choice of 'accumulative' units (where the dividends are reinvested) or 'income' units (where you receive a dividend in cash).

ETFs

Exchange traded funds (ETFs) are new products. They originated in the United States. There is only one provider of ETFs currently in the UK (Barclays Global Investors, trading as iShares). ETFs are very similar to OEICs, the only difference being that they are limited to 'tracker funds' (see below).

With-profits

With-profits policies are financial products that have been much criticized in the last couple of years. This is largely because they have failed to be as low-risk as they set out to be, but also because their very name makes them more confusing and obscure than they need to be.

Essentially with-profits policies are investment funds which provide a way for you to save for the future. They are most often used for saving to purchase an annuity on retirement (for pensions), or a lump sum at another specified date (to pay off an endowment mortgage, for example). They frequently also have a life insurance element built in to them: that is, if you die during the term of the policy it pays out a guaranteed sum, which could be substantially more than you have invested, although this is rarely the prime reason to take them out.

Where they differ from other types of investment fund is that the profits you make every year are 'locked in'. In a unit trust or investment trust the value of your holding is essentially linked with the current market value of the units or shares that you have bought. So if you buy, say, £100 of shares every month for a year and the price of the shares is £1, you will own £1,200 of shares at the end of the year. If the price of the shares then rises to £1.25 over three years, your shares will be worth £1,500. This is clearly good. However, if on the day you retire or wish to pay off your mortgage the stock market falls dramatically and your share's price falls to £0.95, your shares will only be worth £1,140. This could well be a problem if you had been expecting their value to have grown by 25 per cent in the period.

With a with-profits fund the managing company 'smooths' the returns the fund earns each year. It promises to pay you a 'guaranteed amount' or 'sum insured' at the contractual date, which could be on your retirement, death or another maturity date. This will usually be slightly less than the total of all your premiums. It then adds 'annual bonuses' each year, which reflect how well the fund has done that year. These bonuses do not represent all that year's profit, since some of it will be kept back to put into the fund on years when the fund does less well. At the maturity date the company will also add a larger final or 'termination' bonus, which often represents a significant proportion of the profit of your investment.

In our example, say the share prices at the end of years 1, 2 and 3 were £1.10, £1.21 and £0.95. This represents 10 per cent growth in years 1 and 2 and then a loss in value of 21 per cent in year 3. The company awards an annual bonus at the end of each year which is guaranteed: in our example, say 5 per cent, or £60, in year 1, and another 5 per cent, or £66, in year two. In year three, when the fund is worth significantly less, because it has held back some of the profit from the two previous years it can still afford to make a small bonus, of say 1 per cent or £10.50. As this is the year your fund matures you will also get your guaranteed amount say £1,050 – plus a termination bonus of 5 per cent or £52.10. So the final value of your with-profits fund is the guaranteed amount £1,050, the termination bonus £52.10 and the three annual bonuses £60 + £66 + £10.50 = £136.50, totalling £1,238.60. This is 8 per cent more than you would have received from an unprotected fund (see Table 16.2).

Table 16.2 How with-profits funds differ from investment trusts

Year	Amount invested	Share price at end of year	Unit trust value	With-profit g'nteed amount	With-profit annual bonus	With-profit g'nteed total	Difference between investment trust and with-profit fund
1	£1,200	£1.10	£1,320	£1,050	£60	£1,110	–£210
2	£1,200	£1.21	£1,452	£1,050	£66	£1,176	–£276
3	£1,200	£0.95	£1,140	£1,050	£10.50 + £52.10	£1,238.60	+£98.60

This example has been simplified for clarity in a number of ways. First, with-profits policies are not usually this short: you are most likely to take them out for from 10 to 30 or more years. Also you are expected to continue adding your monthly contributions or 'premiums' to them throughout the term of the policy, and not just pay for one year and then sit back and wait! Finally, if the policy has worked as expected then the termination bonus will usually be much larger than a normal annual bonus. Here we used 5 per cent for the annual bonus in the good years and also for termination. It is only when your policy matures in a bad year that you might find your termination bonus is reduced to these levels. Typically a termination bonus would be 20 per cent or more.

The problems with with-profits

With-profits policies have been considered to be lower risk investment products because of the effects of 'smoothing' and the guaranteed elements of the product. You will not lose everything with a with-profits policy, and the longer you hold it for, the greater returns you should acquire.

However, as most with-profits funds are invested in stock markets their fortunes are closely tied to how those markets perform. It is very rare for stock markets to lose value in three consecutive years (it has only happened three times since the early twentieth century), so most managers did not reckon on this happening when projecting the performance of their funds. The three years of stock market falls since 2000 have wiped out all the carefully saved extra profit in these funds, and prevented them from making significant annual bonus payments, or in some cases any payment at all. What is worse is that the termination bonuses have also been drastically reduced.

Many people who took out with-profits policies 25 or so years ago were told that the policy would reach a certain figure, such as the capital repayment on an endowment mortgage or a specific sum to purchase a pension annuity, and that in all likelihood the actual payout would be greater. In the last three years this has been turned on its head, and the actual final policy payment has been less than that promised, so mortgage owners and pensioners have had to find money from elsewhere to fund the missing part of their repayments. As this mostly affects the elderly who have less chance to make up the loss, it can have devastating effects.

For people with more than a few years left of their policy to run there is a choice between cashing in the policy and investing in something more profitable, or sticking with the policy and hoping that as stock markets improve, the returns will as well. However, the effect of three years of low or no bonuses will be very hard to make up.

What to do with with-profits shortfalls

If you already have a with-profits policy you should have already been contacted by the provider alerting you to whether your policy will meet the target amount or not. It should also have set out various options for you should it believe you will not achieve the target amount. If you are in any doubt you should contact your adviser immediately. If you have an endowment mortgage your provider should have sent you the FSA fact-sheet 'EMT1: Your endowment mortgage – time to decide'. If you have not received it ask your provider why it has not sent it to you, and request that it do so straight away. You can also get the factsheet directly from the FSA (call 0845 606 1234 or go to www.fsa.gov.uk/consumer).

Disposing of a with-profits policy

With-profits policies are designed as long-term investments, and disposing of them before maturity usually involves some form of penalty. The most frequent methods of disposing of a with-profits policy are:

- Surrender the policy. You do this by giving it back to the provider. It will repay you your contributions less a charge (especially if you surrender early in the policy term). You will receive the guaranteed annual bonuses and might or might not receive a termination bonus. Each company calculates surrender rates differently.
- Trade the policy. There is a second-hand market for policies, where you might be able to get a better price than that offered for surrendering it. It is known as the traded endowment market. Your policy will have to be reasonably mature before it will be marketable, with at least five years of premiums paid.
- Have the policy designated as 'paid up'. This means that you stop paying any more into the policy, and at maturity you get whatever it has earned with the limited contributions made to it. There will usually be a penalty for doing this, to cover the administration and management charges that are no longer covered by continued premium payments.
- Transfer the policy. For pension with-profit policies you should be able to transfer the fund to an alternative pension fund. The value will be calculated as with surrendering it, although if you transfer it to another product from the same company you might get better terms.

▨ Take out a loan against the policy. Some policies allow you to take out a loan against the policy's future value, as long as you do not stop making the premium payments into it.

Factors affecting pooled funds performance – discounts, charges and tax

While investment trusts, unit trusts and OEICs can all hold exactly the same portfolios, should they choose to do so, and therefore have the same intrinsic investment performance, the final result as far as the investor is concerned can be quite different.

Discounts

As investment trusts usually sell at a discount to their NAV you might not see the full benefit of any increase in the portfolio performance, if there are not enough other investors also seeking to buy the shares. Generally, investment trust shares move in line with their investment performance but at a discount to it. If you bought at a discount, then as long as the discount does not increase this should not affect you too much. And of course the discount could always diminish or even turn to a premium if sufficient demand exists for the shares.

Unit trusts, give or take the spread and delayed pricing, and OEICs trade very near their NAVs, so you should always be rewarded for the performance of the portfolio.

Charges

The price you pay for having a professional (and very highly paid) fund manager look after your money through a pooled fund is applied in charges. With investment trusts, there is a board of directors who run the company, and they appoint managers who manage the portfolio. The directors can change managers if they wish, but in general this rarely happens. The managers charge the company a fee for their expertise, and this is passed on to the investors in the form of a levy each year on the fund. The Association of Investment Trust Companies (the industry-funded trade body for investment trusts: tel 020 7282 5555) lists the investment trusts available in the UK on its Web site, www.aitc.co.uk. It gives the particulars of each trust, and under the financial profile section it shows the total expenses ratio (TER) that managers charge each trust. (For more information on TERs see the box.) The average TER for investment trusts is not listed by the AITC, but you can expect to pay under 1 per cent of funds under management, and frequently closer to 0.5 per cent. Some highly geared or small specialist funds may be more expensive.

Pooled fund charges, total expenses ratios (TERs) and reduction in yield (RIY)

The price you pay for a fund manager's expertise in selecting shares and administering a pooled portfolio takes the form of charges levied by the manager on the fund. These charges reduce the performance of the fund. The charges can vary greatly from one fund manager to another, thus affecting the performance of the different funds greatly.

Not surprisingly the fund managers of investment trusts, unit trusts and OEICs do not shout about the level of the charges that they levy on their funds, although they are required to publish them – especially in the Key Features document they are required to send you with your application. However, the presentation of these charges is often elusive, and even when you locate the details you may find they are not always a picture of clarity. Often just the management fee is listed, and not any of the other costs levied on the fund, such as administration/share registration, custody/ trustee, audit and legal fees.

For this reason independent consultants have created a business in calculating all the levied charges that fund managers use, and creating a standard method to measure these charges. This is the total expenses ratio (TER).

The impact of such charges can be huge on your investment's long-term performance. Fitzrovia, an independent fund consultant that specializes in measuring TERs and has its results used in the Association of Investment Trust Companies Web site, cites the following example:

"A £5,000 investment growing by 7 per cent a year should grow to be worth £19,348 after 20 years (with no annual expenses). But if the annual expenses (or TER) are just 1 per cent these will drag down the performance to £16,036. An extreme example of a TER of 3 per cent drags it down even further to only £10,956 – around £8,400 has been taken in charges."

For further information visit Fitzrovia's Web site at www.fitzrovia.com.

A second measure of how managers' charges reduce the return to the investor is return in yield (RIY) ratios. These measure the percentage point amount that explicit fees and charges subtract from the gross return to a fund. In contrast to TERs, RIY includes the initial charges levied by unit trusts and OEICs, so it gives a better overall indication of managers' costs. Unfortunately there is no current provider of these statistics across the fund management sector.

A final point to note is that neither of the above measures takes into account dealing costs when analysing fund expenses. All funds will inevitably have to buy and sell shares as part of their normal routine, but those that do so more frequently will incur greater dealing expenses. This increased dealing frequency does not necessarily lead to better performance. No clear data is provided by fund management companies on their dealing frequency or costs.

Unit trusts and OEICs charge investors twice for their services. Normally there is an initial one-off fee, which can typically be 5 per cent of your initial investment. This is followed by annual management charges. These will usually be between 1 and 2 per cent but can sometimes be more or less than this. These fees can make an enormous difference to the performance of your investment. The FSA suggests that a typical long-term annual return from your investment should be around 7 per cent a year. With a 5 per cent initial fee and 2 per cent annual fee, your first year's potential growth is wiped out regardless of whether the fund performs or not. The further fees every year, often at 2 per cent, could reduce the growth of your investment by nearly 30 per cent a year if you expect a 7 per cent return. Unit trusts incorporate some of their charges in the prices they give for the units.

The FSA provides very useful tables on its Web site (www.fsa.gov.uk/tables) that enable you to compare the charges of many different unit trusts and OEICs. Currently the tables are only set up for those funds that are provided in an ISA, but you will see the impact of the charges all the same. Some of these charges are very large – with an initial investment of £5,000 and holding the fund for 10 years with an average of 7 per cent growth per year, the FSA tables show you can expect to pay the fund manager anywhere between £1,500 and £2,800 during the period, with the average being around £1,850. Note that funds that operate to the government's CAT standard are significantly cheaper.

Tax

There are no special tax advantages to holding your investment in a pooled fund. You are liable for income tax and CGT unless you hold the shares in an ISA (see below). However, the managers do not have to pay CGT on any gains they make on holdings within the funds.

Buying your shares – broker, fees and stamp duty

Purchasing shares through a broker is quite straightforward once you have registered with it (which must be done for money laundering reasons). Brokers' fees can vary widely. Online brokers (see Chapter 21) often offer fixed-price dealing regardless of the amount you want to trade. Traditional brokers may also do this, but if you also want advice, they are likely to charge you a percentage fee. See Chapter 1 for more details on brokers.

All shares bought on the London Stock Exchange are subject to a purchase tax called stamp duty. It is currently 0.5 per cent of the transaction value. Shares purchased on foreign exchanges may have other taxes applied to them.

Measuring your fund's performance – indexes and tracker funds

There are so many different pooled funds to choose from that it can be bewildering trying to tell one fund's performance from another's. Many will give you ranking figures showing that they are in the 'top quartile' of funds in their sector, or such like. These figures are rather meaningless unless you know exactly the criteria used to categorize the sectors and grade the ranks. A useful way of benchmarking how your investment is doing is to compare it not to other similar funds but to an index (see the box).

Financial indexes (or indices)

Indexes are notional portfolios of all the shares in a sector or grouping of companies. They measure the performance of that sector or group to show its average performance over time. There are a large number of indexes available to investors today. By comparing the performance of their own portfolios with the performance of one of the stock exchange indexes, investors can see how well they have done from a comparative point of view.

In the UK the most widely noted index is the FTSE 100. This monitors the performance of the 100 largest quoted companies on the London Stock Exchange. It accounts for around 80 per cent of the value of the London Stock Exchange. The index was started in 1984 with a base of 1000, and it reached a peak on the last day of 1999 at 6930.

Other FTSE indexes include:

- FTSE 250 – the next 250 largest companies, representing around 18 per cent of the capitalization of the London Stock Exchange.
- FTSE 350 – the FTSE 100 and FTSE 250 together.
- FT Actuaries All Share – the top 800 companies, accounting for 98 per cent of the capitalization of the London Stock Exchange.
- FTSE Smallcap – the companies in the All Share Index not included in the FTSE 350.

The indexes are updated every quarter, with companies that have grown or shrunk in capitalization coming into or being ejected from the relevant index.

For further information about FTSE indexes visit www.ftse.com.

All major stock exchanges around the world have similar indexes.

United States

The Dow Jones Industrial Average Index (known as the Dow Jones) measures the 30 largest companies on the New York Stock Exchange. For further information and other indexes visit www.djindexes.com.

For a broader measure of how US stocks are performing, Standard & Poor has the S&P 500. See www.spglobal.com.

The Nasdaq is a newer exchange that has its own index. Companies quoted on it are generally younger than on the NYSE and frequently tech-oriented. See www.nasdaq.com.

Japan

The Nikkei measures the Tokyo Stock Exchange. See www.nni.nikkei.co.jp.

Germany

The DAX measures the Frankfurt Exchange.
See www.deutsche-boerse.com.

France

The CAC 40 measures the Paris Exchange.
See www.bourse-de-paris.fr.

The index will show you the average performance of the sector or grouping over a period of time. While an index is only a theoretical portfolio, and therefore does not carry any administration costs or buying and selling costs, it should show you what kind of return you could expect from a broad holding of shares in that sector. In practice it appears that it is very difficult to consistently achieve the returns of an index, and harder still to outperform it. The highly paid fund managers are not fools, and they would all dearly love to outperform the indexes, but in fact according to several studies the majority of fund managers fail to achieve the index performance. There are several reasons for this. On the one hand it is caused by a mixture of lack of sufficient skill in asset allocation (which types of asset to hold the investment in); poor stock selection (choosing the best shares, bonds and so on within that asset type) and timing, making the overall portfolio performance only at best close to the index's performance. And on the other hand the imposition of the managers' fees reduces unspectacular returns by a further couple of percentage points.

A study by the WM Company, a respected financial consultancy, for Virgin Direct (a company that sells tracker funds) in 2001 showed that 76 per cent of fund managers failed to beat the FTSE All-share Index over the 5 years to 2000. Over a 20-year period this increased to 80 per cent of funds. It also highlighted that many fund managers, although they charged 'active management' fees, actually only varied their portfolio holding very slightly from the composition of the index. The study went on to suggest that 'it is questionable whether any investor should pay active management fees for a manager who does not deviate substantially from benchmark weights'. Other studies by organizations such as the Office of Fair Trading, the Consumers' Association, the Department of Social Security and the Financial Services Agency have also questioned the performance versus cost of active fund managers. The government-commissioned Sandler Report in 2002 noted that 'Taken together, the impact of undisclosed costs and unsuccessful stock selection were substantial (2.5 per cent per annum, over the period studied) and considerately greater than the explicit charges'. (See the box.)

The Sandler Report on *Managed Funds and Investment Advice*

In June 2001 the government asked Ron Sandler to examine the retail savings and investment industry in the UK. His remit was to:

'identify the competitive forces and incentives that drive the industries concerned, in particular in relation to their approaches to investment, and, where necessary, to suggest policy responses to ensure that consumers are well served.'

When it came to examining the sector of managed funds he noted the following points.

Advised sales, those where the investor was guided by a professional adviser, were peculiarly slanted towards actively managed funds (93 per cent of such sales). Where the adviser was an IFA the figure rose to 97 per cent. Meanwhile institutional investors (professionals investing for pension funds and insurance companies) only had 75 per cent of their managed funds actively managed, and had 25 per cent as tracking funds. It was also observed that private investors who did not seek financial advice and followed their own judgement were similar to institutional investors in their split of funds, 75 per cent active to 25 per cent tracker. Sandler concluded that investors that did not seek advice were generally confident of their knowledge bases, and probably more sophisticated investors than those seeking advice. As such they made the same decisions on fund managers as the institutional investors had. In the United States, Sandler noted, institutional investors split their funds 60 per cent active to 40 per cent tracking.

Sandler reckoned that institutional investors logically ought to be more likely to trust their own judgement and expertise, and therefore sector and stock-picking abilities, than private investors – yet they still preferred to hold more of their portfolios in tracking funds than private investors did.

The reasons for private investors being attracted to actively managed funds were felt to be the marketing of these funds and the emphasis on past performance. Past performance was always the foremost reason given for choosing a fund. Fund charges were only cited as a reason by 14 per cent of respondents. However, past performance has clearly proved not to be a reliable guide to future performance. The report states, 'Identification of likely future out-performance requires highly sophisticated and time sensitive analysis of performance data and fund manager styles. Only a tiny minority of consumers have access to this sort of analysis. Yet without doing so, simply looking at past performance is of minimal value.'

On choosing between active and passive (or tracker) funds the Sandler report notes:

One of the key decisions an investor must make is whether his investments should be managed actively or passively. Active management is appropriate where the investor believes that:

- there are systematic inefficiencies in the market concerned that can be exploited;
- he can identify those investment managers capable of doing so; and
- the benefits available outweigh the incremental costs involved.

'It follows that the choice between active and passive management must be made on a market-by-market basis. There will be no hard and fast rule as to which is more appropriate, though broadly speaking, the more liquid and well-researched a market is, the less likely it is that these criteria apply and therefore the harder it is to make the case for active management (although it should be noted that some active management is necessary for efficient equity markets).'

On the basis that UK and US shares are very liquid and extremely fully researched, and that European, Japanese and even many emerging economies' shares and bonds are only slightly less so, Sandler's judgement that 'the more liquid and well-researched a market is, the less likely it is that these criteria apply and therefore the harder it is to make the case for active management' is as close as government advice can come to recommending passive management over active management without breaking its own rules on the provision of financial advice!

For more information on the Sandler Report visit: www.hm-treasury.gov.uk/Documents/Financial_Services/Savings/fin_sav_sand.cfm

The alternative to 'actively' managed funds is 'passively' managed ones. These are funds that build a portfolio to mirror the performance of particular indexes and track their performance. They do not try to do better than an index – and indeed never will, because of transaction and administration costs and 'tracking error' (although this could be on the upside); they will usually underperform the index by half a per cent or so. As they do not rely on the expertise of individuals but rather on computer modelling programs they are much cheaper to run. Such funds are called 'tracker' funds – as sold by, amongst others, Virgin Direct, which is why they were no doubt happy to pay for the research mentioned above!

ISAs

The government is keen for us all to save money. From time to time it creates opportunities that make saving more worthwhile. It is the nature of governments to change the rules over time, and often these savings opportunities are whittled away little by little over successive years and governments. Gordon Brown has continued this process, perhaps partly out of a belief that it is in fact only the medium to better-off members of society who actually use these savings opportunities, and that he can spend tax more redistributively to the benefit of the poorer members.

Whatever the reason, tax breaks for holding cash, bonds and shares have all diminished from their high point in the early 1990s. Then we had TESSAs (tax exempt special savings accounts) and PEPs (personal equity plans). Both have been stopped, although existing TESSA accounts were allowed to continue, as were existing PEPs. They were replaced in 1999 with ISAs, individual savings accounts. See the box for more information.

ISAs

The old regime

When ISAs were introduced in April 1999 to replace PEPs and TESSAs they came in two options. The first was mini-ISAs, which you could hold in three different asset types: cash, life insurance or shares. In theory you could take out each of these mini-ISAs each year, and invest up to £3,000 in the cash and the shares ones but only £1,000 in the life insurance one.

Maxi-ISAs allowed you to invest up to £7,000 each tax year in a mixture of assets, as long as the cash and shares element was not more than £3,000 and the life insurance not more than £1,000. Alternatively you could invest all of the maxi-ISA in shares. If you wished to invest in a maxi-ISA in any one tax year, you could not invest in any mini-ISAs that same year.

Note that ISAs are not investments themselves, they are just 'wrappers' for your investments. That is, you hold your investments in them and so protect the investments from tax liability.

The benefits of ISAs were that you were not liable for tax on any income that the investments produced, and that the ISA manager could reclaim the 10 per cent dividend tax on dividend income. Also ISA investments were not liable for capital gains tax (CGT) when you came to sell them.

The new regime

From April 2004 ISA managers will no longer be able to reclaim the 10 per cent dividend tax. This means that the only people who benefit from income tax savings with ISAs will be higher rate tax payers – who will continue to avoid the additional 22.5 per cent tax levied on top of the 10 per cent.

From the tax year beginning April 2005 the amounts you can invest in mini cash ISAs and maxi ISAs will be reduced to £1,000 and £5,000 respectively.

There is no guarantee from the government that ISAs will continue beyond 2007.

You must be 18 or over to have an ISA.

Despite the reduced tax incentives and amounts, ISAs are still useful vehicles to hold your investments in. The cumulative effect of no extra income tax (for higher rate payers) and no CGT is still attractive. Further, many fund managers offer lower charges for ISA users.

CAT standards

In an attempt to make the world of personal finance less complicated and easier to deal with, the government introduced the concept of CAT standards in April 1999. CAT stands for charges, access and terms, and to gain the CAT standard a provider has to meet certain criteria in these three areas. Currently CAT standard products are available for the three different types of ISA (cash, shares and insurance) and for mortgages. The criteria they have to meet are set out in the box on page 289.

The Sandler Report (see page 284) recommends a number of simple financial products for the private investor that will come with CAT standards, to remove uncertainty whether the charges and structure of investment products mean they give value for money.

It is important to note that CAT standards do not form any recommendation or guarantee about the future performance or suitability of a financial product. They only indicate that it conforms to a minimum set of requirements on its charges and terms.

Investment strategy

From what has been said above it might appear that actively managed funds are to be avoided at all costs. This is not our view. Investors' investment strategies should be planned to provide them with a balanced mix of risk and return to meet their investment goals. As was stated above, the first important decision is to identify what you are investing for. Having done this you will be able to choose more clearly what levels of risk and return you are prepared to accept, or need.

In our opinion, for the many people who are happy to accept the higher risk of investing in shares in order to gain the better returns they can offer, a central core of index-based (tracker) funds may well be enough. However, a portfolio of tracker funds can never, by definition, outperform the market. For potentially higher returns, whether you are looking for income, capital growth or both, a selection of carefully selected single stocks or truly actively managed funds (those that have real stock selection rather than shadowing the market as pseudo-trackers) may be suitable. It could also be a good option to invest a proportion of your portfolio in income-generating securities (bonds or bond funds).

It is critical to understand the risk/return ratios of the different asset types you hold across your entire finances. You should always have enough accessible cash held in low-risk deposit-style accounts to enable you to pay off unexpected expenses. This is your emergency fund. If you

Existing criteria for CAT Standard Products

Charges	Access	Terms
Cash ISAs • No one-off or regular charges, such as ATM withdrawals • Charges for replacement statements, cards etc are permitted	• Minimum transaction size no greater than £10 • Withdrawals within 7 working days or less	• Interest rates no lower than 2% below Base Rates • Upward interest rate charges to reflect base rate changes within a calendar month Downward changes may be longer • No other conditions
Shares ISAs • Total charges no more than 1% per year of fund value • No other charges to be paid by investor	• Minimum saving no more than £500 pa or £5 per month	• Investments must be in unit trusts, OEICs or investment trusts • Fund must be at least 50% invested in UK or EU shares • Units or shares must be single priced (no spread) • Investment risk must be highlighted in Key facts literature
Insurance ISAs • Total charges no more than 3% of fund value • No other charges allowed	• Minimum premium £250 pa or £25 per month	• Surrender values should reflect underlying asset values • No specific surrender penalties • After 3 years surrender values should at least return premiums paid

Mortgages
See chapter 6

can get credit easily (such as on a credit card) this money need not be instantly available. It could be in a better-paying notice account, for instance. You should then have some low to medium-risk assets such as bonds or shares which are slowly accruing earnings on your behalf. Only when you feel comfortable with this cushion of resources should you start to take on riskier (but more rewarding) investments.

The economist J K Galbraith said, 'there are two types of forecaster, those "who don't know" and "those who don't know they don't know"'.

For forecaster, Galbraith presumably meant economist, but it can read equally well for investor. Future returns on investment are inherently risky, as Galbraith sagely noted. You cannot know what will happen, and it is the fools amongst us who do not realize that and think they can tell what is going to happen. This is why it is important to have that cushion of resources before investing in more risky assets.

With this depressing advice in the background, it is clear that investing in shares is the best way to make money. Figure 16.2 shows the different returns from different asset types over the last century. Shares lead the pack by a full length and a half on investment periods of over 10 years (and the 1990–2000 period caught the stock market at the beginning of a crash and the bond market consequently on a rise). But remember this huge outperformance included reinvesting all your dividends, which most investors do not do.

This brings us to the issue of timing. Making money in the stock market is probably more a factor of timing than stock selection. If you get in and out at the right time you can make huge sums very quickly, but for most investors this is lucky chance rather than something carefully planned. The real art to timing your share purchases is to get in early and stay there for a long time. Yes, money can be made quickly on the stock market, but that is not how an average investor should look at it. The stock market is there to be used slowly over the long term.

If you think you may need to get your money out within two to five years, shares are unlikely to be the best place to put it. This is because at the moment you need to get your money, the market might be going through a temporary slump, and your shares could easily be worth less than when you bought them. Over a period of 10 or more years this is very unlikely to be the case. Over a period of 20 or more years it is unlikely that the stock market can be beaten in terms of average returns.

One way of reducing your potential risk of investing at a peak in the continuous stock market cycle is to invest a small to moderate amount of money on a continuous and regular basis. Whether it is £25, £50, £100 or £500 a month, if you keep dripping this into the market every month you will catch it when it is at its lows as well as its highs, but over time you will start to really achieve significant growth.

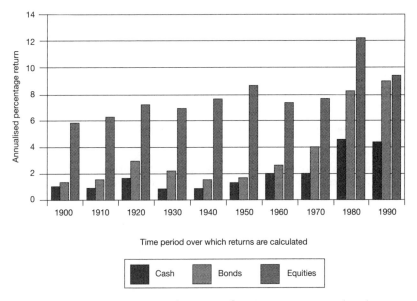

Figure 16.2   Historic performance of equities, government bonds and cash in the UK

Fund managers offer regular savings plans so that you can drip your investment in continuously and buy a diversified spread of shares at the same time. From time to time you should reassess your investments' performance and change funds, and even managers, if you feel they are no longer maximizing your risk/return expectations. You should perhaps change your funds for diversification's sake occasionally anyway. But if possible keep the regular savings going all the time.

It is important to discuss your individual situation with a qualified broker or financial adviser before making any investment allocations unless you are confident that you fully understand the factors affecting your investment decisions and the full range of options available to you.

Derivatives and other types of securities

We have only examined the basic options available in the two main security types, bonds and shares, in this chapter. In the next chapter we look briefly at property investment.

Table 16.3 Summary of the main types of share-based investments

	Single shares	Investment trusts	Unit trusts and OEICs	ETFs
Risk rating	High	Medium–high	Medium–high	Medium (depends on breadth of index)
Income rating	Nil–high	Nil–high	Nil–high	Nil–medium
Amount*	Min: £25 Max: unlimited	Min: £25 Max: unlimited	Min: £25 Max: unlimited	Min: £25 Max: unlimited
Time	Medium to long term	Medium to long term	Medium to long term	Medium to long term
Tax	Dividends paid already taxed, except for higher-rate tax payers. CGT payable on capital gains	Dividends paid already taxed, except for higher-rate tax payers. CGT payable on capital gains	Dividends paid already taxed, except for higher-rate tax payers. CGT payable on capital gains	Dividends paid already taxed, except for higher-rate tax payers. CGT payable on capital gains
Cost	Brokers' fees and stamp duty	Low management fees. Brokers' fees. Stamp duty	Initial fee, management fee – often high. Brokers' fees Stamp duty on OEICs	Low management fees. Brokers' fees

* £25 tends to be the smallest monthly amount most savings plans will accept. For one-off lump sum investments £500 is probably the lowest economic amount.

There is a whole range of complex financial products based on bonds and shares available to the more sophisticated investor. These are increasingly becoming more easily accessible to private individuals. These products include hedge funds and derivative products such as options, forwards and the more old-fashioned debentures.

It is not possible in a guide this size to cover these complex products in a manner that would be both comprehensive and comprehensible. However, hedge funds and split-capital trusts are now relatively common. They have also had their share of notoriety, as people have invested in them without fully understanding the risks attached, so a short description of each is provided below.

Split-capital trusts

Split-capital trusts are not new products, but they have become much more accessible to the average investor in recent years. They are more complicated investments than conventionally structured trusts, and have a range of different share types available to invest in – each providing different rights and returns. Split trusts can split their shares up in a number of ways; the important thing to note is that should the trust not perform as well as expected there is a strict order which determines which types of shares get repaid first. Obviously the lower on the list a share type is, the riskier it is – but this risk is rewarded by higher returns if the trust performs well.

Traditionally 'splits' had only two types of shares: income-bearing and capital growth. This was easy to understand, and the choice was simple for investors looking for either of those qualities. All split trusts have a fixed lifespan. The income shares receive all the income from the trust, and at the end of the trust's life their holders get a fixed redemption price for the shares. Obviously these shares can be bought and sold during the life of the trust, and their price varies in the same manner as do bond prices. The capital shares receive no income, but at the trust's winding-up their holders receive all the remaining assets after the income shares have been paid off. This could represent a considerable return if the assets have performed well.

Recently further classes of shares have been used, such as zero income preference shares, annuity income shares, stepped preference shares and ordinary shares. The repayment order of shares is normally: zero income preference shares; annuity income shares; stepped preference shares; income shares; ordinary income shares; capital shares. Not all share types are available in every split trust. Zero income preference shares offer no income and a fixed redemption price on winding-up. Annuity income shares offer just income and a nominal (for instance 1p) redemption price, the capital value having been paid out as income. Stepped preference shares offer a combination of fixed redemption price and fixed annual interest. Ordinary income shares offer all the income plus a share of the capital value on winding-up.

The problems with split-capital trusts is that many of the trusts also borrowed heavily from banks to buy extra shares for their portfolios in the expectation that this would increase their performance. This back-fired during the share slump following the dot.com bubble and the loans could not be repaid. Many investors did not realize that the trusts were borrowing money, and that those loans always had to be repaid ahead of any shareholders. Thus some investors owning preference shares which were described as very low risk discovered that the trust could not repay even them.

The worst managed funds have now been revealed, and it is thought that the split-capital trusts trading now are much better run and well funded. However, good research and a full understanding of where your shares lie in the repayment schedule is still critical before you invest in these trusts.

Hedge funds

Hedge funds are clever beasts: they should make money whether the market is rising or falling. In crude terms the fund's managers make bets that the market, or at least the shares they are investing in, will either rise or fall. If they think it will rise they 'buy and hold' in the normal way; if they think it will fall they 'sell short', borrowing shares to sell in the expectation of buying replacements later at a lower price. Obviously if the 'bet' goes wrong the managers have to pay out even more on a short sell than they would have had to pay had they acted conventionally.

Conventional managed funds are limited in their ability to short sell, and are not allowed to use most derivative products, but hedge funds can. Hedge fund managers claim that they can reduce the risk exposure of portfolios substantially. However, some hedge funds have gone very wrong, suggesting that because of the gearing associated with such funds, although they might not get into trouble very often, and frequently avoid it because of their clever use of derivatives, when they do get into trouble it tends to be big trouble!

17

Property investment

The third major investment-type asset is property. For most people who own a home, their house is their single biggest asset. This is worth bearing in mind if you are tempted to invest further in property. Currently residential property has experienced a sustained boom, with prices increasing by above trend levels for nearly a decade. Everybody knows that this cannot continue for ever – the big question is whether property prices will slow down to below trend increases (but still continue rising each year) or will crash.

If you know that residential property prices are going to stop rising as quickly, or even to start falling, why should you consider investing in property at all – especially if you already have the bulk of your assets tied up in your own home? This is a perfectly reasonable question, and it may well be that the answer is that you should not be looking at property investment. That said, there are still reasons to invest in property:

- You do not have to invest in residential property. Commercial property works on a different cycle to residential property and has different sets of advantages and disadvantages.
- Private residential property investment is largely 'buy-to-let' which is capital growth-driven. Even if the capital growth element has diminished, the 'income' element can still sometimes be found.
- Property development still offers opportunities – although it is more a business proposition than a personal finance one.

- Overseas residential property is more a lifestyle choice than an investment one, but in many places it can offer you some capital growth as we\ll as days in the sun.

In this chapter we look briefly at residential and commercial property investments. We cannot hope to cover all the details, and if you are interested in pursuing any of these options further you should seek out more details from the vast array of specialist books, Web sites and agents that cover this area.

Advantages and disadvantages of property investment

There are certain real advantages in investing in property over shares, as well as some equally significant disadvantages. The main advantages are:

- You can leverage your investment in a simple way – by using a mortgage. This means that you can buy a property (and its attached income and growth prospects) without having to pay for it all up-front. See Chapter 6 for a fuller explanation.
- As long as you take out insurance, it is very unlikely that your property will lose all its value. It might fall substantially in value, but it is rare for that fall to be more than 25 per cent, and extremely rare for the property's value to disappear all together. Total loss of capital is much more possible in the stock market – ask anyone who held shares in the UK's General Electric Company (a cash-rich, blue-chip engineering stock) in the late 1990s and discovered after it changed into a technology company and rebranded itself as Marconi, that the shares were worth only a few pennies.
- Property also provides some financial flexibility, in that you can raise money against the property while still retaining ownership. If you need extra cash for any reason you can use the capital in the property asset as se\curity against which to borrow. While this is also possible for a share portfolio, the terms attached to such loans are usually much more onerous.

The disadvantages of property investment are:

- It is a much less liquid investment – you cannot buy and sell property in a single day.
- It is not easy to sell fractions of the property as you might do with a shareholding.
- The transaction costs of buying and selling property are high (survey costs, conveyancing fees, estate agent fees and stamp duty).

Residential property

Buy-to-let

Buy-to-let has become a commonplace investment decision in the last 10 years. It started to take off at the end of the 1990s in tandem with the stock market boom, and when share prices started their long fall many more investors switched their share portfolios into residential property. As with all such investment trends, the returns available today are much less than when the 'fashion' started.

The main reason to acquire 'buy-to-let' property is for capital growth. With a steadily rising market it is possible to achieve huge amounts of capital growth with only a little capital outlay from putting down a small mortgage deposit. The rental income then covers the mortgage repayments, and the increasing value of the property soon makes the mortgage an insignificant sum – leaving a substantial capital profit.

Although the residential property market is still rising (more in the north than the south of the UK these days), the 'entry price' for buy-to-lets has risen significantly in recent years. Whereas in the mid-1990s a two-bedroom flat in London cost around £60,000 and so could be bought for a 10 per cent deposit of £6,000 and a mortgage of £54,000, today the same property might cost nearly three times as much, so the investor would need to pay out £18,000 in cash and then fund a £162,000 mortgage. He or she would also be paying more in transaction charges, with higher stamp duty and professional fees.

To make a buy-to-let property work requires a regular and steady rental income. Due to the increase in supply of buy-to-let properties, tenants have found themselves with more properties to choose from, and therefore have been able to negotiate rents – to the detriment of the landlord's income. With rental incomes at best steady, and in many places falling, and with mortgage interest rates now rising, the easy returns that buy-to-let offered have now largely disappeared.

However, if you have a significant lump sum to invest and wish to keep it invested as a long-term investment, buy-to-let can still be attractive. If you can afford to put down a significant percentage as a deposit and have the mortgage only covering, say, 50 per cent of the property value, you should be able to easily make your mortgage repayments, even if interest rates increase a few points. What is more is that, barring a property crash, your investment should still appreciate to keep in line with inflation, and you might even see some excess over the mortgage payments to provide a small income stream.

Buy-to-let administration and costs

Unlike investing in securities, where you make the transaction and then have no more calls upon your time other than notifying the tax inspector of any income or gains liabilities, buy-to-let investments are small businesses. You can outsource the management to an agent who will not only find and vet tenants for you (make sure any agent is a member of ARLA, the Association of Residential Letting Agents: www.arla.co.uk) but can also manage the property. Agents will normally charge you around 10 per cent of the gross rental for finding the tenants and a further 5 per cent for managing them. On top of this they will bill you for any expenses incurred. All these charges could total 20 per cent or more of your rental income, before you even consider paying your mortgage. Of course, if there is major repair work required the cost could be much more. The good news is that all these repairs and agents fees are tax deductible – you can remove them from the rental income before working out your tax liability.

If you live close to the property you could choose to manage the property yourself, and even advertise for and select tenants yourself.

Clearly this will reduce your costs considerably, but it will also mean having to make yourself available to the tenants should problems arise – at times of their choosing, not yours.

Whichever approach you select, you must have a valid rental agreement. The standard 'assured shorthold tenancy agreement' is simple and straightforward, but it needs to be properly drawn up, and these days also requires a stamp duty payment each year. This is usually only £5 – but it is still required.

Other legislation you should be aware of is that all residential properties that have gas appliances are required to have them checked each year by a qualified CORGI engineer, who will issue a Landlord's Gas Safety Certificate. While a similar certificate is not legally required for electrical appliances and fittings, it can also be a good idea. All furniture supplied with rented accommodation must meet Furniture and Furnishings (Fire) (Safety) Regulations 1988. For more information on this, visit www.tradingstandards.gov.uk and see its leaflet, *Consumer Safety in Rented Accommodation for Tenants*, or call your local trading standards office.

Tax implications

As we noted above, many of the costs associated with buy-to-let properties are deductible as legitimate business expenses. You can also deduct a percentage of your rental income against ongoing 'wear and tear'. While general repairs to the fabric of the property and its decoration are tax deductible, any upgrading of the property is not. There is a grey line where one stops and another starts – if you are in doubt consult your accountant or an agent.

The interest charge on your mortgage is also tax deductible, but the capital repayments are not.

Overseas property

Increasing numbers of Britons are buying property abroad. For many it is a fresh start or a sunny retirement, and the house in the sun is their only property. For many others it is a second home, for holidays and renting.

It is unlikely that a foreign property will be a sound investment for financial purposes alone. If you include the 'lifestyle' benefits, it might be a sounder decision. The problems you might encounter in purchasing and renting a house in the UK are inevitably increased when you try to do the same abroad. Not only are you unlikely to be 'on site', but you may well be negotiating in a different language or through unknown intermediaries, and you will undoubtedly be conducting all these processes to a background of a different legal system and cultural processes. All these issues make buying a property abroad a more challenging experience than doing it in the UK.

It is for this reason that many people buy foreign properties in 'new build developments' where the developer is specifically attracting foreign buyers and tries to make the whole process as straightforward as possible. This is a good solution as long as the developer is trustworthy – but they frequently are not. The opportunity to beguile a sun-dazzled buyer from wet Britain is very tempting to the less scrupulous developers. Whether you choose a new development or to restore an old farmhouse in the countryside, it is your responsibility to ensure that you understand all the local laws and procedures.

Foreign property frequently is not as cheap as it first appears, either. Although the price of the building itself might be low, you may well find that local taxes and duties are levied on the purchase, and that annual service charges and rates all start to make the process an increasingly expensive one. Add to that the 'hassle factor' of having things repaired when you have returned to the UK, and worse, having to sort things out when you are on holiday there, and you may feel that it is no holiday at all.

If you are intent on renting out your overseas apartment or house to cover its running costs or even make a small amount of income, you will have to first assure yourself that there is a good demand for such holiday rentals in that area, then find a good agent or reliable locals to manage the property in your absence, and be able to pay them. If this all works successfully you will also need to arrange your rental income so that it is not taxable in both the foreign country and the UK (where overseas rental income is taxable).

As stated above, renting out a foreign property is not likely to make you rich, but it may be a way of having a foreign holiday home and keeping the costs down. The added administration that is involved will be considerable from time to time, and this should not be overlooked.

Commercial and agricultural property

If the property is not residential, it is likely to be either commercial or agricultural. Investing in these areas does not mean you have to become a shopkeeper or a farmer.

Commercial property

Commercial property covers a wide range of non-residential uses from Class A office space (as might be used for the headquarters of a large company) to single shops or light industrial developments. Class A office and large retail space is very expensive and not a realistic objective for an individual investor. However, small offices and shops do appear for sale occasionally. Often you will hear about them through word of mouth, or you can approach a local estate agent or chartered surveyor. The major difference between renting out commercial property and residential property is that the terms are usually harsher on the commercial tenant. While no standardized rental agreement exists and the contract is open to negotiation within the existing legislation, generally commercial tenants agree to longer lease terms. Leases can be any length, but 5, 10 and even 25-year leases are common. The rent will be fixed for longer periods, with reviews every few years. The commercial tenant is often obliged to keep up the fabric of the building as part of the rental contract. All these factors make the renting of small commercial property less of a hassle for the landlord as long as things run smoothly. As with all rented property, bad relations with a tenant can lead to many problems.

Agricultural property

The attraction of investing in agricultural property is the tax advantages it provides. Agricultural property currently has 100 per cent relief from inheritance tax. This is a specific benefit given by the government, rather than a loophole, to help the agricultural sector. The reason it is given is that there are so many other uncertainties and financial difficulties facing farmers. As a result buying agricultural land as an investment might well be ill-advised, although having it as a shelter for your assets at death could be worth considering. Professional advice is essential if you wish to pursue this.

Forestry

In the 1980s forestry had very advantageous tax incentives for higher rate tax payers. Much of this was abolished in 1988, but it is still beneficially treated by the tax authorities. Principal amongst these advantages are 100 per cent income tax relief on timber sales and certain forestry grants. CGT is not applied to commercial timber assets, although the underlying land is taxable. VAT is chargeable. Commercial forestry attracts 100 per cent IHT relief through business property relief scheme if it has been owned for more than two years; amenity woodland can claim agricultural property relief in certain circumstances. Ancient woodland might gain relief from IHT through its heritage value. Obviously professional advice is needed if you wish to invest in this area.

Pooled property investment – and a caution

As with securities (shares and bonds), it is possible for the investor to take advantage of the income and growth opportunities offered by property without actually building up an individual portfolio of residential, commercial or agricultural holdings. However, the FSA has very strict rules about the marketing of such funds to retail investors, and almost all property funds are only made available to institutional investors. The

FSA is considering relaxing these rules. The Chancellor in his Pre-Budget Statement in March 2004 announced a public consultation on the introduction of REITs (Real Estate Investment Trusts) in the UK in the near future.

This strictness highlights the fact that property investment is a very different animal from other security investments and should be treated with great caution.

18

Saving for children

Whether the government has realized that saving for your children is actually quite tricky, or whether the new 'child trust funds' are going to be as complex to administer as existing schemes, it is currently hard to tell. What is certain is that trying to save a significant amount of money for your own children is not as straightforward as it should be.

Child savings accounts and educating children about money

It is an important parental task to educate children how to save money and so see the effects of the personal finance motto of 'little and often and starting now'. There are a large number of child-oriented bank accounts, and National Savings and Investments (NSI) has some special rates for children's savings products. These can be useful products, although some of the specifically child-oriented bank accounts provide more in the way of gimmicky names, gifts and booklets than any real saving benefits in the form of higher rates. Indeed, some of these child accounts are less flexible (in the amounts and notice periods for withdrawals) than standard adult bank accounts.

Saving to learn the process or saving for a purpose?

These saving accounts for children are exactly that – products aimed at getting the children themselves to save money. And as most children only have very small amounts to save, they are geared to only receiving and holding relatively small amounts. If, however, your objective as a parent is not only to educate your children as to the benefits of saving, but also to build up a fund for them that they can use in early adulthood to go towards repaying some student debt, or providing a little supplementary income while studying, or as part of a deposit on their first flat – that is, a sum of money which will make a difference to their lives when they are starting out on their own – your opportunities to do so become hampered by the tax authorities.

An ideal savings period

This is frustrating, because the 18 to 25 year period that you could be putting money into a child's savings is ample time for real gains to be created from the 'little and often and starting now' approach. The compounded benefits of, say, 252 small monthly payments, that is every month between birth and a 21st birthday, are startling. If you were to put £50 aside each month from the month your child was born until his or her 21st birthday, and it grew at the cautious stock market dividend-reinvested level of 7 per cent a year, it would be worth just under £29,000 – which will always be appreciated as a 21st birthday present. If you had also put in lump sums of larger amounts from time to time, this figure would be even larger. If your child reinvested this amount in a high-income-earning product while he or she was at university, say, he or she could receive perhaps £1,450 income from the investment to reduce his/her loan needs, and still have a nice lump sum for a deposit on a house or starting a business or whatever, after leaving university.

The problems

There are two problems with this model. The first one is that you must be over 18 to invest in most pooled funds (investment trusts, OEICs and so on). If you, the parent, have a fund which you are keeping separate from the rest of your finances specifically for your child or children, the tax authorities, not totally unreasonably, do not trust you enough not use some of its gains for your own purposes – so they will tax you as if the gains are your own (which legally they would be).

The second problem with this model is that even if you could separate your child's fund from your own in some way, any money you have given directly to your child that produces an income of over £100 a year is taxed as if it is your own. So the dividend income would begin to be taxed at the parents' higher rate of tax maybe as soon as there was £3,000 of capital. This would severely diminish the dividend reinvestment amounts and so slow the growth of the fund.

Partial solutions

You can create a trust to separate the money (see Chapter 13). However, as noted in that chapter these are often expensive to run. The simplest, and cheapest, is a 'bare trust', but this will only exist until the child's 18th birthday, after which the money becomes his or her own, and if the capital is gifted by the parent the £100 income rule still operates, so the income will then be taxable at the parents' rate. Essentially this is no different from the money being in the child's name all the way through. However, the act of the trust being wound up, and previously 'untouchable' money being 'released' to an 18-year-old, might be more temptation than he or she can bear! And those carefully saved assets could all disappear on something less worthy than had originally been intended.

Other more complicated trusts are only really suitable for large lump sum investments of considerable amounts (£50,000 upwards), as the administration costs are usually high in terms of the income any smaller trusts would generate, and so these are not suitable for the average parent.

The child trust fund

The government has announced that all children born on or after 1 September 2002, who receive child benefit (which is the vast majority of British children), will have a child trust fund (CTF) set up for them by the government. Not only will they have this tax-efficient vehicle set up for them, but the government will also kick it off with an initial amount of £250 and a further (as yet to be decided how large) amount on their seventh birthday.

The CTFs will appear for the first time in April 2005. All children born between 1 September 2002 and that date will receive a voucher for £250 that can be invested in a CTF. The CTFs can be accessed through a financial institution that provides them, in the same way as ISAs are now provided. The parent can present the voucher and start the CTF for the child. If the voucher is not invested within one year, the government itself will start a CTF on the child's behalf.

Once the CTF is started, the child's family can invest a further £1,200 a year in the fund each year until the child is 18. Any income the fund generates will be reinvested and is tax-free. There is no restriction on where the additional investments can be provided from: that is, parents, grandparents, other relations and friends are all free to provide the money up to the annual limit.

Voucher amounts

Children from low-income families that receive child tax credit may receive a further £250 initial amount in their CTF. Children who were born before April 2005 may receive larger voucher amounts to reflect the lost growth incurred between their birth and the CTF being set up.

CTF costs

The CTF is part of the government's scheme for savings. Providers of CTFs will therefore be expected to offer CAT standard CTFs (see page 293 for an explanation of CAT standards). However, at the time of writing the details of these are unknown, except that unlike with pensions where management fees are capped at 1 per cent, it looks as if with CTFs the cap will be at 1.5 per cent of funds. The reason is that the amounts involved in a CTF are much smaller than those in a pension.

As with ISAs, CTFs will be able to be invested in a range of different asset types. You will also be able to invest your child's CTF in funds that do not meet the CAT standards. As with pensions this does not necessarily mean they are bad value, just that they may be more specialized and therefore more costly to run, but perhaps potentially more lucrative. For most people, though, the CAT standard products are likely to be the best long-term choices.

Children born before 1 September 2002

For families that have some children born before 1 September 2002 cut-off date and younger children born after it, the older children do miss out. The government states:

> "You can still save for these children's futures too. There is a wide range of accounts on the market for children. And although these accounts are not tax exempt as such, in most cases the income will be free of tax and where that is the case the accounts will not suffer tax. This is because children (like adults) are entitled to a personal allowance (£4615* for the current tax year). This means that they do not have to pay tax if their taxable income is less than £4615 per annum."

*Note that the personal allowance is now £4745 for 2004/05

This is slightly disingenuous, as 9 times out of 10 it is going to be the child's parents who provide the original investment, so the £100 income threshold will come into operation, as mentioned above, and not the personal income threshold of £4,745. A partial solution is probably to set up a bare trust for any children born before 1 September 2002, as that is effectively what the CTF amounts to. Although the income will still be taxable at the parents' rate if it produces more than £100 per year, it does remove the money from many IHT liabilities.

The CTF at this stage looks like a good solution to the problem of saving significant amounts for children, except that it may split siblings into CTF 'haves' and 'have nots', and that the money becomes available at 18, as with a bare trust, with the same problems that opens up.

Other child savings options

Savings

If we use the same criteria to differentiate between savings and invest-ments as in Chapters 15 and 16, in the short-term, low-risk savings category there is a wide range of savings products available for children. Often it is better to open adult savings accounts in a child's name rather than children's savings accounts, which often focus more on gimmicks and gifts than on a good interest rate. The adult-oriented accounts may give better flexibility and rates.

NSI offers three products recommended for children. Child bonus bonds are bonds that anyone can buy for a child. They come in bonds of £25 that pay a fixed rate of interest over five years. (They can be redeemed early, but with an interest payment penalty.) A child can only hold a maximum of £1,000 of these bonds. The interest is tax-free. The other two products are index-linked savings certificates and premium bonds: see Chapter 15 for more details.

Investment

Children cannot have ISAs – you have to be 16 before you can open one (which is a step forward as before 2001 it was 18!). A similar alternative are tax-exempt friendly societies. Friendly societies are rather unglam-orous financial institutions these days – but none the worse for that. They can offer tax-exempt savings products for children, in which regu-larly deposited sums are invested in either a cash-based account or a shares-based fund. The limitation is that you can only invest up to £25 per month for each child, and the deposits must be made continuously over several years, otherwise the tax advantages are lost. Visit www.friendlysocieties.co.uk for a list of them or call the Association of Friendly Societies for more information on 0207 397 9550.

You can of course invest for children through other adult-type products as discussed above (investment trusts and OEICs), but there are real tax disadvantages for both the parent and the child. Alternatively you can often buy shares and funds directly and hold them as a 'designated plan' for a child. The tax liabilities will remain those of the parent or original investor (not the child) for both income and capital gains, and should the original investor die before the fund is transferred to the child, the asset remains part of the original investor's estate. However, it does keep the holding neatly separate from your own portfolio.

Stakeholder pensions remarkably are available to children – with all the associated tax advantages. (Remember that the government adds basic rate tax back to the first £3,600 of annual pension contributions regardless of whether the stakeholder pays any income tax or not. See Chapter 4 for more information on stakeholder pensions.) It is perfectly possible for parents to have built up a private stakeholder pension for their child by the time he or she leaves school, which would pay out somewhere around £25,000 come the child's retirement age. However, it is more likely that your children will prefer money they can reach before they are 65! This is long-term financial planning at its most extreme – although one effect of using the stakeholder pension scheme for your children is that the money they should be putting into their pension when they are in their twenties and thirties can be reduced a little if they already have a significant pension fund, allowing them to use it for other things.

Conclusion

As we can see there are plenty of options for saving for your child – and using the child's personal tax allowances (£4,745 threshold on income and £8,200 CGT, tax year 2004/05) can allow for significant tax-free investing, as he or she is unlikely to have any other forms of income. However, these tax allowances are severely diminished if the original investment money comes from the child's parent. A child would most likely need a share portfolio of over £150,000 to achieve an income of over £4,745, and even then he or she would only be taxed at the basic dividend rate of 20 per cent.

If, however, the initial funds have come from the child's parent, the child only needs a portfolio of £3,000 to earn over £100 income, and above that rate all further income is taxed with the parent – possibly at the higher rate of 40 per cent.

This means you must find generous grandparents, uncles, aunts or godparents and friends to provide the money. Note that giving the money to one of these people for them to reinvest is still considered to be giving the money yourself.

Failing this the simplest solution has been to set up a bare trust as a tax-efficient vehicle to put any significant savings in. With the arrival of the CTF a simpler and more straightforward system appears to be on the way – at least for children born after 1 September 2002.

For smaller sums of money the NSI products and friendly society accounts are useful from the earliest months. When the child is old enough to begin to understand the concept of saving, opening a simple savings account may be a good educational tool.

19

Tax

We have tried to outline tax-efficient ways of dealing with your personal finances throughout this book. We believe that the best way to keep your tax exposure to a minimum is to deal with each separate financial product or action on its own merits, balancing the financial costs and benefits of each product or process you are interested in as and when you deal with them. Obviously, tax implications will be part of this procedure.

The truth is that for most individuals the opportunity to create hugely advantageous tax-reducing schemes is very small. While we may aspire to clever 'offshore companies' and 'tax trusts' the reality is that the costs of administering such schemes often outweigh the tax benefits. These types of schemes only really work when the sums involved have at least four but probably five or six noughts attached to them. As a result the average taxpayer is limited to using well-known tax-free schemes, such as ISAs or friendly societies, or to maximizing his or her annual personal allowances. These better known schemes are in essence created by the government, and they are usually limited to maximum annual amounts, rarely more than a few thousand pounds of capital – so saving only a few hundred pounds of tax, at most, each year.

That said, we should still make the most of them – although many people do not. The compounded benefits of these savings over a number of years can make a real difference to the long-term totals.

The Scottish judge, Lord Clyde, Lord President of the Court of Session in Edinburgh, stated in a leading case in 1929:

...no man in this country is under the smallest obligation, moral or other, so to arrange his legal relations to his business... as to enable the Inland Revenue to put the largest possible shovel into his stores.... The taxpayer is... entitled to be astute to prevent, so far as he honestly can, the depletion of his means by the Inland Revenue.

This principle, that we all have a right to minimize our tax liabilities within the remit of the law, still stands. It is a foolish person who either through idleness or ignorance then allows the Inland Revenue to take more than its fair share. This in no way suggests that we should evade paying tax: tax evasion is illegal (that is, hiding money from the Inland Revenue that you should rightfully be paying), but taking measures to minimize what you should pay is perfectly legal – and within your rights.

Because we have so little room to manoeuvre when it comes to paying taxes, many of us just close our eyes to them. This works to the politicians' advantage as many of us feel we pay too much, but do not know enough to make a fuss about it. The flip side of this argument is that without taxes the government would not be able to provide the huge number of services it does provide – and as road and rail infrastructure, hospital demand and procedures and educational requirements all continue to need higher levels of expenditure (not to mention defence, social security, foreign aid and all the other branches of government) the need for a tax input never seems to get any smaller.

On the basis that you can deal with things better, the more you know about them, this chapter outlines the basics of many taxes not already dealt with earlier in the book.

Benjamin Franklin's famous line that 'in this world nothing can be said to be certain, except death and taxes' is as true today as it was in 1789. For the most part we can do nothing to avoid everyday taxes. The current Chancellor of the Exchequer, Gordon Brown, has been particularly effective at slipping in taxes that we do not notice, although from time to time he has overstepped the mark and uproar has ensued.

Indirect taxes

Some indirect taxes that we pay all the time include:

- Unleaded petrol: road fuel duty is just under 50p per litre plus 17.5 per cent VAT. So the price of a 75p litre of unleaded petrol breaks down to 11p VAT, 50p duty and 14p to the petrol company.
- Spirits: these are taxed by their alcohol content. Each litre of pure alcohol carries £19.56 duty, so a 70 cl bottle of 40 per cent whisky will carry a charge of £5.48 duty, but a 60 per cent whisky has £8.22 duty. VAT will be charged on this, and the distillers charge as well.
- Wine: is taxed according to volume. A standard litre of wine (alcohol between 5.5 and 15 per cent) has duty of £1.63 per litre, or £1.22 per 75cl bottle. Again VAT is also charged. Note that you will therefore pay less duty as a percentage for more expensive wine!
- Beer: is taxed by volume. Beer attracts just over 12p per litre of duty, or 7p per pint. Again VAT is added.
- Cigarettes: have a complicated charge, of just under 10p per cigarette plus 22 per cent of the retail price, again plus VAT.
- Other tobacco: cigars, hand-rolled tobacco and other tobacco have duties applied by weight per kilo.
- Insurance premium tax: introduced in 1994 at 2.5 per cent it has steadily increased to 5 per cent, except for travel and some insurance for vehicles and domestic/electrical appliances where it is levied at 17.5 per cent.
- Air passenger duty: all flight departures (domestic and foreign) from the UK have a tax applied per ticket. Most European destinations attract a £10 charge, and intercontinental flights attract a £40 charge. (Some airports have reduced charges to attract business – only Inverness is free!) VAT is applied to this, so a 1p promotional ticket will cost you £11.76.
- Vehicle excise duty (also known as vehicle road tax or the road fund licence): nearly all vehicle owners must pay this annual charge. Most private cars are now licensed according to their carbon dioxide emittant level. The charge currently ranges from £55 to £165. It is

administered by the DVLA, a part of the Department for Transport. For more detailed information contact 0870 240 0010 or visit www.dvla.gov.uk.

▨ Television licence: this is one of the very few 'hypothecated' taxes levied in the UK, where the money raised goes to a specific activity – in this case the BBC. From April 2004 the standard television licence costs £121 a year. It is collected by TV Licensing, part of the BBC. For more details call it on 0870 241 6468 or visit www.tv-l.co.uk.

▨ Stamp duties: when certain items are purchased the government applies stamp duties. The largest of these is when purchasing a house, when different rates are levied depending on the price of the house:

  – Up to £60,000: no levy.
  – £60,001 to £250,000: 1 per cent of purchase price.
  – £250,001 to £500,000: 3 per cent of purchase price.
  – Over £500,000: 4 per cent of purchase price.

Stamp duty is also applied to buying shares, at 0.5 per cent of the purchase price, to the nearest £5.

Rental leases also attract stamp duty. It is levied according to the length of lease and any premium paid, and the rates range from £5 to 24 per cent of the rent.

▨ VAT: as we have noted above VAT is often applied to goods that have already been taxed, so it is effectively a tax on a tax. The standard rate is currently 17.5 per cent, but certain goods attract different rates. Some are zero rated: newspapers, books, children's clothes and basic foods.

Tax Freedom Day

The Adam Smith Institute, a right-wing think tank, monitors how many days each year 'we are working for the government' – that is, what percentage of our average income goes to the government through both direct taxes (income, National Insurance (NI), capital gains tax (CGT), inheritance tax (IHT) and corporation tax) and indirect taxes (the list above and others). It expresses this percentage in terms of days of the year. In 2004 it calculated that we will be 'working for the government' until 30 May: that is all the money you earn up to that date in the calendar year will be paid in taxes – and all the money in the rest of the year is yours! Go to www.taxfreedomday.co.uk for more information.

Direct taxes

There are four central-government-levied direct taxes people are likely to face at some point: income tax, NI, CGT and IHT. In addition to these most adults have to pay council tax, which is levied by local authorities.

Income tax and self-assessment

For the vast majority of taxpayers in the UK, contact with the Inland Revenue is very limited. If you are employed and have no other source of income, your employer will deal with your income tax liabilities through the PAYE (pay as you earn) scheme. Your main responsibility is to check that the correct tax code is applied to your earnings (see the box). If your tax code is wrong you might have the wrong amount of tax deducted from your pay.

Income tax numbers and codes

There are three numbers that are applied to you to enable the Inland Revenue to correctly identify you and work out your tax liabilities and benefits:

- Your tax reference number, a 10 digit number that is unique to you, although it can change if you move tax offices. (It will be given to you the first time you make a tax return.)
- Your NI number, an alphanumeric number, typically in the format AB 12 34 56 C, which is unique to you. It is used by the Inland Revenue and the Department of Work and

Pensions (DWP). It is the closest thing to a national identity number that exists in the UK, and stays the same throughout your life. (If you do not have an NI number you can apply for one from your nearest Social Security office.)

▓ Your tax code, an alphanumeric code. The format can change depending on your tax status. This identifies your tax status, from which your tax calculations can be worked. It will change as frequently as your status changes. It is used by your employer to deduct the correct amount of tax from your pay. If you think it is wrong you should tell the Inland Revenue straight away.

The main factors that affect your tax code are:

▓ whether you are single, married or separated;
▓ whether you have children;
▓ if you are receiving a pension;
▓ your income level.

If your tax code is a number followed by a letter, the number is used to work out the tax due on your income from your employment or pension. The letter simply shows how it should be adjusted following any changes announced by the Chancellor. It does not affect the amount of tax you pay.

This is what the letters mean:

▓ L is for a tax code with the basic personal allowance.
▓ P is for a tax code with the full personal allowance for those aged 65–74.
▓ V is for a tax code with the full personal allowance for those aged 65–74 plus the full married allowance for those born before 6 April 1935 and aged under 75 who are estimated to be liable at the basic rate of tax.
▓ Y is for a tax code with the full personal allowance for those aged 75 or over.

▪ T is used if there are any other items the Inland Revenue needs to review in your tax code, or if you ask it not to use any of the other tax code letters listed above.

If your tax code is a letter 'K' followed by a number, it means that the total allowances in your code are less than the total deductions to be taken away from your allowances.

The codes BR, D0 and 0T are mainly used where you have a second source of income and all your tax allowances have been included in the tax code applied to your first or main source of income. They simply tell your employer, pension payer or benefit office how much tax to deduct.

These codes can change slightly each year. (The explanation above is for tax year 2003/4.)

Your tax code is notified to you in a coding notice, form P2. Further explanations can be found in the leaflet *Understanding Your Tax Code* (P3) from the Inland Revenue (www.inlandrevenue.gov.uk/pdfs/p3_2003.pdf).

The government requires those who are self-employed, freelance, have capital gains to declare, have second sources of income or are higher rate taxpayers to fill in a self-assessment tax return each year. Whether you have to fill-in a self-assessment tax return or not, it is important that you keep safely all relevant forms and records, in case you need to fill in a return at a later date. The Inland Revenue publishes a leaflet, *A General Guide to keeping Records*, which can also be found online at www.inlandrevenue.gov.uk/pdfs/sabk4.htm.

The main records an employee receives from his or her employer are:

▪ Form P60, a certificate your employer gives you after 5 April (the end of the tax year) showing details of pay and tax deducted. Your employer must give this to you by 31 May of the relevant year.
▪ Form P45 (Part 1A), a certificate from an employer showing details of pay and tax from a job you have left.

- Form P160 (Part 1A) is the form you are given when you retire and go on to a pension paid by your former employer.
- Your payslips or pay statements (you will also need certificates or other proof of any foreign tax you have paid on your employment income).
- A note of the amount of any tips or gratuities, and details of any other taxable receipts or benefits not included in forms P60, P45 (Part 1A) or P160 (Part 1A). You should record these as soon as possible after you receive them, and not simply estimate them at the end of the year.
- Forms P11D or P9D or equivalent information from all the employers you have worked for during the year, showing any benefits in kind and expenses payments given to you, such as company car and mileage, health insurance or tied accommodation. Your employer must provide you with these forms by 6 July after the end of the tax year.
- Information on any share options awarded or exercised or any share participation arrangements.
- Certificates for any Taxed Award Schemes in which you have participated.
- Information from any person or company, other than your employer, who provided you with benefits in kind in connection with your employment.
- Information about any redundancy or termination payment.

It is also sensible to keep your forms P2 and P2K (PAYE coding notices), as they may help you to keep track of any earlier underpayments of tax that are being collected through PAYE.

You must notify the Inland Revenue of any potential tax liability within three months of becoming self-employed or by 5 October if you have other taxable income, such as rental income or capital gains. You will then be sent a self-assessment (SA) form to fill in. This must be handed in with a cheque for the appropriate amount of tax by 31 January of the year after the tax year you are filing for. That is, for tax you are liable for in the tax year 5 April 2003 to 4 April 2004, your tax return must be handed in (with payment) by 31 January 2005.

People with large and regular tax bills are expected to 'pay on account': that is, they pay half in January and half in July. However, the January sum is a forward payment against the current year's liabilities and the July payment occurs after the tax year has finished. The next January any extra tax or rebate required to correct those payments can be added in or deducted, at the same time as tax is paid for the succeeding tax year.

If you are late with your payments you will be fined £100, plus 5.5 per cent interest if you still have not paid by the end of February. Further fines can be levied for even later payments and also for non-disclosure of income.

If you fill in the appropriate figures by the end of September preceding the January deadline, the Inland Revenue will calculate your tax liability for you. Alternatively, if you fill in the SA form online (for which you must apply to the Inland Revenue for a user code: go to http://www.inlandrevenue.gov.uk/sa/) you can have the calculation made instantly. Otherwise you must do the calculations yourself or employ someone to do them for you. Use a qualified tax adviser.

The Inland Revenue will check your calculations and can inspect your return up to a year after it has been made, after which you can consider the tax year closed. You will be notified if an inspection is being carried out. Only a small percentage of returns are inspected, and most of those are clarifications of particular parts of the return rather than the whole thing. There were only 400 serious tax fraud investigations in the last tax year.

Reducing your income tax

The self-employed, company directors and shareholders of small companies are probably in the best position to put in place individual schemes and processes to reduce their tax burden. The manner in which they pay themselves, through salaries, bonuses, or dividends can be carefully balanced to minimize the tax liability, and the judicious sharing of costs and expenses through such firms can also help. Each circumstance will be different, so you should consult a professional tax adviser.

For the rest of the working population the opportunities are reduced. If you are married and only one partner works it is tax-efficient to transfer any income-generating assets (shares, bonds or rented properties) into the name of the spouse who has little or no taxable income, thus utilizing his or her tax-free threshold or lower tax rates.

Make sure you use your annual ISA allowances to build up tax-free investment funds.

If you work from home be sure to deduct any legitimate business expenses from your house bills. See Kogan Page's *A Guide To Working For Yourself.*

If you are in doubt about your tax return you should consult a qualified tax adviser, such as a qualified accountant. Contact the Chartered Institute of Taxation to find a tax specialist. See www.tax.org.uk or call 020 7235 9381.

National Insurance

See page 78 for basic NI information.

Capital Gains Tax

CGT is charged against any profit you have made from selling an asset. You must declare it in a self-assessment form, even if you have no other tax liabilities or if your income tax is dealt with through PAYE.

Currently individuals have a tax-free capital gains allowance of £8,200 in the tax year 2004/5. Any amount 'gained' above this must be declared. Note it is only the gain that is taxed, not the whole amount paid. So if you bought an asset worth £15,000 and sold it for £20,000, that would be a gain of £5,000 only – and if that was your only gain in that tax year, you would have no CGT to pay as it is less than your £8,200 allowance. If on the other hand you had already made gains in that tax year of £4,000, you would only have £4,200 left in your allowance, so £800 would be liable for CGT at 40 per cent. This means you have to pay the Inland Revenue 40 per cent of £800, or £320.

Some assets are exempt from CGT, the main one currently being your principal residence. Calculation of CGT can be more complex than at first appearance, as the Inland Revenue allows some assets to be index-linked and offers relief on others if they have been held for a long time. If you are in any doubt contact a qualified tax adviser.

As with income tax, if you are married and one spouse has not used their CGT allowance, then as spouses can transfer assets freely between each other, you could transfer the asset before selling it. If in doubt seek professional advice from a tax adviser.

Inheritance tax

See Chapter 13 for details on this.

Council tax

Council tax is levied by and paid to your local authority. The council tax has become more controversial recently as local councils have tended to raise the tax by well above the rate of inflation each year. The Audit Commission in its report on the 12.9 per cent average council tax increase of 2003/4, reported in January 2004 that:

> The increases were caused by a variety of factors, but there were two principal reasons. First, spending by councils went up by more than had been allowed for in the grant settlement. Second, the effect of the grant regime – whereby 75 per cent of funding comes from central government – was that each 1 per cent councils added to spending above amounts allowed for in the grant settlement increased council tax by 4 per cent.

The government has indicated that it might change the structure of council tax but has publicized no actual proposals. The Liberal Democrats propose a local income tax, which they say would be fairer, but their opponents criticize it as being too simplistic.

The council tax is levied through eight tax bands. Houses are allocated to one of these bands on the basis of their value when the tax was introduced in 1993. Although the bands bear no relevance to the real current value of houses, they should still roughly indicate the proportionate value of the house compared with other houses in the district. While the band applied to your house remains the same year-in and year-out, the tax applicable to that band can increase every year. Council tax is often considered unfair, as pensioners and people on low incomes who happen to live in larger houses, either inherited or since increased in value due to external factors, have found themselves suddenly burdened with extremely high council tax bills.

Discounts are usually available for single-occupancy houses, disabled people, students, members of the armed forces and so on. Contact your local council for details specific to your area.

For general information on council tax contact the Valuations Office: visit www.voa.gov.uk, or call 020 7506 1700 to obtain details of your nearest office.

Tax planning – making the most of your allowances

We have already noted that individual SA tax returns must be notified to the Inland Revenue by 5 October and handed in by 31 January. There are a number of other dates that you should keep an eye on.

The tax year runs from 5 April of one year to 4 April of the next year. This means that to receive your tax-free allowances and other annual entitlements you must complete your transactions by the end of 4 April. Important amongst these are:

- Your *ISA investments*. Make sure you have used up your £7,000 (in 2004/5; £5,000 thereafter) annual ISA investment entitlement by 4 April each year.
- Those people entitled to make *private pension contributions* (whether stakeholder or not) must have invested their money in their pension scheme by 4 April. Remember that you can put in between 17.5 and 40 per cent (depending on your age) of your best year's salary from the last six years, including the current one.
- The tax-efficient investment vehicles, such as *venture capital trusts* and *enterprise investment schemes,* work on tax year bases. If you have

invested in them or wish to do so, take action before the end of the tax year.

- If you intend to make *Gift Aid* donations and are a higher rate taxpayer, remember that they can be offset against your earned income.
- Your annual allowance for *CGT* will be lost if you do not use it in the tax year. 'Bed and breakfasting', where you sell shares late one day and buy them back early the next, so taking your gain, and restarting your base value at the new higher price, was made illegal in 1998. You must now leave 30 days between sale and repurchase to claim the CGT allowance. But you can vary the process by buying a similar stock or 'bed and ISA-ing' your holding, where you sell and then rebuy in an ISA wrapper. Remember that this process still incurs buying and selling costs and stamp duty.
- Finally you can lessen your future *IHT* burden by fully utilizing the tax-free annual gift allowance, currently £3,000 per giver (if you did not use it in the previous year you can double it to £6,000) to pass on money to your children. The £250 gift allowance per person receiving per tax year to any number of individuals can also be used.

For those people with small businesses, particularly property rentals, there is a range of allowances on capital expenditure, office equipment and so on. Refer to your tax adviser or a small business guide for more details.

20

Complaining

Dealing with finance is often complicated, and mistakes will happen now and again. Whether this is a computer clerk inputting the wrong number, a document going astray, or a more serious problem such as poor advice being given, it is up to the individual whose money it is to keep an overall check that his or her assets are being looked after properly.

If you do spot a mistake, you must notify the organization concerned immediately. If you feel you have a more serious problem, whether that is in the advice you have been given, the manner in which you have been treated or something else, you should report it to the organization concerned straight away. It is your right to do so.

Having taken the problem up with the organization concerned, you might still feel that the issues you have raised have not been dealt with adequately. It is at this stage that you should consider taking a complaint further.

The finance industry in the UK is very tightly regulated. The regulatory structure is becoming simpler, although the regulations themselves are getting more complicated.

The FSA: the regulator – not the judge

The FSA regulates the widest range of financial services in the UK, but not all of them. The FSA has four main objectives, the third of which is:

> *Securing the right degree of protection for consumers.* Vetting at entry aims to allow only those firms and individuals satisfying the necessary criteria (including honesty, competence and financial soundness) to engage in regulated activity. Once authorized, we expect firms and individuals to maintain particular standards set by us. We monitor how far firms and individuals are meeting these standards. Where serious problems arise we investigate and, if appropriate, discipline or prosecute those responsible for conducting financial business outside the rules. We can also use our powers to restore funds to consumers.

The FSA supervises:

- deposit takers (banks and building societies);
- the insurance industry including Lloyd's of London;
- investment firms (fund managers, investment banks, UK stock-brokers, independent financial advisers and so on);
- pension providers;
- mortgage providers.

But while the FSA writes the rules and oversees that firms adhere to them, it does not get involved with individual complaints.

The Financial Ombudsman: the judge

An ombudsman is a government official whose role is to investigate complaints and mediate a fair settlement between two parties. The Financial Ombudsman is an independent arbitrator between individuals and financial firms. You do not have to use the Ombudsman service, you are always at liberty to take the matter to court if you so wish. However, the Ombudsman is a less aggressive and usually more effective way to resolve a complaint, and critically it is free to consumers. You do not have to accept the Ombudsman's decision, but if you do accept it, it is binding on both you and the other party.

The Financial Ombudsman can intervene on all matters that the FSA regulates. The service lists the following as its areas of competence:

- banking services;
- credit cards issued by banks and building societies;
- endowment policies;
- financial and investment advice;
- health and loan protection insurance;
- household and buildings insurance;
- investment portfolio management;
- life assurance;
- mortgages;
- motor insurance;
- personal pension plans;
- private medical insurance;
- savings plans and accounts;
- stocks and shares;
- travel insurance;
- unit trusts and income bonds.

It also points out that they cannot intervene in matters concerning:

- personal loan and credit-card providers that are not banks or building societies;
- most general insurance brokers;
- most mortgage brokers;
- firms' proper use of their 'commercial judgement' (for example, deciding whether to give someone a loan, what insurance premium to charge, or what surrender value or with-profits bonus to pay);
- the actions of someone else's insurance company (for example, after a car accident);
- the way an investment has performed.

You must always have tried to sort out the problem with the company concerned before the Financial Ombudsman can become involved.

To complain to the Financial Ombudsman you must follow a set procedure. See the box for the suggested way to complain to the firm, and then what the Financial Ombudsman might be able to do for you.

Financial Ombudsman advice on complaining

Complaining to the firm

1. It is usually best to complain to the firm in writing, but if you phone, ask for the name of the person you speak to. Keep a note of this information, with the date and time of your call – and what was said. You may need to refer to this later.

2. Try to stay calm and polite, however angry or upset you are. You are more likely to explain your complaint clearly and effectively if you can stay calm.

3. If possible, start by contacting the person you originally dealt with. If they cannot help, say you want to take matters further. Ask for details of the name or job title of the person who will be handling your complaint, and for details of the firm's complaints procedure.

4. When you write a letter of complaint, write 'complaint' at the top. Set out the facts as clearly as possible and keep your letter short and to the point. Say why you are not happy and what you want the firm to do about it. This will make it easier for the firm to start putting things right.

5. Write down the facts in a logical order and stick to what is relevant. Remember to include important details like your customer number or your policy or account number. Put these details at the top of your letter.

6. Remember to enclose copies of any relevant documents that you believe back up your case. Keep a copy of any letters between you and the firm. You may need to refer to them later.

Involving the Financial Ombudsman

If you are not satisfied with the response from the firm you can then approach the Ombudsman. You will need to send it your complaint on its own complaint form. You can get one of these by calling 0845 080 1800 or downloading it from the Web site www.financial-ombudsman.org.uk.

The Ombudsman will consider your complaint. If it feels it can help it will try to resolve the problem informally, and failing that will make a formal approach to the firm requesting specific details and paperwork as appropriate. Normally the procedure is completed within six months. The Ombudsman will keep you informed during that time. Most complaints are settled informally by the service; however, if a formal procedure is taken, a final decision will be made by an ombudsman (who has a legal position, rather than the complaints service as a whole) and his decision is final.

Generally you must make your initial complaint to the Financial Ombudsman within six months of your last correspondence with the firm you are complaining about. Anyone can make the complaint to the Ombudsman, either you or someone on your behalf. You do not need a solicitor to go to the Ombudsman. For more information contact the Financial Ombudsman service and ask for its leaflet *Your Complaint and the Ombudsman*, or go to its Web site.

Consumer credit complaints

As was noted above, the FSA and the Financial Ombudsman do not get involved in cases dealing with loans or credit not provided by a bank or building society. The provision of loans and credit by other organizations, including both credit brokers and retail firms, is controlled by the Office of Fair Trading (OFT).

Any business that offers its customers credit or loans must have a Consumer Credit Licence provided by the OFT. The OFT will only issue a licence if it considers that person to be a 'fit person'. In assessing fitness it will:

> take into account anything we consider to be relevant to a person's fitness, in particular evidence of: fraud, dishonesty, violence, discrimination, breaches of consumer protection law, or business practices that are oppressive or improper (even if they don't break the law). If we receive evidence that a licensee is not a fit person after a licence is issued, we can revoke, suspend or change the terms of the licence.

However, as with the FSA, the OFT is the regulator, not the judge. The OFT does not take up individual consumers' complaints. There is no statutory body that deals with loan and credit disagreements. If you have a complaint or problem with a loan or credit product (other than from a bank or building society) you should take it up with a solicitor or the Trading Standards Service. Alternatively you can ask the local Citizens Advice Bureau to intervene.

Citizens Advice Bureaux work through local offices, so you must get their number from your local telephone directory or go to www.citizensadvice.org.uk/cabdir.ihtml.

The Trading Standards Authority is the national umbrella for each local authority's trading standards service. Individual consumer complaints must be handled by the local authority trading standards service. Its number will be in the telephone directory, possibly listed under the name of the local authority. If you have access to the Internet you can get the details of your local trading standards service by going to www.tradingstandards.gov.uk.

Trade associations

Almost all sectors of the finance industry, especially those dealing with retail consumers, have trade associations. We have tried to highlight the relevant associations throughout this book. Most trade associations have strict codes of conduct their members must adhere to, in addition to any legal regulations. If you believe you have a legitimate complaint it can often be helpful to contact a trade association (if the firm belongs to one) to see what action it advises. The threat of involving a trade association may prompt action from otherwise awkward firms, and is less significant a step than involving more legally empowered bodies such as the Ombudsman or trading standards.

On this basis it is always worth noting whether a firm you are planning to deal with is a member of a recognized trade body before you get involved with it.

21

Using a PC and the Internet

If you have access to a computer and are happy with using it, keeping track of your personal finances can be made simpler. With access to the Internet this process is made even better, and an untold range of useful services and information can open up to you.

At its simplest a computer can help you file any correspondence you send to companies and keep records. With the use of spreadsheets you can track your own accounts and portfolios, and work out future values of products more easily. However, all these things can be done without a computer as well – if not necessarily as neatly or efficiently.

The computer really comes into its own with the use of personal finance software. For many people, keeping an overall track of their finances is made much simpler, and the information is presented much more clearly in graphs and charts that show how much of their income they are spending where, what rates of growth they are getting and so on, through the use of these comprehensive programs. The most commonly used are Microsoft's Money program and Quicken from Intuit. There are also packages that focus specifically on tax matters, such as Tax Calc, also from Intuit. Note that these packages need to be updated each year to have the correct tax information on them – and clearly if you are an UK resident you need to purchase the UK editions.

The Inland Revenue can provide you with an online self-assessment return for free. See www.inlandrevenue.gov.uk/sa/.

All these software packages work best if you can update prices and information through an Internet connection. With access to the Internet, researching and controlling your finances is taken to a different level of ease and sophistication.

Internet research

Whether you are trying to compare savings rates at different banks and building societies, find the cheapest car insurance or discover a historical share price, the Internet can help you source this information in a matter of minutes, where it might have taken you hours or even days before.

The Internet is full of financial resource providers. As with all things provided on the Internet, the variation in quality of the information provided can be enormous from one site to another. Some sites are very specialist, focusing on just one aspect of financial products; others are designed for professionals rather than consumers; others present information that really is only there as promotion for their products; and some are excellently impartial and clear. Also many sites are not relevant to the UK, although they appear in UK search engine findings. It is always worth checking to see if the site's figures are quoted in dollars or pounds, or if any contact telephone numbers are described as 'toll free', which would indicate it is a US site rather than a UK one. Any site that has a .co.uk suffix is fairly likely to be UK-specific.

Other than looking at the address, there is little way of telling whether a site is going to be useful other than by visiting it. It is usually pretty easy to spot if the site is going to be impartial or sales-led once you have got there, but it always pays to be critical at this early stage.

By going to official sites you can be reasonably certain of impartiality. Some of the best official sites offering financial information in the UK are government and trade association sites. We list a few below:

www.fsa.gov.uk (Financial Services Authority).
www.oft.gov.uk (Office of Fair Trading).
www.financial-ombudsman.org.uk (Financial Ombudsman Service).
www.thepensionservice.gov.uk (Pension Service).
www.bsa.org.uk (Building Societies Association).
www.bba.org.uk (British Bankers Association).

www.investmentfunds.org.uk (Investment Management Association).

www.apcims.org (Association of Private Client Investment Managers and Stockbrokers).

www.nationaldebtline.co.uk (National Debt Line).

Listed below are some general financial information sites that may be useful to you:

www.ft.com (The *Financial Times's* site).

http://news.bbc.co.uk/1/hi/business/your_money/default.stm (an unwieldy address for the BBC's straightforward online personal finance section).

http://uk.finance/yahoo.com (the ISP Yahoo's site for current financial data).

www.fool.co.uk (a down-to-earth and slightly irreverent site with impartial advice: note that it is easily confused with the US site at www.fool.com).

http://money.msn.co.uk (Microsoft's UK finance site, which has a range of online calculators to work out your likely mortgage and other loan payments, tax payment estimates, pension estimators and other such planning tools).

http://money.guardian.co.uk (the *Guardian* newspaper's money information site).

www.hemscott.net (independent financial data provider).

There are many financial product comparison sites. The ones below are well known and widely used:

www.moneysupermarket.com (independent financial data provider).

www.moneyfacts.co.uk (independent financial data provider).

www.moneynet.co.uk (independent financial data provider).

www.moneyextra.com (run by Chase de Vere financial advisers).

Internet banking

Internet banking evolved out of the concept of branchless telephone banking, with the Nationwide offering the first UK Internet banking facility in 1997. Now nearly all banks offer an online facility of one type or another. This may be connected to your normal account at a branch, to allow you to manage your money from home (or anywhere else), or it may be an account only accessible over the Internet.

The online access to normal branch accounts enables you to transfer money between your own accounts and to other people's accounts, and to pay bills and check if payments have been made or received without having to visit your branch. It allows much closer control than monthly bank statements ever did, and importantly allows you to do your banking at times convenient to you, and not necessarily in normal banking hours.

Online savings accounts, where you can only access your account details through the Internet, are also widely available these days and often offer the best savings rates. As you rarely have to deal with a real person, but rather everything is administered by you through your computer, the bank's costs are kept to a minimum, and as a result they tend to offer better savings rates than otherwise similar (but not Net-based) savings accounts.

In addition to the main high street banks, there are a number of exclusively Internet-based banks, although many have close connections with the high street banks even if their names do not suggest it:

First Direct (www.firstdirect.com) is the branchless banking arm of HSBC.

Egg (www.egg.com) currently has Prudential Insurance as its largest shareholder.

Smile (www.smile.co.uk) is the branchless banking arm of the Co-operative Bank.

Cahoot (www.cahoot.com) is a division of Abbey plc.

Intelligent Finance (www.if.com) is a division of the Halifax, part of HBOS.

The well-known high street banks all have their own online sites as well. They also have corporate Web sites, so for example www.barclays.co.uk takes you to the main Barclays home page, from where you can go to its personal banking site as well as its business banking, investment banking, stockbroking and other functions. The same applies for most of the other main high street banks.

All these personal online banking organizations offer a wide range of financial products, from current accounts and saving accounts to mortgages and loans.

Internet stockbroking

It is very easy to buy and sell shares over the Internet. To do so you must register with one of the many online stockbrokers that now exist. Online stockbrokers tend to be 'execution only', where no advice is given: all the service provides is the ability to buy and sell through the site. These tend to have fixed prices for each transaction and are generally pretty cheap. They also offer more sophisticated facilities for regular investors, and those wanting to buy and sell foreign currency or some simple derivative products.

Online stockbrokers will allow you to monitor your portfolio, with the prices being updated either each day or in real time depending on the level of service you subscribe to. Some of the better known companies include:

E*trade (www.etrade.co.uk) one of the original online brokers in both the UK and the United States.
Stocktrade (www.stocktrade.co.uk) a division of the stockbrokers Brewin Dolphin.
Ample (www.iii.co.uk) is an independent broker in its own right.
Sharepeople (www.sharepeople.com), part of American Express.
Hargreaves Lansdown (www.h-l.co.uk), large independent stockbrokers based in Bristol.
Comdirect (www.comdirect.co.uk) is part of Germany's Commerzbank and Europe's biggest broker.

The difference between these dealers is fairly minimal, often down to presentation and ease of use more than speed of execution or commission fees. Most of the large traditional stockbrokers offer some form of access to your portfolio online these days as well, if not the ability to carry out transactions.

Other Internet facilities

The Internet's reach for organizing and administering your personal finances is growing all the time. Beyond the services mentioned above, you can also research and arrange your pension online, buy and manage your household, car and travel insurance, arrange private healthcare and so on. There are a vast number of sites offering you loans and credit, some reputable, but plenty less so.

Beware!

It is relatively easy to set up a Web site and start trading – what is more, it is difficult to track down the owners and managers of sites if they wish to keep themselves hidden. This ability to reach people easily while remaining unreachable themselves makes Internet-based businesses very attractive to the unscrupulous trader. For this reason you must always assure yourself of the bona fide credentials of any company you do business with online. Check that it provides a believable and reachable postal address and telephone numbers. Check that it is regulated by the FSA if appropriate, and double-check it from the FSA's firm check service (http://www.fsa.gov.uk/firmcheckservice/index.html) if you are uncertain. Most sites have an 'About us' section which gives some background to the company and people that run it. The more reputable sites will have easily found 'About us' sections with straightforward and clear information about themselves.

Financial advisers

Throughout this book we have often stressed that there is only so much you can do yourself, and some professional guidance from an impartial and independent expert may be necessary to help select the right particular product for your particular needs. If you get in touch with an IFA this can be done quite easily. As set out in Chapter 1 there are a couple of Internet sites that have IFA directories and advice – which can lead you to IFAs' own sites. In early 2004 www.adviser300.com was launched, which is the first site able to give advice directly over the Internet.

Appendix

Useful contacts

Advice

Advisers

IFA Promotions
2nd Floor, 117 Farringdon Road
London EC1R 3BX
www.unbiased.co.uk
0800 085 3250

Society of Financial Advisers
www.sofa.org

Solicitors for Independent Advice
www.solicitor-ifa.co.uk

Benefits

Child benefit
www.inlandrevenue.gov.uk/
childbenefit
0845 302 1444

Child Support Agency
PO Box 55
Brierley Hill
W Midlands DY5 1YL
www.csa.gov.uk
08457 133 133

Entitled To
www.entitledto.co.uk
Online only service

Charity

All About Giving
Charities Aid Foundation
Kings Hill, West Malling
Kent ME19 4TA
www.allaboutgiving.org
01732 520 055

Inland Revenue – Gift Aid (England)
St Johns House, Merton Road
Bootle
Merseyside L69 9BB
www.inlandrevenue.gov.uk
0151 472 6055/6

Inland Revenue – Gift Aid (Scotland)
Meldrum House,
15 Drumsheugh Gardens
Edinburgh EH3 7UL
www.inlandrevenue.gov.uk
0131 777 4040

Consumer

Buy.co.uk
Portland House, Stag Place
London SW1E 5BH
www.buy.co.uk
0845 601 2856

EnergyWatch
Regional offices – call for your local
address
www.energywatch.org.uk
08459 06 07 08

Trading Standards
www.tradingstandards.gov.uk
Online only service

uSwitch
PO Box 33208
London SW1E 5WL
www.uswitch.com
0845 601 2856

Debt

Consumer Credit Counselling Service
Wade House, Merrion Centre
Leeds LS2 8NG
www.cccs.co.uk
0800 138 1111

Debt Advice Centre
Haywards Heath Debt Advice Centre
Elizabeth House, Heath Road
W Sussex RH16 3AX
www.debtadvicecentre.co.uk
01444 441 893

Equifax Credit File Advice Centre
PO Box 1140
Bradford BD1 5US
www.econsumer.equifax.co.uk
0845 600 1772

Experian Consumer Help Service
PO Box 8000
Nottingham NG1 5GX
www.experian.co.uk
0870 241 6212

National Debtline
The Arch, 48–52 Floodgate Street
Birmingham B5 5SL
www.nationaldebtline.co.uk
0808 808 4000

Debt/consumer

Citizens Advice Bureau
   See local telephone directory
www.adviceguide.org.uk

Disability

Department of Work and Pensions –
Disability Rights
Level 6, Adelphi Building
John Adams Street
London WC2N 6HT
www.disability.gov.uk
0800 88 22 00

Disability Advice Network
(DIAL UK)
St Catherine's, Tickhill Road
Doncaster
S Yorks DN4 8QN
www.dialuk.info
01302 310 123

Disability Rights Commission
FREEPOST MID02164
Stratford-upon-Avon
CV37 9BR
www.drc-gb.org
08457 622 633

Education

Department for Education and Skills
Sanctuary Building
Great Smith Street
London SW1P 3BT
www.dfes.gov.uk
0870 000 2288

Independent Schools Council
Information Service
Regional offices – call for your local
address
www.iscis.uk.net
020 7798 1561

Student Loan Company
100 Bothwell Street
Glasgow G2 7JD
www.slc.co.uk
0800 40 50 10

UK Nurseries
www.uk-nurseries.com
020 8580 2922

Universities UK
Woburn House, 20 Tavistock Square
London WC1H 9HQ
www.universitiesuk.ac.uk
020 7419 4111

General

Community Legal Service
www.clsdirect.org.uk
0845 345 4345

Consumer Association
2 Marylebone Road
London NW1 4DF
www.which.net
020 7770 7000

Financial Services Authority –
Consumer Advice
25 The North Colonnade,
Canary Wharf
London E14 5HS
www.fsa.gov.uk/consumer
0845 606 1234

National Consumer Council
20 Grosvenor Gardens
London SW1W 0DH
www.nationalconsumercouncil.org.uk
020 7730 3469

General/benefits

Advice-UK
12th Floor,
New London Bridge House
25 London Bridge Street
London SE1 9ST
www.adviceuk.org.uk
020 7407 4070

Health

NHS Direct
www.nhsdirect.nhs.uk
0845 46 47

Insolvency

Association of Business Recovery
Professionals
8th Floor, Aldersgate House
London EC1A 4JQ
www.r3.org.uk
020 7566 4200

Insolvency/redundancy

Insolvency Service
21 Bloomsbury Street
London WC1B 3QW
www.insolvency.gov.uk
0845 145 0004

Long-term care

IFACare
37–38 The Old Woodyard
Hagley Hall, Hagley
Worcs DY9 9LQ
www.ifacare.co.uk
01562 881888

Mortgages

The Mortgage Code
University Court
Stafford ST18 0GN
www.mortgagecode.co.uk
01785 218200

Pensions

Pension Advisory Service
11 Belgrave Road
London SW1V 1RB
www.opas.org.uk
0845 6012 923

Pension Credit Advice
Check for local address
www.thepensionservice.gov.uk/
pensioncredit/
0800 99 1234

PensionCheck
www.pensioncheck.co.uk
01625 576 576
The Pension Service
Check for local address
www.thepensionservice.gov.uk
0800 99 1234

Pensions/benefits/
long-term care

Age Concern (England)
Astral House, 1268 London Road
London SW16 4ER
www.ace.org.uk
020 8765 7200

Age Concern (Scotland)
Leonard Small House, 113 Rose Street
Edinburgh EH2 3DT
www.ageconcernscotland.org.uk
0800 00 99 66

Help the Aged
207–221 Pentonville Road
London N1 9UZ
www.helptheaged.org.uk
020 7278 1114

Savings and investment

Association of Friendly Societies
10/13 Lovat Lane
London EC3R 8DT
www.friendlysocieties.co.uk
020 7357 9550

Bank of England Brokerage Service &
Registrars
Southgate House, Southgate Street
Gloucester GL1 1UW
www.bankofengland.co.uk/registrars/b
rokeragehome.htm
01452 398333

CREST
33 Cannon Street
London EC4M 5SB
www.crestco.co.uk
020 7849 0000

Debt Management Office
Eastcheap Court, 11 Philpot Lane
London EC3M 8UD
www.dmo.gov.uk
020 7862 6500

Fitzrovia
Corinthian House,
279 Tottenham Court Road
London W1T 7AX
www.fitzrovia.com
020 7307 1444

FTSE Indexes
St Alphage House, 2 Fore Street
London EC2Y 5DA
www.ftse.com
020 7448 1800

National Savings and Investment
Depends on the product – call for
correct address
www.nsandi.com
0845 366 6667

TrustNet
www.trustnet.com
01483 783 908

Tax

Tax Aid
Room 304, Linton House
164–180 Union Street
London SE1 0LH
www.taxaid.org.uk
020 7803 4959

Tax/benefits

Inland Revenue – Tax Credits
www.taxcredits.inlandrevenue.gov.uk/
0845 300 3900

Trusts

Society of Trust and Estate
Practitioners
26 Dover Street
London W1S 4LY
www.step.org
020 7763 7152

Unemployment

New Deal
www.newdeal.gov.uk
0845 606 2626

Government and regulation

Consumer

Trading Standards – Consumer
Complaints
www.consumercomplaints.org.uk

Investment/pensions

Government Actuaries Department
Finlaison House
15–17 Furnival Street
London EC4A 1 AB
www.gad.gov.uk
020 7211 2600

Tax

Council Tax – Valuations Office
New Court, 48 Carey Street
London WC2A 2JE
www.voa.gov.uk
020 7506 1700

Bank of England
www.bankofengland.co.uk

Continuity
www.financialsectorcontinuity.gov.uk

Department of Trade & Industry
(DTI)
DTI Enquiry Unit, 1 Victoria Street
London SW1H 0ET
www.dti.gov.uk
020 7215 5000

Financial Ombudsman Service
South Quay Plaza, 183 Marsh Wall
London E14 9SR
www.financial-ombudsman.org.uk
0845 080 1800

Financial Services Authority (FSA)
25 The North Colonnade,
Canary Wharf
London E14 5HS
www.fsa.gov.uk
0845 606 1234 (+44 20 7066 1000)

Financial Services Compensation
Scheme
7th Floor, Lloyds Chambers
Portsoken Street
London E1 8BN
www.fscs.org.uk
020 7892 7300

Government Services Directory
www.open.gov.uk
Online only service

HM Customs & Excise
www.hmce.gov.uk
0845 010 9000

HM Treasury
Correspondence & Enquiry Unit
2/S2 HM Treasury,
1 Horseguards Road
London SW1A 2HQ
www.hm-treasury.gov.uk
020 7270 4558

Inland Revenue
www.inlandrevenue.gov.uk
0845 302 1455

Office of Fair Trading
Fleetbank House,
2–6 Salisbury Square
London EC4Y 8JX
www.oft.gov.uk
08457 22 44 99

Office of National Statistics
Customer Contact Centre,
Room 1.015
Cardiff Road
Newport NP10 8XG
www.statistics.gov.uk
0845 601 3034

Trade associations

Advisers

Association of Chartered Certified
Accountants
ACCA Connect,
64 Finnieston Square
Glasgow G3 8DT
www.acca.co.uk
0141 582 2000

Association of Independent Financial
Advisers
Austin Friars House,
2–6 Austin Friars
London EC2N 2HD
www.aifa.net
020 7628 1287

Association of International
Accountants
South Bank Building, Kingsway
Team Valley
Newcastle-upon-Tyne NE11 0JS
www.aia.org.uk
0191 482 4409

Chartered Institute for Public Finance
and Accountancy
3 Robert Street
London WC2N 6RL
www.cipfa.org.uk
020 7543 5600

Institute of Chartered Accountants in
England and Wales (ICAEW)
Chartered Accountants Hall,
PO Box 433
London EC2P 2BJ
www.icaew.co.uk
020 7920 8100

Institute of Chartered Accountants of
Ireland
CA House, 87/89 Pembroke Road
Dublin 4
www.icai.ie
+353 1637 7200

Institute of Chartered Accountants of
Scotland
CA House, Haymarket Yards
Edinburgh EH12 5BH
www.icas.org.uk
0131 347 0100

Debt

Association of British Credit Unions
Holyoake House, Hannover Street
Manchester M60 0AS
www.abcul.org
0161 832 3694

Consumer Credit Trade Association
www.ccta.co.uk
01274 390380

Credit Services Association
(Debt Collectors)
3 Albany Mews, Montagu Avenue
Newcastle-upon-Tyne NE3 4JW
www.csa-uk.com
0191 213 2509

Finance and Leasing Association
2nd Floor, Imperial House
15–19 Kingsway
London WC2B 6UN
www.fla.org.uk
020 7836 6511

Mortgages

Council of Mortgage Lenders
3 Savile Row
London W1S 3PB
www.cml.org.uk
020 7437 0075

Savings and investment

Association of Investment Trust
Companies
Durrant House, 8–13 Chiswell Street
London EC1Y 4YY
www.aitc.co.uk
020 7282 5555

Association of Private Client
Investment Managers
114 Middlesex Street
London E1 7JH
www.apcim.co.uk
020 7247 7080

Association of Solicitor Investment
Managers
Riverside House, River Lawn Road
Tonbridge
Kent TN9 1EP
www.asim.org.uk
01732 783548

Building Societies Association
3 Savile Row
London W1S 3PB
www.bsa.org.uk
020 7437 0655

Tax

Chartered Institute of Taxation
12 Upper Belgrave Street
London SW1 8BB
www.tax.org.uk
020 7235 9381

Index

NB: page numbers in *italic* indicate figures or tables

Index of Advertisers